humor

 Other titles in this
series include:

humor

A READER *for* WRITERS

Kathleen Volk Miller
Drexel University

Marion Wrenn
NYU Abu Dhabi

New York   Oxford
Oxford University Press

Oxford University Press, publishes works that further Oxford University's
objective of excellence in research, scholarship, and education.

Oxford   New York
Auckland   Cape Town   Dar es Salaam   Hong Kong   Karachi
Kuala Lumpur   Madrid   Melbourne   Mexico City   Nairobi
New Delhi   Shanghai   Taipei   Toronto

With offices in
Argentina   Austria   Brazil   Chile   Czech Republic   France   Greece
Guatemala   Hungary   Italy   Japan Poland   Portugal   Singapore
South Korea   Switzerland   Thailand   Turkey   Ukraine   Vietnam

Copyright © 2015 by Oxford University Press.

Published by Oxford University Press.
198 Madison Avenue, New York, New York 10016
http://www.oup.com

Oxford is a registered trademark of Oxford University Press

Library of Congress Cataloging-in-Publication Data
Humor : a reader for writers / [editors] Marion Wrenn, NYU Abu Dhabi; Kathleen Volk
Miller, Drexel University.
     pages cm
   ISBN 978-0-19-936268-4
   1. American wit and humor. 2. Wit and humor--Authorship. I. Wrenn, Marion,
editor. II. Volk Miller, Kathleen, editor.
   PN6165.H77 2014
   808.7--dc23
                                                                                    2014033951

Printing number: 9 8 7 6 5 4 3 2 1

Printed in the United States of America
on acid-free paper

brief table of contents

contents

1 Expository 1

"The ladies won, slapped all the men's butts, but then what to do?"

"One week, we made online dating profiles that were deliberately opaque and misleading."

"If I had had them, I would have been a completely different person. I honestly believe that."

"In a recent global poll, Abu Dhabi took first place in a list of cities ranked alphabetically."

"Comedy in a foreign language is tricky business."

"The drug convinced its user, whatever his height, that he was three inches taller."

"I remember thinking I wish I knew what my secrets were, what I really thought."

"On the boat, we did laundry like this. You wore your underwear until you felt you were no longer a member of the human race. Then you turned it inside out and wore it some more."

"DAD: (laughing) There are actual monsters in the world, but when my kids ask I pretend like there aren't."

2 Analytical 89

"The fact that contemporary adult Americans also tend to associate the word 'pamper' with a certain *other* consumer product is not an accident, I don't think, and the connotation is not lost on the mass-market Megalines and their advertisers."

"On the one hand, that clip of those gauntish pale bodies being steamrolled while fat German ladies looked on chomping gum. On the other hand, sometimes rural folks, even if their particular farms were on hills, stayed up late filling sandbags."

3 Persuasive   173

"Why are men, taken on average and as a whole, funnier than women?"

"There was nothing we needed more in 2005 than an attractive, leggy brunette who was willing to brazenly undermine her would-be hotness."

"This is a super model, people. Do you know what that is? It's like a regular model . . . only *super.*"

"For we judge between the plate that is unclean and the plate that is clean, saying first, if the plate is clean, then you shall have dessert."

"Who could tell what the next moment would hold?"

"The 'h' is in the same place, decade in, decade out. The g is fixed, eternally. It makes you, like, *thirsty*."

"A liberal joke, at present, is no laughing matter."

"People sat up and took notice. They laughed. Then they Googled. Then they got angry. Then they got active."

". . . and I say/ 'Wester.'"

"Out of instinct I almost try to press the text of the deckle-edged pages, hoping something will pop up, a link to something trivial and fast."

thematic contents

what's funny?

what's funny about politics?

what's funny about language?

what's funny about culture?

what's funny about technology?

what's funny about gender?

what's funny about travel?

what's funny about death?

what's funny about families?

preface

Listening to someone explain a joke can be boring. But trying to figure out how a joke works, or how a humorous essay is constructed, can teach you fascinating things about the art of crafting powerful, purposeful, college-level writing.

What's funny? Your answer says as much about who you are and where you grew up as your taste in food or clothing. What we laugh at is tied directly to our culture and identity.

Kathleen cracks up at David Sedaris; Marion thinks Dunn's "If a Clown" is a howler. And there were moments when we were mutually baffled by each other's sense of what's funny. This collaboration not only taught us about each other's different comic sensibilities, it taught us about empathy.

We hope you come to the project of reading funny work, reading how scholars and comics (re)assess what makes something funny, not only with your own sense of humor but with an open mind. You will learn about these sources, yourself, as well as the significance of what the folks around you find funny.

Understanding what makes another person laugh helped us better see where each other stood, and also made us better comedy scholars. Humor studies and humor theory is a rich and well-established field of inquiry. Classicists have studied ancient satires and comedies; anthropologists have looked at humor across different cultures. Psychoanalytic critics have analyzed the relationship between humor, the self, and the subconscious. Postcolonial and critical race theorists have looked at racial humor and the social construction of race, racism, and power. Racial humor, to dwell on a key example, has received in-depth scholarly attention elsewhere. We acknowledge that rich body of interdisciplinary literature (and encourage you to explore it!), but it is beyond the scope of this book. We give you, instead, the tip of the comedy studies iceberg in the work we've compiled.

We hunted and gathered for this anthology in (at least) two ways: We each came into the project with much-loved pieces we felt strongly about including, and then we also looked for topics and categories we felt should be included. We not only gathered sources that made us laugh; we practiced the art of describing them to each other, naming key patterns and features inside the sources, interpreting how these texts work, then making an argument about where they fit in the arc of this anthology—expository, analytical, or persuasive.

A word about the organization of the book: Separating these essays, articles, short stories, and poems in rhetorical strategies was extremely difficult and sometimes even felt forced, like we were imposing labels on these readings when they should not be limited to a particular rhetorical category. Analysis, persuasion, and exploration dovetail and overlap: No piece of writing is **one** of those things. But, funnily enough (ha ha), we chose rhetorical mode as the primary categorization for some of the same reasons that made it so hard: Those three basic divisions take personal "taste" out of the mix. Rhetorical mode offers readers a neutral stance, a high plateau, a wide lens through which to look at the work. We hope our headnotes and questions help you look closer.

That closer look might also involve our secondary organization: themes. Which is to say that if comedy depends on context, and we've "decontextualized" pieces in order to gather them here, then we thought we owed it to you to "re-contextualize" them, too. Our secondary Table of Contents echoes the broader themes signaled by the other readers in the Oxford series—identity, culture, and language, to name a few. Half the fun of editing the book was in discussing the way these pieces echo not only at a rhetorical level but also fit together thematically. So we decided to "go with it" and you'll see certain pieces listed more than once in multiple places in the thematic table of contents.

Due to the import of context, we made sure to describe the venue in which each piece was first published. Different venues target different audiences, exactly like you do when you chose not to tell the same joke at your family's holiday table that you would to your peers at a party. Think about it: You are probably a member of several separate groups who have their own "inside jokes." You have probably seen the same joke or bits of the same movie with different groups and witnessed as people reacted quite differently to the same image or words. We're hoping to help you make sense of those different reactions, as a way to help you become even more aware of audience in your own writing and other forms of communication. We've included some information on many of the original publication venues so that you have a deeper understanding of the rhetorical relationship between the writer and his or her audience (and maybe you'll be intrigued enough to go check out other work at the venues we describe).

We are not arguing that you have to agree with us, or laugh with us, bowing to either of our senses of humor. It is perfectly fine if you roll your eyes at Barthelme, groan at Schneiderman. What we are asking is that you trust the comic event—in other words, some people laugh at some things, others at others—and trust that the comic event is worth interpreting. The trick is to be curious about how the joke is constructed, how the humor works on the page, how it imagines its audience or viewer, and the way it engages our hearts and our heads (not to mention triggering a good belly laugh or two).

The fascinating fact is that the humor comes from the text and from the context in which it is produced and consumed. Is the comedy coming from the persona or the punchline? The comic or the audience? And how does the range of understanding of "what's funny" shift, change, and reflect the cultural values surrounding the comic event? The answers are varied and are often likely "both." Anything worth thinking about always means more than one thing. That's what makes "humor" such a rich, robust topic for the Oxford Reader Series.

Humor: A Reader for Writers is part of a series of brief single-topic readers from Oxford University Press designed for today's college writing courses. Each reader in this series approaches a topic of contemporary conversation from multiple perspectives:

- **Timely** Most selections were originally published in 2010 or later.
- **Global** Sources and voices from around the world are included.
- **Diverse** Selections come from a range of nontraditional and alternate print and online media, as well as representative mainstream sources.
- **Curated** Every author of a volume in this series is a teacher-scholar whose experience in the writing classroom as well as expertise in a volume's specific subject area informs his or her choices of readings.

In addition to the rich array of perspectives on topical (even urgent) issues addressed in each reader, each volume features an abundance of different genres and styles—from the academic research paper to the pithy Twitter argument. Useful but non-intrusive pedagogy includes the following:

- **Chapter introductions** that provide a brief overview of the chapter's theme and a sense of how the chapter's selections relate both to the overarching theme and to each other.
- **Headnotes** introduce each reading by providing concise information about its original publication, and encourage students to explore their prior knowledge of (or opinions about) some aspect of the selection's content.
- **"Analyze" and "Explore" questions** after each reading scaffold and support student reading for comprehension as well as rhetorical considerations, providing prompts for reflection, classroom discussion, and brief writing assignments.
- **An appendix on "Researching and Writing About Humor"** guides student inquiry and research in a digital environment. Co-authored by a research librarian and a writing program director, this appendix provides real-world, transferable strategies for locating, assessing, synthesizing, and citing sources in support of an argument.

about the authors

Kathleen Volk Miller is co-editor of *Painted Bride Quarterly*, co-director of the Drexel Publishing Group, and a Teaching Professor at Drexel University. Volk Miller writes essays and fiction, with work in publications such *Salon.com*, *The New York Times*, *Family Circle*, *Drunken Boat*, and other venues. She wrote weekly for *Philadelphia Magazine*. She is currently working on *My Gratitude*, a collection of essays, and *Ramp Agent Parenting*, a memoir/self-help guide. She speaks about various aspects of running a literary magazine, especially collaboration and working with students. She coordinates an annual writing conference at Drexel University and bimonthly literary events in Philadelphia. For more information, see kathleenvolkmiller.com.

Marion Wrenn is a media critic, cultural historian, and literary editor who writes essays and creative nonfiction. Her essays have appeared in *American Poetry Review, South Loop Review*, and *Poetics*. She earned her PhD from NYU's Department of Media, Culture and Communication and has received grants and awards from NYU, the AAUW, and the Rockefeller Archive Center. She is currently completing her book *Inventing Warriors*, the story of America's Cold War initiative to reorient international journalists. She co-edits *Painted Bride Quarterly* with Kathleen and has taught writing at NYU, Parsons, and the Princeton Writing Program. She currently directs the Writing Program at NYU Abu Dhabi.

acknowledgments

We've worked together on *Painted Bride Quarterly* for twenty years, but the experience of putting together an academic text was brand new and terribly rewarding. Can we thank each other here? Plus, without Carrie Brandon, this book would not exist, and for that, and her, we will be forever grateful. The team at Oxford deserves accolades for the beauty and freshness of this series. Thanks much to the writers who let us reprint their work: a book on humor was, appropriately, so much fun to thread through with questions and commentary.

Drexel University has been KVM's academic home for the past nine years, and the support they give PBQ, DPG, and KVM's own career leaves nothing wanting. Thanks especially to KVM's department chair, Dr. Abioseh Porter, and her dean, Dr. Donna Murasko, for having imbued the department and college with an energetic spirit. MCW thanks friends and colleagues at NYU, the Princeton Writing Program, and NYU Abu Dhabi. We'd also like to thank all of our students for making every day a new challenge, in the best of ways. You make us better teachers and better thinkers.

Finally, thanks to our personal tribes. KVM thanks her lovely and loving family, especially Michael and her children Allison, Hayley, and Christopher. MCW thanks her mother, Mary R. Wrenn, and her husband, Jonathan Burr, finally and always.

Nudnik, Nastya. "Summer Evening," from the "emojination" project. Reprinted by permission of the artist.

1 Expository

"Experience is something you don't get until just after you need it."
—Steven Wright

What do ping-pong paddles, sitcoms, and breasts have in common? Each one makes a crucial appearance in the following seemingly discombobulated collection of humorous essays. But the real punch line? This gathering of sources hangs together via their driving rhetorical mode: exposition. The expository impulse—where a writer is driven by a need to explain or narrate or describe—is at the heart of these pieces and what holds them together in this chapter. The authors set out to richly describe and thoroughly render a range of texts, patterns, and cultural practices they have noticed—from non-native-English-speaking comics on the Edinburgh comedy circuit to the imagined life-world of an ex-president at the dentist's office.

These pieces make us pay attention. Each, in its own way, helps a reader understand the significance of this thing that fascinates the author via writing that dwells on details. They cut through the clutter and noise of daily distractions and focus in on what we might otherwise take for granted or might otherwise have ignored. You will find lists, categories, narratives, and explanatory theories of how funny stuff works. Meta-essays on craft (ironic and otherwise) sit alongside short stories and poems fueled by an explanatory impulse.

We all know the fastest way to kill a joke is to try and explain what's funny about it. But these exemplary explanations don't kill the comedy; instead, they show us how to think in more robust and complex ways about the work of comedy—and about how comedy works.

Dan O'Shannon
What Are You Laughing At?
A Comprehensive Guide
to the Comedic Event

Dan O'Shannon is most famous for his work in television. Currently an executive producer of the ABC show *Modern Family*, he is an American writer and producer who has worked on such classic shows as *Newhart*, *Cheers*, and *Frasier*. This excerpt from his book, *What Are You Laughing At? A Comprehensive Guide of the Comedic Event* (Continuum 2012), offers a readable summary of comedy theories as well as his own framework for understanding the way we experience humor. We admire the basic framework he sets up for how to make sense of what we experience as "funny."

Introduction

If you're looking for a book that will teach you how to write comedy, I suggest you keep moving. You still have time to pick up a copy of *Writing Big Yucks for Big Bucks* before the store closes. However, if you want to understand the bigger picture—what is comedy, why do we respond to it in the way we do—then you've come to the right place.

I've always been what you might call a comedy detective. I observe and create comedy and I study the laugh. That's the true mission of the comedy detective: understand the laugh. What's really going on? What invisible factors are shaping the response?

The answers haven't always come easily. In one instance a single laugh became a 15-year riddle.

I heard it on March 12, 1977. I was barely 15 years old, living in rural Ohio. It was a Saturday night, and like most of America, my family was watching *The Mary Tyler Moore Show*. The episode, called "Lou Dates Mary," chronicles an awkward date between Mary Richards and her boss, Lou Grant. The show builds to a moment on Mary's couch, where the two characters slowly go in for a kiss—only to start laughing as they realize how silly it is for them to try to turn their relationship into something it's not.

> "Comedy appears to be a shape shifter."
> —Dan O'Shannon, *What Are You Laughing At? A Comprehensive Guide to the Comedic Event*

The climactic moment felt slightly off to me. But it wasn't the scene. The actors were brilliant and the situation was genuinely funny. It was the studio audience. The laugh started out loud and full, but there was an odd quick taper to it. The moment left me hanging somehow. 5

I didn't think about it again until years later, when I was writing and producing *Cheers*. (Coincidentally, one of the writers on the staff was David Lloyd, who wrote many episodes of *The Mary Tyler Moore Show*, including "Lou Dates Mary.") We were filming an episode in which the less-than-ambitious Norm does a joke where he starts to talk about taking his career and marriage seriously, but he's only kidding and can't even complete the sentence without cracking himself up. At this I heard a familiar response from the studio audience: a shriek of laughter followed by a too-quick taper. And suddenly I had the answer. I now understood the laugh I'd heard 15 years earlier.

The first step toward understanding the laugh is to understand what comedy is and how it works. Unfortunately, there's one tiny problem:

Nobody agrees on what comedy is or how it works.

For centuries, theorists have argued over comedy's unifying link. Incongruity, superiority, aggression, surprise, and relief keep popping up, either singly or in combinations. I've seen the amateur expert analyze the linguistic structure of a few jokes and extrapolate their conclusions to account for all of comedy. The true amateurs, meanwhile, divide comedy into various "forms" (satire, farce, insult humor, wordplay, gross-out humor, etc.) and proceed from there, not knowing that they've already lost the battle.

10   And so we come to the purpose of this book: the creation of a new and comprehensive model of comedy; a model upon which any joke or humorous incident (along with the reaction it gets) can be examined effectively.

This model will allow for any variation in comedy's arsenal; linguistic jokes as well as slapstick, intentional comedy along with unintentional. It accounts for the decay of old jokes, the nature of practical jokes, and the existence of meta-comedy. It will also catalog the variables of transmission that are so crucial to comedy response.

I'll be presenting new ideas in this book, as well as rearranging some old ones. By the end, you'll have a true understanding of what happens when man meets comedy. You'll see how every comedic experience is unique, and you'll understand the possible factors that go into every laugh.

Think of it as *The Comedy Detective's Handbook*.

Who Am I and Why Should You Listen to Me?   Before plunging into a book of this size, you may want to know why you should trust me. Fair enough.

15   For me, the road began in 1970. I was sitting on a gymnasium floor with the rest of my class for a school assembly. There was a man on stage and he was making us laugh. I have no idea what he was doing; in fact, I have no recollection of the day at all except for the moment when the man paused. He was waiting for us to catch our collective breath, and he leaned against the microphone stand and mused, "There's nothing like the feeling of making people laugh."

The click inside of me was deafening. I remember looking around the room to see if anyone else had heard what I heard; or rather, connected with it like I did. Amazingly, the remark had passed over them. But they were changed, because in that moment I saw them as people, but maybe they could also be . . . audience. I was eight years old, and I'd found my calling.

I was going to be funny.

Thus began the loneliest period of my life. I was full of enthusiasm but didn't have the slightest clue how to be funny. I just knew what made me laugh. Back then it was Jerry Lewis, so I became Jerry Lewis. I learned quickly and painfully that there is also nothing like the feeling of not making people laugh. I was too young to understand the enormous difference between a character doing comedy in the context of a made-up movie and someone enacting the same behavior in real life.

In my teens I was studying sitcoms on TV, recognizing joke patterns. I analyzed cartoons. In the library I found and devoured James Thurber and Robert Benchley, trying hard to duplicate their styles in my writing. The problem? I had no perspective, no point of view. I was simply too young to generate credible material. And let's remember: my audience was mostly other kids—not exactly the kindest crowd.

Unencumbered by popularity, I began to discover books about comedy. The first one I ever read was Steve Allen's *The Funny Men,* written in 1956. A revelation. Around this time Leonard Maltin was writing about cartoons, comedy teams, *The Little Rascals* . . . everything I watched on TV that no one wanted to discuss with me on any real critical level. I read books by Joe Adamson, George Burns, Milt Josefsberg, Walter Kerr, everything I could lay my hands on.

At age 19 I started doing stand-up comedy with original material. And I found out that indeed, there is nothing like the feeling of making people laugh.

This book is the result of what I learned over the next 30 years.

(Are you still reading this in a bookstore? Are you trying to decide between this book and *Being Funny for Money* by that guy who wrote for *My Little Margie*? Did you flip ahead and see all the diagrams I have?)

You'll notice that there's almost no citing of other comedy research in these pages. The contents are based on my observations, first as a stand-up comic and then as a sitcom writer and producer. Fortunately, I was able to work on some of the best shows in television: *Newhart, Cheers, Frasier, Modern Family,* and many more. I worked alongside brilliant writers, actors, and directors, and I kept my eyes and ears open the whole time.

25   I've written thousands of jokes and attended thousands of rehearsals. I've taken part in endless rewrites, all in the service of making scripts funnier. The stage has been my laboratory, and I've witnessed the reactions of hundreds of thousands of people to joke after joke after joke, every variation imaginable. I learned that we can use jokes to trigger every feeling in the psyche. It got to the point where I could hear when the laugh was off; I could hear when we got the right response but for the wrong reason. I learned the language of laughter, not by reading about it in a book, but by immersion. I lived there.

Before Embarking . . .   If you're going to plow ahead, there is one rule:

Lose your comedy prejudice.

There are readers who will go into this book with preconceptions. Some believe that All Comedy is About Truth or that The Job of Comedy is to Provoke. I would urge you to not confuse your preferred use of comedy with the definition of comedy itself. Comedy is flexible. It can be a sword, it can be a Band-Aid. It can make us think, it can distract us from thinking.

Also:

30   We all have individual senses of humor. This means that there will naturally be comedic examples in here that you do not find funny. Some are old-fashioned, others may just not do it for you. This does not diminish their value as examples. They have all been found funny by individuals or audiences at some point, and that's enough.

The study of comedy is not limited to that which is currently popular, critically embraced, or personally favored. We'll pull comedy from silent films to *South Park,* from people getting hit in the groin in home videos to mash-ups on YouTube.

And for an eight-year-old I used to know, we'll even find a little Jerry Lewis.

Overview

1 Common Comedy Theories

Comedy appears to be a shape-shifter. It comes at us in so many ways and attaches itself to so many emotions that it's difficult to pin the thing down to a single, workable model. Is it really possible for the humor of Mark Twain to be related to the sight of the Three Stooges slapping each other senseless? A collection of Calvin and Hobbes can elicit laughs. So can a man falling downstairs, or a co-worker doing an impression of the boss, or a toddler swearing, or a joke that's so unfunny it becomes hilarious, or an outlandish drawing of genitalia, or a song parody, or *His Girl Friday,* or a dog trying to eat peanut butter, or the fact that some people still use the word "outlandish."

So what is the unifying link? There are several well-known theories as to just what comedy is. Since many of these come up routinely in comedy discussion, and because you don't want to look like an idiot if you get trapped in one of these conversations, here is a brief rundown of the more familiar schools of thought. But I'm not going into a lot of detail—what am I, Wikipedia?

Comedy Is Pain   "When I fall down, it's tragedy. When you fall down, it's comedy." This is the old adage that describes pain theory. We get to laugh at the misfortune of others from a safe distance, say, a theater seat or across the street.

Time can also be the safe distance that allows us to laugh at pain. From the comfortable seat of adulthood we can laugh at the gut-wrenching emotional pain we suffered as children and teenagers.

There's another old saying: "Tragedy plus time equals comedy." Few people would think to make a joke about the sinking of the Titanic in April 1912. The tragedy needed to be a safe distance away, the victims less real. (As a side note, our society has, over the years, shortened the time between a tragic event and the inevitable jokes. There are two reasons for this. First, there seems to be a race to get the first joke out, as though a tragedy is now a challenge to see who can cause the most shock. Second, our technology enables everyone to have a national spotlight. Even if people made a Titanic joke in 1912, no national outlet would ever think of printing it, so those jokes never registered on the public radar.)

The value of the safe distance allows us to enjoy pain on several levels. If we see Moe smack Curly with a tire iron, distance allows us to absorb the shock of the blow vicariously. We can identify with Curly; we can be shocked by the violence, all without feeling the pain. There may also be an unconscious element of relief in the laughter, in the sudden realization that we can be close to this experience and not be hurt.

Or maybe we identify with Moe, which leads nicely into . . .

40   **Cruelty/Aggression**   This school of thought states that we can enjoy aggression toward others safely through comedy. We sublimate aggression in real life, and seeing it happen safely can be a release. This would contribute to the popularity of insult humor. But then, so does . . .

Superiority   There are those who believe that all comedy creates feelings of superiority. Seeing someone painted as a buffoon can cause us to feel a sudden jolt of elevation in our own status, which is then expressed as laughter.

Identification   Identification is recognition of our own traits, history, or emotions in the comedy. Identification is the bread and butter of observational humorists who go on and on about relationships and the differences between men and women. Since the audience is generally made up of men and/or women, this kind of humor is very relatable.

Subversion   This is laughter at the inappropriate. We may find great joy in railing against authority through comedy, or enjoy comedy that pushes the boundaries of social acceptability. We may be shocked into laughter or enjoy comedy that we also find off-putting. Dark humor may be included here. Perpetrators of this type of comedy are surrogates for the sides of ourselves we know we shouldn't express. When we see our sublimated feelings or desires expressed, we may also feel . . .

Relief   Freud believed that laughter is the result of a release of tension. This can be the dramatic tension built up within the joke or within the narrative surrounding the joke (as in the comedy relief that pops up in a dramatic situation). It can also refer to a release of social tension, such as when we break the ice with humor or use comedy to approach subjects and behaviors that are uncomfortable to bring up. The relief caused by the use of humor is a release of tension.

45   **Irony**   Irony is often confused with coincidence. While sheer coincidence is random, irony is based on goals. For example, if a character (or a society) needs to accomplish a specific goal, an ironic twist may determine that it is achieved in an unexpected way, or that the goal is achieved but produces the opposite of the intended effect. It may also be that what the character really wanted all along can only happen when the stated goal fails. Take all

those old pulp fiction stories in which an obsessed character finally gets everything he wanted ... forever ... because he's actually in Hell! Now there's some irony for you.

Here are two examples of coincidence, only one of which results in irony:

1. I have a daughter, named Chloe, from my first marriage. After my divorce I married a woman who has a daughter named Chloe. Friends have called this ironic, but it's only a coincidence.
2. When I was in my twenties I decided to see a therapist (never mind why). I didn't have much money, so I went to a low-budget counseling center where I could be interviewed and then assigned to a therapist based on my problems and goals. I asked for a female therapist, because I didn't want to feel like I was talking to my father, who was the source of some of my problems. They assigned me to a young lady named Terry—which is my father's name. This is more irony than coincidence, since I was now using a Terry to try to overcome the effects of another Terry.

It's coincidental, rather than ironic, that both stories have to do with the duplication of names.

In comedy, there are two kinds of irony:

50

1. Irony within the narrative: in this case, all the pieces that create irony exist within the story being told. O. Henry wrote stories with ironic twists and endings.
2. Ironic laughter, or ironic comedy: here, the irony does not exist within the dramatic structure. If we hear a joke so awful that we laugh at how bad it is, we are taking part in the irony; in other words, the joke did not contain irony; irony was provided by our response. Why is it ironic? Because the intent of the joke was to get laughter, and it did—but for the wrong reason.

Disappointment   In the broadest sense, disappointment theory is based on the premise that we laugh at the unexpected. Some have referred to this as thwarting of expectation. In many jokes, a set-up leads us one way, and the punch line takes us in an unexpected direction. A man is walking across the street. Suddenly, and without warning, he drops into an open manhole. The surprise short-circuits us in some way, shocking us into laughter.

Incongruity   Incongruity is the joining together of two or more disparate ideas for humorous effect. This may be as basic as a photo of a man with a baby's head superimposed over his own, or the old commercial in which a man sings in a beautiful operatic voice about his lack of Rice Krispies. The brilliant silliness of *Monty Python's Flying Circus* mines incongruity over and over with dazzling effect—listing examples would fill up this book. One of my personal favorites: the gathering of Karl Marx, Vladimir Lenin, Che Guevara, and Mao Zedong into a panel where they are asked questions, not about communism, but about sports and pop music for prizes.

55   **Parts in Search of an Elephant**   There is an old story about a group of blind men who touch an elephant to learn what it is like. One who touches the tusk concludes that elephants are like pipes. Another, touching the tail, believes that elephants are shaped like ropes. The man who puts his hands on the side of the animal announces that the creature is like a wall.

When we gather these basic theories together, it begins to look as though people have been approaching comedy from different directions. Some theories concern the comedy's content, others are based on the feelings that arise from the comedic experience, and others are process-related.

The problem is this: Every one of these theories can account for the primary cause of laughter in thousands of jokes. Therefore, they would seem to be canceling each other out as candidates for the "root of all comedy."

We need to step back and see these ideas as components of a larger, more comprehensive model.

For now, file these theories in the back of your head. You'll see them all again.

60   We're going to build an elephant.

WARNING: BEWARE THE BAD LISTS

A common approach to defining comedy is to start by breaking it into categories, then distracting everybody by defining the categories. If you Google "forms of comedy" you will find a number of charts and lists, some made by serious students of comedy, others by casual observers. Often, these lists seem thrown together with no clear parameters: one entry may be based on linguistic structure, while another is based on the effect it has on the audience. Still others are based on content. The result is that we have awkward stews of qualities and styles blended together and served up like so:

Types of Comedy

Farce
Slapstick
Wordplay
Parody   65
Satire
Drawing-room comedy
Shock/gross-out humor
Insult humor

This list is virtually useless. How, for example, is one to categorize a gross   70
insult that relies on wordplay occurring in a farce?

· ✦✦ ·

2 The Comedic Event

Based on what we observe in our daily lives, we can easily surmise that an encounter with comedy goes something like this:

1. A receiver (this can be anyone—you, me, Mr. Stec next door) comes into contact with . . .
2. comedic information (a joke or any comedic stimulus), and has a . . .
3. response (laughter, a smile, the rolling of eyes, whatever).

Graphically, we may depict the incident as in (Figure 1.1):   75

RECEIVER ⟶ △ COMEDIC INFORMATION ⟶ RESPONSE

Figure 1.1

Comedic information refers to anything we find funny, whether it's a formally structured joke or witnessing an amusing occurrence, or even the random funny thought. In this book, comedic information is represented by a triangle.

Using this diagram as a starting point, we can plug in any joke and note the response. And here's a joke now:

> Did you hear about the Polish airline disaster? A two-seat Cessna crashed into a cemetery. So far they've recovered over 300 bodies.

You, the reader, may have had a response, but I don't know what it was (Figure 1.2):

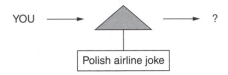

Figure 1.2

80   So I've called my Aunt Rita and told her the joke. This was her response (Figure 1.3):

Figure 1.3

Perhaps Mike from next door will react differently (Figure 1.4):

Figure 1.4

In these examples the joke is the only consistent element. Therefore, one might assume that different responses must be due to individual tastes. You, Aunt Rita, and Mike may simply have dissimilar senses of humor.

The truth, however, is more complicated. The receiver's journey through a joke is loaded with variables, any one of which can greatly alter the response. Without knowledge of these variables and how they work, the comedy detective simply flails around in the dark.

Expanding Our View: The Comedic Event   First, we must accept that comedy is an experience. A joke written on a piece of paper is not comedy, any more than a stick of dynamite is an explosion. At best, information by itself can only be intended comedy. In order for it to work, it has to be activated by the receiver.

Let's go back to the Polish airline joke. You came across the words in a book written by a stranger who was not present to influence your response. On the other hand, Aunt Rita heard the joke from someone she loves, who was on the phone waiting for a reaction. You both encountered identical comedic information, but took part in very different comedic experiences. 85

This is why a good comedy detective doesn't attribute the laugh solely to the comedic information. He attributes it to the comedic event.

Using the above diagrams as a simple representation of the comedic event, our next step is to zoom in and take a closer look—particularly at those arrows, because it's within those arrows that so many variables come into play.

So let's chart the receiver's journey.

Part One: Elements of Context (Reception Factors)   These are the elements of the joke's context, the pre-joke conditions that can affect our level of readiness to take in and appreciate comedy. Here are a few examples:

1. A great joke told by your best friend may provoke a different response from you than the same joke told by someone you despise. 90
2. If you're watching a movie in a crowded theater, you may be more likely to laugh than if you're watching it by yourself.
3. If you're drunk, any comedy may be extra funny or not funny at all.
4. A joke on a sitcom may annoy you, while the same joke in a play may earn your applause.

Some basic reception factors are shown in their place on the model (Figure 1.5):

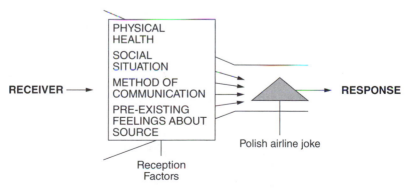

Figure 1.5

95   **Part Two: Completion of the Incongruous Picture**   Here we get to the
triangle that represents the joke.

Back when you read about the Polish airline you took in the information, which made you fill in logical gaps to figure out that people were digging up bodies from a cemetery. Once the idea was assembled, you were free
to enjoy (or not) the incongruities in the completed image (Figure 1.6):

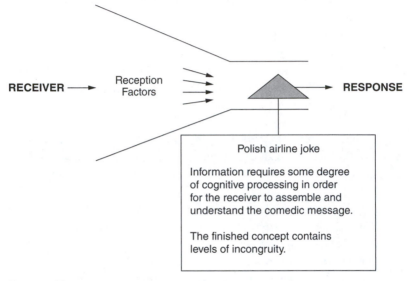

Figure 1.6

All comedic information has two core variables:

1. The amount of cognitive work it takes to assemble the incongruous
   concept.
2. The level of incongruity contained in the completed image.

100   Notice I'm saying "amount" and "level." Not all incongruity is equal, and
not all comedic information requires the same amount of work to assemble
or decode. Later on we'll discuss ways to estimate these levels, and see that
their interaction has a significant effect on the nature of the receiver's
response.

Don't be misled. While incongruity is a component in all comedy, not
all comedy is incongruity. That would be like stating that tires are an element of all cars; therefore all cars are tires.

While we often laugh at high incongruity, it can also be overshadowed by other factors, such as when a joke triggers strong feelings of superiority or shock. These feelings can be so powerful that their impact dominates the experience in our minds—we're barely aware of the incongruity.

In addition, note that the level of incongruity in comedic information may be exceedingly low, to the point at which it is not a primary factor in the response. There is much to explain in this department, and we'll get to it all in Part Two.

[*Note for any ringers out there*: You may suspect that I'm heading in the direction of incongruity resolution theory, but rest assured: I'm not. As will be discussed in Chapter 6, incongruity resolution is based on flawed principles— I'll even go so far as to say that it's one of the biggest road-blocks to understanding comedy ever created.]

Part Three: Enhancers/Inhibitors and Aspects of Awareness   Now that   105 the brain has worked out the joke, the finished thought can trigger emotions in the receiver. These emotions can either enhance or inhibit the receiver's response to the incongruous picture (Figure 1.7):

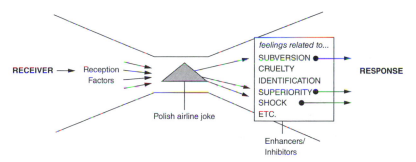

Figure 1.7

You'll recognize some of these feelings as being core components in those standard comedy theories from a few pages ago. In this model, they are triggered by recognition of the comedic idea.

A receiver hearing the Polish airline joke may have a response that is enhanced by the subversive nature of using a fatal plane crash as comedy. He may also enjoy feelings of superiority over the protagonists, as well as the shock value. Another receiver's response may be inhibited owing to the morbid nature of the material or indignation at the slight on the Polish.

As I write this, there has recently been an actual plane crash in a cemetery in Montana—talk about an inhibitor.

Examples of enhancer/inhibitors:

1. A receiver's reaction to foul language can enhance or inhibit his response to a joke.
110
2. A joke may cause an audience member to change his feelings for, or gain insight into, the character or person who delivered it. This may enhance or inhibit the response.
3. If the joke is about, say, a political figure or celebrity or family member, the joke will be enhanced or inhibited by the audience's feelings for that target.
4. Someone hearing an inside joke may have his or her appreciation enhanced simply by being aware that only a few people get it.
5. A receiver's appreciation for the execution of the joke may enhance the response.

Remember the old joke "Your mama's so fat she has her own ZIP code?" Once we figure it out, we're left with the image of a woman as large as a city. This is an impossible image—a highly incongruous one—and the enjoyment may be enhanced by the fact that it has some cruelty in it. Cruelty is an enhancer; it is not the joke. If someone simply says, "Your mama's very fat," we have cruelty but no discernible incongruity to make it comedically viable.

115   And of course, this very cruelty can be an inhibitor. If we have struggled with weight all our lives, we may not enjoy the incongruous picture of a woman as large as a city.

Reception Factors vs. Enhancers/Inhibitors   The kid in the back of the room has a question. He wants to know if reception factors are the same as enhancers and inhibitors. Good question, kid in the back.

Reception factors are contextual variables, and indeed they trigger emotions that enhance or inhibit the experience, but their effect is at work before the joke can make an impact. We may call them pre-joke enhancers/inhibitors if we wish, but we note them separately, for two reasons:

1. To reinforce the idea that these factors are in play before the joke, giving us a state of mind prior to contact with the comedic information.

Reception factors set the stage for the joke, which is different than reaction to the joke itself.

2. The way reception factors trigger feelings is fairly straightforward, as we'll see. However, once we've encountered the joke, all hell breaks loose. We are cognizant of the joke in multiple aspects of awareness.

Aspects of Awareness   We not only experience the joke, we experience *the experience* of the joke. We do this in multiple aspects of awareness, any   120
of which may trigger an array of feelings.

We are aware of the joke's internal reality (a man walking into a bar, a sitcom scene, whatever), while we are simultaneously aware of the joke's existence in our own reality. We have a critical appreciation of the joke and its execution. We may even have a response that is shaped by our awareness of other receivers' responses. Any strong feeling in any of these aspects of awareness can make or break the experience.

With this last set of variables in place, our simple diagram of the comedic event now looks like this (Figure 1.8):

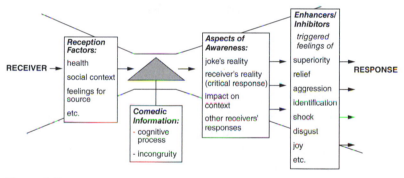

Figure 1.8

A More Fluid Approach   By understanding the nature of the comedic event, we don't tangle ourselves up in the "all comedy is this" and "all comedy is that" debate. Any enhancer or inhibitor triggered by any element of the comedic event may be the dominant factor in the receiver's response. In other words, there's room for everybody.

To illustrate the point, let's resurrect comedy detective Arthur Schopenhauer, who, like many others, believed that all comedy is incongruity. Schopenhauer went so far as to say that the more incongruous a concept, the more explosive the laugh. This is simply not true.

125   The lower the incongruity of a joke, the more it resembles reality, and thus the more we can relate to it. Identification is a strong enhancer. This is why some people laugh more at the soft comedy of *The Andy Griffith Show* than at the high incongruity of *Monty Python's Flying Circus*.

(I should point out that *Monty Python*'s comedy, as highly incongruous as it could be, was often enhanced by subversiveness, and shock, as it poked fun at many sacred cows.)

Throughout this book, we'll see many examples of low incongruity humor that triggers strong enhancers. These enhancers provide the necessary wattage for low incongruity to succeed.

Notice that Schopenhauer also does not take into account any contextual variables, such as the receiver's feelings for the source of the comedy, or even whether or not the receiver is having a bad day. He is trying to create a direct correlation using only the joke and the laugh. This only works if:

1. Every joke is floating in space with no context.
130   2. Every receiver has the same comedic preferences.

Oh, Schopenhauer!

This is, of course, a simple overview.

3 Documenting the Comedic Event

Creating a Comedy Diagnostic   Let's say you want to know why a certain joke got the response it did from a single receiver or from multiple receivers. Or perhaps you heard a laugh that was way out of proportion to the joke being told, and being a good comedy detective your curiosity is stirred.

How do we examine the event? How can we haul it up on the rack and take a good look at it?

135   Naturally, you would want to have as much information about the event as possible. That's where our handy checklist comes in. We're going to build it as we make our way through the book. It will contain every important variable in comedy, and with it, we can record the details of any comedic event and theorize as to the likely primary factors motivating the response.

Think of it as documenting the scene of a crime.

This list will be in the form of a chart as seen here:

	ELEMENTS OF COMEDIC EVENT	INFLUENCE ON RECEIVER
VARIABLE		
VARIABLE		
VARIABLE		
VARIABLE		

Figure 1.9

Someday, a chart such as this may serve as the basis for a working comedy diagnostic—a standardized data-gathering tool for noting comedy response. Amassed on a large scale (millions of jokes, millions of receivers), these data would give us a virtual topography of humor preferences in this country. We could track preferences by age, ethnicity, socio-economic status, geographic region. We could chart comedic evolution over time, as well as identify regional migrations in mass comedy preferences. Eventually, one could even create a test for measuring senses of humor based on national averages.

But we're getting ahead of ourselves.

[*Note:* Don't drive yourself crazy splitting hairs and trying to get the charts perfect. Their use in this book is primarily for idea reinforcement; to get you used to thinking in terms of these variables. You are not expected to actually carry a chart around with you.]

By merely understanding the nature of the variables, you will be equipped with enough information to give you probable answers as you learn the language of the laugh.

Expanding the Definition of "Joke"   To make things easier, the word "joke" will be taken to mean *any* comedic information, whether it is a self-contained language-based structure, or a bit of physical business, or an amusing thing you saw out of your window the other day, or a toddler pronouncing words in a funny way.

Those who study jokes may find themselves uncomfortable with the idea that a dog trying to bite a flashlight beam is a "joke" because it isn't self-contained comedy; no set-up has been provided to make the punch line clear. As we'll see, we can always find the set-up and we can always find the punch line. We just have to know where to look.

"Laugh" vs. "Response"   I tend to use these terms somewhat interchangeably, but I should be clear on this. A successful joke need not necessarily elicit a physical laugh—I've often heard people respond to comedic information with a nod and a muttered "that's funny." A lack of laughter does not mean failure as comedy. And, as we'll learn, laughter can also exist for reasons that have little to do with how funny the information is to the receiver.

Analyze

1. Irony is often confused with something else. What? Explain the distinction O'Shannon points out.
2. What is "comedic information"?
3. Name three "enhancer/inhibitors" for the comedic event.

Explore

1. O'Shannon writes: "We not only experience the joke, we experience the experience of the joke." What does he mean? Can you come up with an example of this experience from your life?
2. Building on Question #1, use an example from your own experience and write an essay in which you critique or refine his idea about "aspects of awareness" and their role in our experience of a comedic event.
3. Watch an episode of one of O'Shannon's shows. Identify a particular scene that grabs your attention. Analyze the humor of the scene by drawing upon the theories O'Shannon briefly summarizes in this chapter.
4. Conduct a viewing experiment. Watch one of O'Shannon's shows at home alone. Make notes about what cracks you up and why. Then watch one as a class. Pay attention to what you laugh at, what the group laughs at, and how it feels to view the show as a group. Discuss the different experiences. What can you make of your discoveries?
5. Elsewhere O'Shannon writes that laughter is "the equivalent of wagging our tails." What does he mean? Free-write a response to his claim.

Felix Clay
"6 Weirdly Specific Characters That Are in Every Sitcom Ever"

Cracked.com (the companion website for the now-defunct *Cracked Magazine*), regularly features humorous list-posts like the one below. List-posts tend to grab a reader's attention with a bold headline and the list-structure makes them super-easy to read (ideal for a small screen!). Note how the author, **Felix Clay**, establishes his authority through the structure of this blog post: the headline promises six character types, and he delivers on that promise.

So you want to do whatever the opposite of cultural enrichment is and make your own sitcom. It's not that hard—look how many shows premiere every fall. Your four major networks will probably pump out at least six sitcoms each, and within a month and a half they'll be gone and your only knowledge of them will be a mild headache when you try to remember what happened last Monday at 9 on CBS. That headache is a little, rotten piece of brain matter that will never fully repair itself. It died so that you might not remember that they tried to make a sitcom out of those cavemen characters from Geico commercials.

Sitcoms are pretty easy to slap together because they're all basically the same, in the way every game of Monopoly will be the same—same pieces, same layout, same sense of impending dread the longer it goes on. To save you some time, I'm going to lay out all the important sitcom characters you'll ever need. Some shows only use a couple; you'll want to take all of them if you want to ensure that your show really lasts. Or fails really fast, it can go either way.

#6. The Horny Character
The horny character is a perennial favorite of sitcoms since the 1970s, when sex was discovered. They exist to make awkward sexual jokes and innuendoes and seem to romp about solely in a world of base, debauched desires.

As Seen In: Blanche DuBois, Sam Malone, Kelly Bundy, Mona Robinson, Sandra Clark, Larry Dallas, Joey Tribbiani, Barney Stinson, G.O.B. Bluth

5   **Why This Character:** Sex is funny to people—just look at all the sex articles on *Cracked*. More importantly, sex should be funny. If sex is too serious, you may be an asshole. Any human who doesn't crack a smile in the face of a queef is a soulless abomination. The horny character is able to express all those perverse inner desires and say those filthy things audience members want to hear but can't express for themselves. Now sure, maybe you're OK with striking up a conversation with a bus driver about fisting, but think of the average shmuck out there who probably gets red in the face when someone says "titmouse." It's for those people that perv characters exist, so they can live vicariously through their TV friend who never gets STDs but has porked the entire greater Los Angeles area thrice this season.

#5. The Crabby Old Fart

Old people are hilariously out of touch and have short tempers. Anger is funny when it comes from someone ineffectual and unimportant, like a grandparent or someone no longer valuable to society. These characters are often irrational and confusing, which is great.

As Seen In: Martin Crane, Sophia Petrillo, Frank Barone, every character Jerry Stiller plays, Mr. Roper, Walter Powell, Pearl Shay, Archie Bunker, Fred Sanford, Uncle Phil

Why This Character: Old people are a necessity because they keep us rooted in our own mortality. Who hasn't watched *Sanford and Son* and thought, "I'm gonna be that asshole and then I'll die." And when you thought it, you thought "gonna," not "going to." Because as an old asshole, you don't care much for grammar anymore.

Old people are hilariously faultless in sitcoms. Because they're from a different time, like back when manners, understanding, empathy, thoughtfulness, and not being shitty didn't exist, they can say and do things the average person would be vilified for. Archie Bunker was a terrible racist and is one of the most beloved sitcom characters ever. How did they ameliorate this? He met a famous black guy in one episode. Somehow that worked.

10   The reason we like cranky old shit characters is because they get their comeuppance somewhere along the line, usually at the hands of a more likeable younger character. If the old person tried to run the show alone, it would suck, and probably alienate everyone. However, pay lip service to the

other side of the coin in a young and therefore correct character, and every-one is happy, because we know the younger star must be right, he's younger. If the old person was right, he wouldn't be so damn old.

Special notice should be paid to *The Golden Girls*, where somehow the younger character was Bea Arthur, who was as old as the sand dunes borne from her aged womb.

#4. The Servant

For reasons never adequately explained, a small but vocal percentage of sitcom producers are fairly certain audiences love rich people. They love them and want to see them abuse and be abused by their hired help, thus the fascination with butlers and housekeepers was born. It doesn't make sense in any way, but maybe in the '70s and '80s every Hollywood writer living out of a shitty basement apartment had dreams of one day verbally abusing Tony Danza.

As Seen In: Mr. Belvedere, Geoffrey the Butler, Benson DuBois, Alice from *The Brady Bunch*, Bertram from *Jessie*, Fran Fine and Niles, Florida Evans, Rosario Salazar, Tony Micelli, Lurch

Why This Character: Servants are a gateway between two worlds that 15 potentially opens up a lot of storylines. A story about rich people is one thing, a story about the working class another, but a servant bridges the gap and lets us see both interact. And, because you're probably working class (the rich have different stations with better shows. *Breaking Bad* has been on rich TV since 1995), you can relate to the butler or housekeeper who, against all odds, is allowed to have a smart mouth and sass her employer, when in real life if a nanny tried to smart off like Fran Drescher, INS would be at the door before she got to the trite punch line. She's not even a for-eigner, but don't you doubt they'd have her cleaning toilets in a Brazilian hostel by week's end.

Smells like beef and ransom.

We like servants because they're us and, even in the face of opulence, they don't take no guff. Again with the poor grammar. Just because they work for a richer person doesn't make them less human and, more import-antly, rich people are dumb dickfaces at least 70 percent of the time and need a servant to keep them in line because if they didn't have one, they'd be wallowing in their own twattery at every turn. Servants keep them real, yo.

#3. The Idiot

Arguably the single most famous and popular character in the entire history of comedy, the idiot is as timeless as it is hackneyed and predictable. But dammit if he still can't make you laugh with his antics. Oh, that idiot and his antics. They are to die for. Take a moment to reflect and, perchance, chuckle. I know I will.

As Seen In: Cousin Balki, Joey Russo, Joey Tribbiani, Dauber Dybinski, Matthew Brock, Woody Boyd and Cliff Claven and Coach, Theo Huxtable for the first several seasons, Mallory Keaton, Rose Nylund, Buster Bluth, Buddy Lembeck

20   **Why This Character:** The idiot is the perfect comic foil. Unlike the aggressive old fart character or the unseemly horny character, the idiot is very often good natured but just so bag of turds dumb that when he falls into misfortune, you enjoy it, because morons fail in ways those of us who don't need helmets and never stab our faces with forks while eating never do.

The key to an idiot is the lack of realism. It's slipping on a banana peel. Have you ever done that? Of course not. First of all, who the fuck leaves banana peels on the ground? Do you live with Donkey Kong? And even if one were on the linoleum, why are you windsprinting through the kitchen in the dark such that you can't even see it in front of you? And then, even if you were so negligent as to not see it, what kind of Teflon-coated floor do you have that a banana peel, a not inherently slippery object, would send you flying? Why, you'd have to be some kind of idiot! Boom! Comedy noose just got tightened, bitches! That feeling in your loins, that's me, breathing deeply, right down there with comedy. In your loins. No need to thank me.

Inhale the funny, exhale the laughs.

We like idiots because they make us feel superior. No one wants to watch a show and feel like Scott Baio is trying to be smug and in charge of them as viewers. I swear to God, if Scott Baio tried to come over and make dinner and tidy up my place, I would end him so hard, he would cease to exist retroactively, and shit he did yesterday would unhappen. That's how much he's not in Charge of my shit.

We need dumbass Buddy Lembeck to come into the kitchen and accidentally eat a dirty sponge because maybe he didn't get enough oxygen when he was a baby or he has a really unfortunate accumulation of heavy metals in his brain. It doesn't matter the reason, it's just funny and allows us to point and laugh and say, "Oh man, I'd never do that. Betty White, you're some kind of chucklefuck!" Of course in this instance we're switching from Buddy Lembeck on *Charles in Charge* to Rose Nylund, or you just get Willie Aames and Betty White mixed up sometimes.

Note: Betty White seems like quite a smart lady in real life, but man was   25
Rose a dummy on *The Golden Girls*.

#2. The Fish out of Water

The fish out of water is a classic character we can all relate to. The out-of-place character is that guy or girl who just never seems to fit in, and because of that, hijinks ensue. Oh man are hijinks fun. It's like when an online comedy writer hangs out with attractive women and people are like "He must have money" or "They must have no self-esteem" or whatever. Hijinks.

As Seen In: Alex P. Keaton, Frasier Crane, Steve Urkel, Will Smith, Tony Micelli, Alf, Webster, Vicki the Robot, Mork, Penny, Charles

Why This Character: Because homogeny is for suckers, you need to throw a monkey into the wrench or a Frasier into a dive bar. It doesn't even need to make sense why that character continually hangs out with everyone who is so very different from them. In fact, it will never make sense, and questioning it will kind of ruin the whole joke. For instance, why is Alex P. Keaton a staunch conservative when the rest of his family are borderline hippies? Why do the Winslows not lock their doors to keep Steve Urkel out? Why didn't Willy sell Alf to the government for a fortune in secret government alien money? Just shut up.

Out-of-place characters draw attention to the problems and weirdness of the "normal" characters. Penny on *The Big Bang Theory* is neither a geek nor physically hideous. She just walks into the room and suddenly a joke is written. Admittedly, it gets old to compare nerds to a hot girl all the time, but still, it's something. Better than what *Homeboys in Outer Space* had, anyway.

#1. The Straight Man

This is the foundation for any comedy, a touchstone to which we all relate   30
and empathize. These characters are the fuzzy, warm center of the sitcom universe that you identify with because they're normal. They may act out on occasion, they may have idiosyncrasies, but that just endears them to you further, because so do you! It's like James L. Brooks and Marcy Carsey peered into your very soul and then cast Valerie Bertinelli and Jim Belushi

as opposite sides of your personality! Amazing! And hey, who the hell is Valerie Bertinelli?

As Seen In: Ross Geller, Chandler Bing, Jerry Seinfeld, Dan Connor, Carl Winslow, Dorothy Zbornak, Danny Tanner, Ray Barone, Tim Taylor, Cousin Larry, Michael Bluth

Why This Character: This character needs to ground the entire sitcom universe and temper everyone else. The idiot is only an idiot compared to this character. The horny guy is only horny compared to this guy. And the straight man may be a complete tool sometimes, or boring, or the smartest, most interesting and enviable human ever, but only because of the nutters he surrounds himself with that make him shine.

The best part about the straight man character is how much you'll start to dislike him over time, depending on the success of the show and, curiously, how much the actor will probably start to dislike the role as well. Do you think Bob Saget is happy about what he did on *Full House*? On one hand, from a career standpoint, it made him a household name and probably paid a lot of bills, but I want to say, with nothing more than a hunch to guide me, Bob Saget fucking hated Danny Tanner. And David Schwimmer probably hated Ross Geller, because everyone hated Ross Geller. The straight man becomes a bit of a wet blanket after six or so seasons and you just wish they'd die already. Like Dan Connor did. Or Cousin Larry. He died, right?

Epilogue

Now that you have an appropriate cast of characters for your sitcom, remember to make storylines that people will find interesting and unexpected, like about in-laws coming to visit, bad dates, getting fired from work, new neighbors, old friends coming to town, a marriage, kids getting in trouble, a misunderstanding that potentially ruins a relationship, and a health scare. No one has ever done any of those stories. Your show is going to be a hit.

Analyze

1. Ross Geller and Chandler Bing are fictional characters from *Friends*. Jerry Seinfeld was the star of a sitcom in which he figured as the central

character. What, according to Clay, do Ross Ge

and Jerry Seinfeld have in common?

2. Clay's list of six character types creates the illusion

prehensive and complete. But did he miss anything

type that you have noticed in the TV shows you wat

leaves off his brief list.

3. Using Clay's list of character types, invent a plot and make a "pitch" for a sitcom.

4. Can we apply the logic of Clay's list to another medium or genre? Do you notice "weirdly specific character types" such as these in video games, for example?

Explore

1. Clay focuses on character types. This move has an ancient legacy that we can trace back to Aristotle's *Poetics*. (Check out Aristotle's *Poetics* for the classic formulation of core dramatic terms such as plot, character, etc.). Which do you think is the key, most formulaic aspect of a sitcom: character or plot? Support your claim with evidence from your favorite sitcoms.

2. *Cracked*, an American humor magazine, was founded in 1958 as a version of the more famous *Mad Magazine*. In other words, *Cracked* was Pepsi to *Mad*'s Coke. Access a digital archive and take a look at several magazine covers from both magazines in the 1950s. What do you notice? What can you make of the similarities and differences between the two print magazines?

3. At the time this anthology went to press, both *Cracked* and *Mad* have online magazines. Visit both websites and compare them. How has each evolved from its print version? How do the online versions of *Mad* and *Cracked* compare to each other now? How has their sense of humor changed—over time and/or across media platforms?

4. Using Clay's column as a model, write and submit a piece for *Cracked*.

olin Nissan
"The Ultimate Guide to Writing Better Than You Normally Do"

Colin Nissan is a writer and humorist with a background in advertising. His creative copy has won awards like *Ad Age's* Campaign of the Year and *Creativity Magazine's* Spot of the Year. This essay appeared in McSweeney's *Internet Tendency*, the digital arm of McSweeney's Publishing, the publishing house founded by Dave Eggers. The punchy headlines for each section of this advice column offer nifty advice to writers—but Nissan's explanations of these "rules" make us love his writing.

Write Every Day

Writing is a muscle. Smaller than a hamstring and slightly bigger than a bicep, and it needs to be exercised to get stronger. Think of your words as reps, your paragraphs as sets, your pages as daily workouts. Think of your laptop as a machine like the one at the gym where you open and close your inner thighs in front of everyone, exposing both your insecurities and your genitals. Because that is what writing is all about.

Don't Procrastinate

Procrastination is an alluring siren taunting you to Google the country where Balki from *Perfect Strangers* was from, and to arrange sticky notes on your dog in the shape of hilarious dog shorts. A wicked temptress beckoning you to watch your children, and take showers. Well, it's time to look procrastination in the eye and tell that seafaring wench, "Sorry not today, today I write."

Fight Through Writer's Block

The blank white page. El Diablo Blanco. El Pollo Loco. Whatever you choose to call it, staring into the abyss in search of an idea can be terrifying.

But ask yourself this; was Picasso intimidated by the blank canvas? Was Mozart intimidated by the blank sheet music? Was Edison intimidated by the blank lightbulb? If you're still blocked up, ask yourself more questions, like; Why did I quit my job at TJ Maxx to write full-time? Can/should I eat this entire box of Apple Jacks? Is *The Price is Right* on at 10 or 11?

Learn from the Masters

Mark Twain once said, "Show, don't tell." This is an incredibly important lesson for writers to remember; never get such a giant head that you feel entitled to throw around obscure phrases like "Show, don't tell." Thanks for nothing, Mr. Cryptic.

Find Your Muse

Finding a really good muse these days isn't easy, so plan on going through   5
quite a few before landing on a winner. Beware of muses who promise unrealistic timelines for your projects or who wear wizard clothes. When honing in on a promising new muse, also be on the lookout for other writers attempting to swoop in and muse-block you. Just be patient in your search, because the right muse/human relationship can last a lifetime.

Hone Your Craft

There are two things more difficult than writing. The first is editing, the second is expert level Sudoku where there's literally two goddamned squares filled in. While editing is a grueling process, if you really work hard at it, in the end you may find that your piece has fewer words than it did before, which is great. Perhaps George Bernard Shaw said it best when upon sending a letter to a close friend, he wrote, "I'm sorry this letter is so long, I didn't have time to make it shorter." No quote better illustrates the point that writers are very busy.

Ask for Feedback

It's so easy to hide in your little bubble, typing your little words with your little fingers on your little laptop from the comfort of your tiny chair in your miniature little house. I'm taking this tone to illustrate the importance of developing a thick skin. Remember, the only kind of criticism that doesn't make you a better writer is dishonest criticism. That, and someone telling you that you have weird shoulders.

Read, Read, Read

It's no secret that great writers are great readers, and that if you can't read, your writing will often suffer. Similarly, if you can read but have to move your lips to get through the longer words, you'll still be a pretty bad writer. Also, if you pronounce "espresso" like "expresso."

Study The Rules, Then Break Them

Part of finding your own voice as a writer is finding your own grammar. Don't spend your career lost in a sea of copycats when you can establish your own set of rules. If everyone's putting periods at the end of their sentences, put yours in the middle of words. Will it be incredibly difficult to read? Yes it will. Will it set you on the path to becoming a literary pioneer? Tough to say, but you're kind of out of options at this point.

Keep It Together

10   A writer's brain is full of little gifts, like a piñata at a birthday party. It's also full of demons, like a piñata at a birthday party in a mental hospital. The truth is, it's demons that keep a tortured writer's spirit alive, not Tootsie Rolls. Sure they'll give you a tiny burst of energy, but they won't do squat for your writing. So treat your demons with the respect they deserve, and with enough prescriptions to keep you wearing pants.

Analyze

1. What should you be on guard against when seeking your muse?
2. What are two things Nissan says are more difficult than writing?
3. Which, according to Nissan, keeps the writer's spirit alive: demons or Tootsie Rolls?

Explore

1. Come up with three more rules for improving your writing. Then spend some time explaining why the rule makes sense. Bonus points if you can break the rule while advocating for it.

2. Which of Nissan's rules is hard for you? Which is easy? Pick one and free-write about your writing process. You might start out with "I am the writer who . . ." or "I am the reader who . . ." See what you can learn about your process.

Jonah Weiner
"Jerry Seinfeld Intends to Die Standing Up"

Brooklyn-based **Jonah Weiner** is a contributing editor at *Rolling Stone* and a contributing writer at *The New York Times Magazine*. He has also written for *Slate* and *The New Yorker*. In this profile of comedian Jerry Seinfeld we learn about the comic's idiosyncratic creative process. The genius of the piece is in the way Weiner takes us "backstage" and reveals Seinfeld's approach to the work of comedy.

Jerry Seinfeld began his commute after dinner, in no particular hurry. Around quarter to 8 on a drizzly Tuesday, he left his Manhattan home—a palatial duplex apartment with picture windows and a broad terrace overlooking Central Park—and made for a nearby garage. Due to tell jokes at a comedy club downtown, he decided to drive what he calls his "city car": a 1998 Porsche 911 Carrera 4S. Stepping into the garage, he tugged a thick fabric cover from the car. The interior was a pristine matte black, and the paint job was a startlingly luminous azure. "It's called Mexico blue—a very traditional Porsche color," Seinfeld said. "In the '70s it looked normal, but now it looks insane."

Jerry Seinfeld's comedic persona is unflappable—annoyed plenty, but unmarked by extremes of emotion, much less tragedy.

Larry David in a scene from Seinfeld's online series, *Comedians in Cars Getting Coffee*: "You have finally done a show about nothing."

Michael Richards in *Comedians in Cars Getting Coffee:* "What is it— coffee, liquor, money? Is that your life now?"

5   His hair, flecked with gray, was buzzed almost to the scalp, and he was dressed in light-blue Levi's, a navy knit polo and a dark wool blazer. Seinfeld, who once said he wore sneakers long into adulthood "because it reminds me I don't have a job," has lately grown partial to Nike Shox, which he likes for their extravagant cushioning, but tonight he opted for tan suede desert boots. When he's in the workplace—on a stage, microphone in hand, trying to make a crowd erupt—the feel of a harder sole helps him get into the right mind-set.

"I just tried a little Twitter experiment," Seinfeld said. His appearance, at Gotham Comedy Club, had so far been kept secret, but just before leaving home, he'd announced the gig online on a whim. "They've only got a half-hour to get there, so I'm not expecting a flash mob," he said. Gotham was an opportunity for Seinfeld to audition brand-new material and fine-tune older bits in a relatively low-stakes context. In two days, he would perform for nearly 3,000 people at Manhattan's Beacon Theater, and that show loomed large. It would be Seinfeld's first performance in New York City since 1998, not counting impromptu club appearances and the odd private event, and it would kick off a citywide tour, with performances in each of the other boroughs. Born in Brooklyn, educated in Queens and famous for a fictional Manhattan apartment, Seinfeld called the tour "a valentine," but he was, on one level, ambivalent about it. "'The Hometown Hero Returns' is not my narrative of being a stand-up," he said. "For me, it's the hotel. It's 'I Don't Belong Here.' It's 'The Stranger Rides Into Town.' That's the proper form of this craft."

Seinfeld wondered if hordes would see his tweet and hustle over to Gotham, but sparse attendance would be fine, too. Several weeks earlier he materialized, unannounced, at the Creek and the Cave, a club in Long Island City, and performed for "14 people." Most comedians dislike telling jokes to empty seats, but at this point Seinfeld enjoys a room that offers some resistance. "I miss opening for Frankie Valli and Ben Vereen, walking out as an unknown and there's no applause: let's get it on," he said. "I once opened for Vic Damone at a nooner on a basketball court in Brooklyn. They're going, Who is this kid? Oh, god! They're sure you're not worth the trouble. But I'd win over some of those rooms." After you've helped create and starred in one of television's best-rated, best-loved sitcoms—a show that, thanks to rampant syndication, is still bursting Kramer-style into people's living rooms 14 years after its finale—tough crowds are tougher to come by. "I would love it if there were only two people there tonight," he said.

To get the Porsche out of the garage, Seinfeld had to execute something like a 12-point turn, somehow managing, as he nudged the car back and forth, not to leave chips of Mexico blue all over an unnervingly close concrete column. Seinfeld is 58, and his face is rounder and more deeply lined than it once was, but it has retained the bright-eyed boyishness of his sitcom days. He smiles readily, either at something someone else has said or—since he is frequently the funniest person within earshot—at something he came up with. His default display of amusement is to squint hard and scrunch up his nose till his front teeth protrude from a rictus grin: a groundhog tickled by the sight of his own shadow.

Tonight he was feeling out of sorts. "My head's spinning a little bit from the travel," he said. He had returned only yesterday from France, where he spent a three-day vacation sightseeing with his family, attending a birthday party and examining a vintage Meyers Manx dune buggy he was thinking about buying. Ever since he began working comedy clubs, in 1975, Seinfeld has considered himself a stand-up above all else, and the other roles he has taken on—sitcom icon, husband, father of three—can come into conflict with the calling. "We did a lot of moving, and we had a lot of fun," he explained, "but I get thrown off easily. If I have one weekend off from stand-up, and I do something weird, I completely forget who I am and what I do for a living."

Because Seinfeld's big post-*Seinfeld* projects have been few and far   10
between—the stand-up documentary *Comedian* (2002), the animated children's film *Bee Movie* (2007), the reality-show misfire *The Marriage Ref* (2010), which he produced and appeared on as a judge—you might assume that he whiled away the last decade on a private island somewhere, racing Spyders and fanning himself with royalty checks. Instead, since 2000, Seinfeld has spent a portion of nearly every week doing stand-up. He is on track to do 89 shows this year, plus private appearances, which shakes out to about two performances a week. He's living the life of a road comic, albeit one who sells out 20,000-seat London arenas and schleps to gigs via chartered planes rather than rented subcompacts.

Earlier this year, Seinfeld started a 10-episode online series, *Comedians in Cars Getting Coffee*, in which he wheels around in gorgeous old Triumphs and Karmann Ghias and cracks wise over mugs of coffee with friends like Larry David, Alec Baldwin and Carl Reiner. The show's intended audience, Seinfeld says, is "this bubble world of people who love funny and want to get into it a little closer." But while he acknowledges the Internet's usefulness in keeping comedy relevant—podcasts, video channels and Web sites devoted to comedy are booming—he sees stand-up as, at bottom, an antidote to technological alienation. "We're craving the non-digital even more these days, the authentically human interaction," he says. "We need to see some schmuck sweat."

For Seinfeld, whose worth *Forbes* estimated in 2010 to be $800 million, his touring regimen is a function not of financial necessity but rather of borderline monomania—a creative itch he can't scratch. "I like money," he says, "but it's never been about the money." Seinfeld will nurse a single joke for years, amending, abridging and reworking it incrementally, to get the thing just so. "It's similar to calligraphy or samurai," he says. "I want to make cricket cages. You know those Japanese cricket cages? Tiny, with the doors? That's it for me: solitude and precision, refining a tiny thing for the sake of it."

When he can't tinker, he grows anxious. "If I don't do a set in two weeks, I feel it," he said. "I read an article a few years ago that said when you practice a sport a lot, you literally become a broadband: the nerve pathway in your brain contains a lot more information. As soon as you stop practicing, the pathway begins shrinking back down. Reading that changed my life. I used to wonder, Why am I doing these sets, getting on a stage? Don't I know how to do this already? The answer is no. You must keep doing it. The broadband starts to narrow the moment you stop."

Gotham Comedy Club was a 15-minute drive downtown. Passing the Museum of Natural History, Seinfeld tuned the car radio to WFAN, where a baseball game was under way. "Do you know this player Adam Greenberg?" he asked. "Seven years ago, he was a rookie, and in his very first at-bat he got hit in the head with the ball—knocked out, concussed, out of the league." Seinfeld raised an index finger from the wheel: "One pitch." The Marlins had agreed to sign Greenberg for a single day after fans petitioned on his behalf. "It might seem a bit Jewy if I get too excited about it—I wish he wasn't Jewish," Seinfeld said. "But it's a fascinating story. One at-bat after seven years. Think of the pressure on this guy!"

15   Seinfeld likes pressure. He describes doing live comedy as "standing against a wall blindfolded, with a cigarette in your mouth, and they're about to fire." His objective at Gotham was piecework. "A lot of what I'll be

doing tonight are tiny things in my bits where I'm looking for a little fix, where something isn't quite smooth," he said. "A lot of stuff I do out of pure obsessiveness." One bit began with the observation that "tuxedos are the universal symbol for pulling a fast one." "That line works," he said. "But I want to get from there to a point about how the places where you see tuxedos are not honest places—casinos, award shows, beauty pageants, the maitre d'— all these things feel shady." He added: "But I've been having trouble getting the audience to that. I'm trying to bring that to a punch line."

Seinfeld likens his fine-bore interest in jokes to his longstanding infatuation with Porsches, of which he owns "a few dozen." "People ask me, Why Porsches? A lot of it is the size, same as with bits. The smaller something is, the harder it is to make, because there's less room for error." In high school he took shop classes, even after a counselor told him that college-bound kids didn't need to, because he wanted to know how machines fit together. "I have this old '57 Porsche Speedster, and the way the door closes, I'll just sit there and listen to the sound of the latch going, *cluh-CLICK-click*," Seinfeld said. "That door! I live for that door. Whatever the opposite of planned obsolescence is, that's what I'm into." Mark Schiff, a veteran club comic and one of Seinfeld's oldest friends, told me: "He's a scientist. When you watch him, he's in the lab, concocting. I feel that way, too, to a degree, but with him every little nuance is so valuable." Sarah Silverman, who has shared bills with Seinfeld and long admired him, agrees: "Whereas most comedians are lazy bastards, he's the ultimate craftsman."

In front of Gotham, six orange traffic cones marked "Con Edison" were arranged in the street. Spotting us, a bouncer built like a bank safe emerged to remove them: when Seinfeld appears here, he calls the owner, who reserves a space. Seinfeld got out, eliciting happy stares and excited murmurs from passers-by. His posture was excellent; his gait leisurely. In Gotham's packed main room, the comic Jim Gaffigan was onstage. Seinfeld remained in the hallway, studying a sheet of yellow paper scribbled with lines he wanted to improve. In the car, he'd warned me, "When I get to the club I'm not going to want to chat until after; I'm in my own world." He made some small talk with the bouncer and the owner about baseball, but he was plainly preoccupied. The bouncer said, apropos of Greenberg's head injury, "My daughter got a concussion, and she still gets headaches." Seinfeld was staring at his notes. "Huh," he replied, no longer listening.

After a few minutes, Gotham's host asked the 300-strong crowd to welcome "a special guest—Jerry Seinfeld!" and if they'd been tipped off on

Twitter, it didn't diminish their enthusiasm. "Yes! Yes!" a burly guy shrieked, grasping frantically for his phone to take a picture. Seinfeld's set lasted 20 minutes and he seemed at ease. The tuxedo bit got medium-size laughs; one of the biggest explosions came when Seinfeld, mulling the topic of goofy outfits that dads wear on weekends, concluded, "All fathers essentially dress in the clothing style of the last good year of their lives"—a joke about aging-male despair couched in a joke about fashion. When Seinfeld recited it, a man in khakis did an actual spit take into his beer bottle. At one point, Seinfeld lost his thread and sighed as he checked his notes; even the sigh got a laugh. He closed to a standing ovation.

Seinfeld retired to a dressing room, plopping down beside a bucket of bottled water. I congratulated him on the performance. "I'd say two-thirds of that set was garbage," he said, matter-of-factly. "Whether it was lines coming out wrong or the rhythm being off." He said he'd counted "probably eight" jokes that failed to get the kinds of laughs he desired. "There's different kinds of laughs," he explained. "It's like a baseball lineup: this guy's your power hitter, this guy gets on base, this guy works out walks. If everybody does their job, we're gonna win." I told him about the khaki guy's spit take, and Seinfeld cracked up, calling this "a rare butterfly." Nevertheless, "there wasn't one moment where I was where I wanted to be. That was just a workout. I had to get it going again."

20   Over nine seasons, *Seinfeld* enjoyed an omnipresent, epochal success: you can draw a line from *Seinfeld* to Larry David's *Curb Your Enthusiasm* to Ricky Gervais's *Office*, *Arrested Development*, *It's Always Sunny in Philadelphia*, the American *Office* and out from there to maybe half the sitcoms currently on the air. In stand-up circles, Seinfeld is a towering figure, revered for the sharpness of his eye as he scrutinizes subjects large (marriage, death) and small (answering-machine protocol, 5-Hour Energy drink). In 2001, George Carlin spoke admiringly of "the little world, the kind of world Jerry Seinfeld investigated to a great, high level." When *Seinfeld* went off the air and Seinfeld began rededicating himself to stand-up, he told *Time* that he didn't consider himself great. When I asked him how he evaluates his talent today, Seinfeld demurred before allowing, "I think it's there now." He says he plans to do stand-up "into my 80s, and beyond."

One afternoon not long after the Gotham gig, Seinfeld invited me to his Upper West Side work space, where he spends most days, writing jokes. Clean, modern and cozy, it resembled some hip therapist's office: a high-ceilinged, poured-concrete box with a long plushy couch, a little balcony and a kitchenette. Framed pictures covered a wall: a production still from the George Reeves *Superman* serial; an original cartoon of Seinfeld and Alfred E. Neuman that ran on the cover of *Mad Magazine* in 1997; a photo of Steve McQueen with a Porsche 917 that the actor owned in the '70s and that today belongs to Seinfeld. A sleek Pinarello racing bicycle, which Seinfeld rides around town, stood against a wall. "It's very addictive, that feeling of gliding through the city," he said. Some Emmys huddled in a corner beside a ventriloquist's dummy, which Seinfeld cherishes more than the awards: "I did a comedy show with that in third grade."

Seinfeld sat in an armchair in a sweater and jeans, resting gray Shox on a footstool. On a typical weekday, after getting the kids (his daughter Sascha, 12, son Julian, 9, son Shepherd, 7) to school and exercising in his building's gym, Seinfeld walks here, grabs a legal pad and a Bic pen and sits at his desk. No street noise penetrates. The pages of the pad are destined for either a wastebasket or a master file containing Seinfeld's entire act, handwritten. The other day, perusing this file, he found a joke in which, discussing touch-screen phones, he likens the act of scrolling through a contact list and deleting names to the effete, disdainful gesture of a "gay French king" deciding whom to behead. Seinfeld wrote the joke a year ago and forgot it; having rediscovered it, he'd be telling it onstage that weekend.

Seinfeld's shows last a little over an hour, but he has about two hours of material in active rotation, so he's able to swap in different bits on different nights. There is a contemporary vogue for turning over an entire act rapidly: tossing out jokes wholesale, starting again from zero to avoid creative stasis. Louis C.K. has made this practice nearly synonymous with black-belt stand-up. Seinfeld wants no part of it. "This 'new hour' nonsense— I can't do it," he said. "I wanna see your best work. I'm not interested in your new work." C.K., who used to open for Seinfeld, has called him "a virtuoso— he plays it like a violin," and the two are friendly. I asked Seinfeld if he thought C.K.'s stand-up hours, widely praised, would improve if he spent more than a year honing each one. "It's not really fair for me to judge the way somebody else approaches it," Seinfeld replied. "I care about a certain level of detail, but it's personal. He would get bored of it. It's not his way. It's a different sensibility." There was another big difference between the two, Seinfeld noted: "Working clean." Almost from the beginning, Seinfeld has forsworn graphic language in his bits, dismissing it as a crutch. "Guys that can use any word they want—if I had that weapon, I'll give you a new hour in a week," he said.

Developing jokes as glacially as he does, Seinfeld says, allows for break-throughs he wouldn't reach otherwise. He gave me an example. "I had a joke: 'Marriage is a bit of a chess game, except the board is made of flowing water and the pieces are made of smoke,'" he said. "This is a good joke, I love it, I've spent years on it. There's a little hitch: 'The board is made of flowing water.' I'd always lose the audience there. Flowing water? What does he mean? And repeating 'made of' was hurting things. So how can I say 'the board is made of flowing water' without saying 'made of'? A very small problem, but I could hear the confusion. A laugh to me is not a laugh. I see it, like at Caltech when they look at the tectonic plates. If I'm in the dark up there and I can just listen, I know exactly what's going on. I know exactly when their attention has moved off me a little.

25   "So," he continued, "I was obsessed with figuring that out. The way I figure it out is I try different things, night after night, and I'll stumble into it at some point, or not. If I love the joke, I'll wait. If it takes me three years, I'll wait." Finally, in late August, during a performance, the cricket cage snapped into place. "The breakthrough was doing this"—Seinfeld traced a square in the air with his fingers, drawing the board. "Now I can just say, 'The board is flowing water,' and do this, and they get it. A board that was made of flowing water was too much data. Here, I'm doing some of the work for you. So now I'm starting to get applause on it, after years of work. They don't think about it. They just laugh."

Seinfeld believes funniness is genetic. When his father, Kalman, was sta-tioned in the Pacific during World War II, he'd transcribe jokes he heard and store them in a box for safekeeping. "In the army, that's kind of how you got through it," Seinfeld says. "People would tell jokes by the score, be-cause what else are you going to do to maintain sanity? The recognizing of jokes as precious material: that's where it starts. If you've got the gene, a joke is an amazing thing. It's something you save in a box in a war."

Born in 1954 and raised on Long Island, in Massapequa, Seinfeld dreamed of growing up to be an advertising man, and he still appreciates commercials for their narrative economy. The Seinfelds were "pretty Jewish," Seinfeld recalls: "Went to temple, kept kosher, two sets of dishes." The younger of two siblings (his sister helps handle his business), he earned his first spit take, as a little kid, while snacking with a pal; Seinfeld told a joke, and the friend burst out laughing, spraying Seinfeld's face with sodden crumbs. His love of comedy matured when he heard Jean Shepherd's epic, askew radio monologues, and when he bought Bill Cosby's 1965 album,

Why Is There Air?. Seinfeld adored Shepherd's knack for "taking something small and making it big," and he marveled at Cosby's "vocal instrument: he can do this person, the sound of chewing gum, the corduroys rubbing together, the other kids—he was all over the keyboard." But the comedian who made Seinfeld think he could actually become one was Robert Klein. "He was a New York, middle-class kid," Seinfeld says, "and through that I could see a path for myself."

Seinfeld's work habits were stringent from the start. Studying communications and theater at Queens College, he arranged an independent study in stand-up, trying club sets, analyzing others' sets and writing a 40-page paper. When he scored his first appearance on Johnny Carson's *Tonight Show,* in 1981, he practiced his five-minute set "200 times" beforehand, jogging around Manhattan and listening to the *Superman* theme on a Walkman to amp up.

We're accustomed to the cliché of the stand-up as sad clown: a racked soul on a dim stage, salving psychic wounds, craving approval. When audiences yell, "I love you," at Seinfeld, he likes to reply, "I love you, too, and this is my favorite type of intimate relationship." He told me: "That's the wiring of a stand-up. This is my best way of functioning." But he sees himself more as exacting athlete than tortured artist. He compares himself to baseball players—putting spin on the ball as it leaves his fingers, trying to keep his batting average high—and to surfers: "What are they doing that for? It's just pure. You're alone. That wave is so much bigger and stronger than you. You're always outnumbered. They always can crush you. And yet you're going to accept that and turn it into a little, brief, meaningless art form." He said: "I'm not filling a deep emotional hole here. I'm playing a very difficult game, and if you'd like to see someone who's very good at a difficult game, that's what I do."

For audiences, Seinfeld's approach has its escapist comforts. In his jokes   30 he often arranges life's messy confusions, shrewdly and immaculately, into a bouquet of trivial irritants. Seinfeld's comedic persona is unflappable— annoyed plenty, but unmarked by extremes of emotion, much less tragedy. "He's the least neurotic Jew on earth," Sarah Silverman says. In a joke Seinfeld told for decades, he called an overflowing toilet "the most frightening moment in the life of a human being," and there's a sense in which his clean, precise bits are marvels of plumbing, keeping abjection at bay. On *The Arsenio Hall Show*, in 1991, Hall told Seinfeld, "We got so much going on in the world; we got this war, the economy, crime." Seinfeld replied,

"It's all going on, but it's not happening right here, right now; it's all going on out there."

This sensibility reached brilliant heights on the sitcom, which featured four gleefully mercenary protagonists for whom New York was a playground of silly social hurdles, warm diner booths and the odd totalitarian soup joint—Seinfeld calls the show "utopian." *Seinfeld* feels so emblematically '90s largely because of its extreme moral disengagement, which rankled some viewers. In a column for *The Times*, Maureen Dowd quoted Leon Wieseltier, the *New Republic*'s literary editor, as saying that *Seinfeld* was "the worst, last gasp of Reaganite, grasping, materialistic, narcissistic, banal self-absorption." She went on to say that the show was a product of "the what's-in-it-for-me times that allowed Dick Morris and Bill Clinton to triumph." (Fittingly, the series ended with the gang imprisoned on good Samaritan laws.)

Seinfeld disagrees that his show was, as the saying goes, about nothing. "I don't think these things are trivial," he says, pointing to how political commentators compared President Obama's renewed bravado the day after his lackluster Colorado debate performance to the *Seinfeld* episode where George, insulted at work, devises a comeback too late. And Seinfeld says that as his act has grown to address marriage and fatherhood, the laughs have deepened. "It hits them in a totally different way," he said. "Once you step into that area, you're in their kitchen, in their bedroom, deep in their life. It's a very intimate and potent comedic thing."

His best jokes, concerned as they are with the ultra-quotidian, have an understated timelessness. Several younger comedians I spoke with described Seinfeld as an ongoing influence. Judd Apatow, who as a kid in the late '70s became obsessed with Seinfeld's stand-up, told me, "From the get-go he was the greatest observational comedian who ever lived—nobody was, or is, as funny as him." In high school, Apatow persuaded Seinfeld to sit for a long interview during which he dissected his bits, methodically laying bare their musculature. Apatow says it was "a lesson in how to write jokes" that he has never forgotten. Kevin Hart, an arena-packing comic, told me that Seinfeld was generous with advice when Hart was starting out, adding that his analytical gift remains unequaled: "He can describe a bouncing ball in a way that changes the way you look at bouncing balls forever."

Seinfeld doesn't chase trends: he is fully content to woodshed up on Mount Olympus. He has only passing interest in topical humor and no time for winking meta-jokes or absurdist non sequiturs. He believes in showmanship, laying out his bits in heavily theatricalized tones and cadences rather than feigning extemporaneousness or a cool deadpan, and when he plays theaters, he wears Armani suits in blacks and grays. "I have old-school values," he says.

This has obvious dangers. The defining comic of a bygone era, as Seinfeld is to the '90s, risks becoming that era's prisoner: out of touch, or worse, obsolete. Seinfeld's style was so distinctly realized so early on that it quickly lent itself to an immortal caricature: "What's the deal with . . . ?" Seinfeld himself poked fun at his association with this construction all the way back in a 1992 *Saturday Night Live* sketch, playing a quiz-show host who began nearly every question with those four words.

But, in almost counterintuitive ways, Seinfeld has dodged self-parody in his act. Avoiding excessive topicality has allowed his jokes to feel evergreen; keeping them a bit square has forced him to keep them sharp; and skipping grand pronouncements for small, finely rendered epiphanies allows the material to seem universal. Aziz Ansari, another young comedian who admires Seinfeld, told me, "You could stick him on some alien planet and he'd have the same brilliant, precise observations about how silly everything they do is."

Since Richard Pryor, at least, confession has been prized in stand-up, and this is as true today as ever. The biggest stand-up story of 2012 came this summer, when the comedian Tig Notaro took a Los Angeles stage and wrung laughs from a saga of personal misery that included the sudden death of her 65-year-old mother followed by a breast-cancer diagnosis. At Seinfeld's office, I asked him what he'd do, onstage, if he had a month like that, and I appended a "God forbid" to the question. "Thank you for 'God forbid,'" he said. "I love it. Hilarious. You have to say that." He clapped his hands with delight. "If I had a month like that, I'd do a whole bit about 'God forbid.'"

Seinfeld's father died in 1985, while battling numerous cancers, "probably ultimately of heart failure," Seinfeld says. (His mother, 98, lives in Florida.) He never told jokes about it, he said, because "it doesn't make me funny. If it makes you funny, that's what you talk about. That bit for Tig Notaro, it decided it wanted to be a bit. The bit is using her to get to the audience, and she's lucky enough to be in the right place at the right time. She's the second baseman in the double play: You've just got to be there to

35

catch it and throw it on. She's a genius for recognizing it and making the move." But he insisted that bloodletting was not requisite for greatness. "What does Don Rickles tell us about himself in his show? Probably not much. He's not pouring his guts out to you, but his craft is so amazing, his skill is so amazing, there's depth in that."

Beneath the surface, Seinfeld says, much of his act concerns "the pointlessness of life itself. I've got jokes where I'm saying your life sucks, your possessions are garbage, you're not important." Larry David, to whom Seinfeld remains close, told me, "Jerry doesn't get enough credit for his misanthropy—it's why we get along so well." In a new bit, Seinfeld likens a man to a balloon. At the outset of a romantic relationship, the balloon is buoyant and beautiful and "the woman holds on tight" for fear he'll fly away. Flash forward, and the balloon's doddering around, off in a corner somewhere, low to the floor, pathetically unable to "even lift up its own string." It's as elegantly crushing a joke about human decay and dashed hopes as has been told.

40   In conversation, Seinfeld describes an offstage "tendency toward depression," accompanied by a lifelong spiritual yearning. "There's always something missing," he said. He has dabbled in Zen Buddhism ("I love the word games, the koans"), Scientology ("I took a couple classes in 1976") and transcendental meditation. He still identifies as Jewish. "I was very flattered recently to hear about a Nazi rally in Florida where they took DVDs of the show, sprayed swastikas on them and threw them through the windows of a synagogue," he said. "That was nice."

He alluded to romantic dissatisfaction as something that used to depress him. On the sitcom, Seinfeld's life was a carousel of beautiful women. "Was that my actual life at the time?" he asks. "Probably." He remained single until he was 45, and in his act today he notes that he clearly had "some issues." After having kids, he told me, he realized "there was this whole other quadrant of my brain lying there dormant. Kids give you something. If it wasn't for my kids, I'm pretty much done with living. I could kill myself. Now there's something else to live for."

One Friday in early October, Seinfeld took a private plane from New York to Kansas City, Mo., told jokes onstage for 75 minutes, then flew to Milwaukee, where he was booked at the Riverside Theater the next night. On Saturday morning he wanted to see *Argo*, so he rented an entire theater at the local movie palace, the Oriental, and watched it with his opening act,

Mark Schiff, and his tour producer. "I liked it," Seinfeld said later on, over coffee at his hotel, "but the ending was a little Hollywood."

He had done two of his five planned performances in New York, one in Manhattan and one in the Bronx. Seinfeld thought they'd gone well, but he confided that the dates might double as a farewell tour of the city. "When Clark Kent turns into Superman, he needs a moment—a phone booth, a storage room!" Seinfeld said, describing the breathing room he relies on to get into show mode. "If I'm at home, I don't have the physical or mental space to don my costume. It's horrible. There's no closing of doors: I have little kids. As soon as you close the door someone's banging on it. And when I'm home, I love that. I don't want any personal space, I want them crawling all over me. But when I do this other thing? I can't tell you I enjoyed it that much."

When Seinfeld isn't on the road, he stays in. He likes *Mad Men*; his wife, Jessica, a cookbook author, likes *Homeland;* the whole family enjoys *The Voice.* Seinfeld does not watch any sitcom regularly, giving up on most after a few minutes. If he happens to catch a *Seinfeld* rerun, he'll watch until he sees himself, then change the channel. He regards his own ubiquity with nonchalance. After his performance at Brooklyn College, in November, when a fan asked him what programs he enjoys, Seinfeld replied: "I don't watch that much television. I *was* television."

Over coffee at his hotel in Milwaukee, Seinfeld talked about his home life, characterizing his children as the opposite of rich brats. His daughter grew upset, he said, upon receiving an iPhone 5 from Jessica, calling it a "mean-girl phone" and requesting something cheaper; his son Julian tells Jerry he's "spoiled" and implores him to sell his cars. The kids have inherited the comedy gene. "I'll say, 'O.K., it's time for dinner,'" Seinfeld said, "and they go, 'Oh, like I didn't already know that.' I say, 'That's me, you can't do me!'"

Comedians in Cars Getting Coffee is an experiment in "isolating the gene," Seinfeld says. "I went out the other night with three comics and a non-comedian, and it was amazing: these are all Jack Russells, and this is a Collie." He's proud of the Web show's finale, in which he and Michael Richards discussed the onstage tirade that Richards delivered in 2006, de-railing his career. Confronting black hecklers, Richards bellowed the word "nigger" seven times, an outpouring caught on camera. In the controversy that followed, it was hard not to see the rant as a moment of unfiltered ugliness, but Seinfeld says this interpretation reflects a category error. Speech on a stage, delivered in a performative context, is unique, he argues, and bits—even those that come off the cuff—are different from straight confessions. "It was a colossal *comedic* error," Seinfeld said. "He was angry, and it was the wrong choice, but it was a comedic attempt that failed. In our culture, we don't allow that, especially in the racial realm. But as a comedian, I know what happened, he knows what happened and every other comedian knows what happened. And all the black comics know it, and a lot of them felt bad about it, because they know it's rough to be judged that way in that context. You're leaping off a cliff and trying to land on the other side. It was just another missed leap."

When we'd drained our cups, Seinfeld stood and, stopping for some photos in the lobby, went to his room for a nap. I met him later in his dressing room at the Riverside, where he was about to take the stage for a 10 p.m. performance. His jacket hung from a rack in the corner, and he was on a couch in shirt sleeves, dipping pretzels into a Skippy jar, watching the Yankees game, feeling good. Schiff, his opener, was there, too. A car commercial featuring Shaquille O'Neal came on. "Look at this horrible sweater they put him in," Seinfeld said. "You can see how his knees are hurting him when he comes down those stairs." O'Neal called the car stylish. "'Stylish?'" Seinfeld repeated. "With your sweater vest on?" The game resumed, and Ichiro Suzuki, the lean Yankees outfielder, approached the plate. "This is the guy I relate to more than any athlete," Seinfeld said. "His precision, incredible precision. Look at his body type—he's made the most of what he has. He's the hardest guy to get out. He's fast. And he's old."

The camera panned across the dugout. "These are young guys, Mark," Seinfeld said. "How could they have these nerves of steel?"

"They do 180 games," Schiff said. "If you did 180 shows in a row, you'd have it."

50   "But this is the postseason, this one counts," Seinfeld said. "If a crowd doesn't laugh, O.K. But this guy gives up the homer, and 60,000 people are weeping!"

Schiff soon disappeared to warm up the audience. Seinfeld fell silent, chewing pretzels and watching the game. In 20 minutes, he was up. He stood, brushed the crumbs from his pants, slid into his jacket and made for the stage, ready to play some ball.

Analyze

1. In what year did Seinfeld start working in comedy clubs?
2. Weiner describes the time it takes for Seinfeld to develop a joke as "glacial." What does that mean? Point to evidence from the profile.
3. What was Seinfeld's major in college?

Explore

1. Go to *The New York Times* website and watch the short video about "The Pop-Tart Joke." What does the clip help you understand about the art and craft of revision? What is your writing and revision process?
2. The celebrity profile is a specific form of pop culture journalism. Take a closer look at the construction of this piece. How would you describe its structure? What is the governing organizational pattern that holds the beginning, middle, and end together?
3. Visit Jonah Weiner's website and read three or four more of his pieces. Work in two ways: Look for complexity within the pieces (patterns and puzzles worth thinking about); then look for complexity across the pieces (note any patterns in his prose that carry across more than one essay). Drawing upon direct evidence from the sources you read, make an analytical argument about Weiner's preoccupations as a thinker and a writer.

Katie Burgess
"How to Read a Poem"

Katie Burgess's sardonic short essay appeared in *The Rumpus*, an online pop culture journal, covering books, music, film, sex, politics, and even comics. Their mission states that what authors and editors have "in common is a passion for fantastic writing that's brave, passionate and true (and sometimes very, very funny)." Burgess makes fun of the clichés we hear about poetry, such as the abstractions, the readers' inability to understand poems, and the rejections poets receive. By making fun of poetry/poets, she is actually teaching us about them.

For thousands—or perhaps billions—of years, poetry has been done by poets. There was Shakespeare, Maya Angelou, and others. To write poetry, to catch the spontaneous overflow of powerful feelings or whatever, one must recollect in tranquility, which is pretty much achieved without a lot of effort. But someone needs to read poetry, to keep it from piling up. How exactly is this accomplished? As Robert Frost, a poet, once said, "A poem begins as a lump in the throat, but most of them are benign."

First, read with a pencil, or if that doesn't work, your eyes.

Look at the format of the poem. Are the lines continuous or broken up? How long are the lines? Are they arranged into dense blocks of text? Could you find a shorter, less crammed poem to read, for example one of those poems shaped like the thing they're about? A poem about oatmeal that is shaped like oatmeal, or a poem about shopping that is shaped like a shoe?

Next read the title. It may tell you exactly what the poem is about, eliminating difficulty. For instance, "Ode on a Grecian Urn" is about an urn that is Grecian, so that takes care of that.

5   To fully understand poetry, familiarize yourself with the elements of a poem, such as meter, which is 3.28 feet. Scan the poem, ideally in Photoshop, so you can correct the color balance and add lens flares, etc. Look for any images (from the French *images*). Images include trees, flowers, moonlight; in some cases all three. Circle each image and write "image" in the margin, so you won't forget them, as to make them memorable. There are similes and metaphors also (you learned about these in third grade and can disregard them). Some poems rhyme—these are what's known as *old-timey poems*. Many poems feature enjambment, which today can be treated with physical therapy.

It is important to nail down the type of poem you have: there are epic poems, limericks, and whatnot. There are villanelles, which are not villainous (only bad at reading social cues), and sestinas, which occur in the early afternoon, often after the midday meal. Most likely there are other types of poems out there, but we may never know for sure.

Now that you know the basics, delve deeper. An effective poem draws you into a conversation, like this:

You: You got anything going on this weekend?

Poem: Not much. Just finishing up my community service for that DUI.

10   Did you know that poetry is actually meant to be read aloud? The louder, the better. Try taking your poem to a coffee shop, library, synagogue, etc.,

and reading it at the top of your lungs. Right away people will take notice of your literary *savoir faire* (literally "I-don't-know-what").

One misconception people have about poetry is that it is written in "code," one they aren't smart enough to understand. In fact, if you do not comprehend a poem, you may return it. Send a SASE and copy of the defective poem to:

> Returns Center
> 1402 Innovation Park
> Suite 138
> Battle Creek, MI 49014

You should receive a new poem in six to eight weeks. The old poem will be delivered by barge to a South American landfill.

With top-notch poetry reading abilities, you will enjoy accompanying wealth and popularity. Forget hiding behind a lamp when your friends discuss "The Raven." Instead you may deduce from context clues, "That's about a scary bird!" Sit back and let the compliments roll in.

We're aware that many people who read poems go on to write them, but   15
with the right medication you can prevent this from happening.

Analyze

1. Is the objective of the piece "How to Read a Poem"?
2. How does Burgess immediately establish her tongue-in-cheek tone?
3. Find one term (of the many) that Burgess wrongly defines and define it correctly.

Explore

1. Can Burgess's tone be interpreted as condescending? Where might you find evidence that this piece is not "Poetry for Dummies" but a statement about those who do not "get" poetry?
2. The entire premise of the essay is that the speaker doesn't know what she's talking about and yet she's giving advice. Find and discuss an example of an "error" that you find amusing.
3. Are there any moments her facetious tone works against the objective of the piece? Find and discuss.

Jennifer L. Knox
"The Best Thanksgiving Ever"

American poet **Jennifer L. Knox** received her BA from the University of Iowa and her MFA in poetry writing from New York University. Her poetry has been widely anthologized—from *The Best American Poetry* (1997, 2003, 2006, and 2011) to *The Best American Erotic Poems: From 1800 to the Present*. Knox has written three books of poems: seek them out. Read them. Laugh heartily at the winking wisdom lurking in these irreverent poems.

This poem is a great example of Knox's work. The piece describes a surreal Thanksgiving meal (where the guests wind up naked) in a voice that oscillates between a kind of breathless enthusiasm and a comic deadpan.

After the meal, Sandy decided we should spice up charades
by slapping the loser's butt with a ping-pong paddle.
Whenever Ed got slapped, he farted because he was so nervous.
The ladies won, slapped all the men's butts, but then what to do?
"Take off your clothes!" I told Sean, who didn't seem like the kind
of guy who'd do such a thing—but he was, and he did. Then Jim
took off his clothes. Then John. And then the other Jim
who brought all the lovely bottles of wine. And finally Ed.
Deb came out of the bathroom and saw five big men naked in the kitchen.
They screamed, "Take off your clothes!" We all figured she would,
and she did. Then Sandy the Slapmaster, then me, then Tomoko
who kept her glasses on. We walked around the house naked,
talking about how it was to be naked with other naked people,
how none of the guys had boners, and how cold it was out in the garage.
Somebody found a big bottle of vodka. We made a no-hugging rule.
John kept trying to open the curtains and show the neighbors
what they were missing. Deb thought an orgy was imminent,
but since we'd all spent a lot of time in Iowa, I didn't think it would fly.
Jim passed out. Ed put a robe on. I passed out. We woke up
the next morning in t-shirts, ate bagels from Bagel Land, and said,
"We all got naked last night." That afternoon, on our way
to the Walt Whitman Mall, the ladies gave each other nicknames
ending with the word "Bitch." Deb was Stupid Bitch,

Sandy was Gentle Bitch, Tomoko was Fucking Bitch and I was Precious Bitch.
All the bitches agreed that slapping people's butts with a paddle
was something we needed to do every weekend, that this was the best
Thanksgiving ever, and that Ed had the biggest dick we'd ever seen.

Analyze

1. Is this a reliable persona? How does the speaker make you doubt or trust her?
2. What is the point of the expletives at the end of the poem? Are they only meant to shock the reader? Or do they help create the poem's universe?
3. What is the name of the mall they head over to the next day?

Explore

1. Instead of situating Knox's seemingly surreal poem in a poetic tradition, consider how it fits in a longer tradition of comedy sketches. Look up Bill Cosby's famous "Chocolate Cake for Breakfast" bit. How are the two texts similar? How are they different? What does the comparison help you see about the craft of comedy?
2. Knox's poem relies on the "carnivalesque," an inversion of conventions and expectations. This is not the typical Thanksgiving Dinner most Americans have come to believe is the norm. But has any family ever really had a "normal" Thanksgiving? Even the most "normal" families have quirky anecdotes and rituals. Although you might not be whacking each other with ping-pong paddles, you might have your own stories to tell. Write a richly detailed description of a holiday gone awry.

Erin Somers
"Modern Vice"

"Modern Vice" is a tongue-in-cheek, very short essay from **Erin Somers**, editor-in-chief of *Barnstorm Literary Magazine*. Somers is currently working on a novel-in-stories about competitive eating. "Modern Vice" first appeared in *The Rumpus*, an online pop culture journal, covering books, music, film, sex, politics, and even comics. Their mission states that what authors and editors have "in common is a passion for fantastic writing that's brave, passionate and true (and sometimes very, very funny)."

W e were tired of being good, so we decided to start sinning. We didn't want to kill anybody or steal anything, so we stuck to modern vice.

It went well at first. We told unfunny stories that came to no real point. Every third get-together, we neglected to bring beer. We put bumper stickers on our cars: "World's Best Uncle," "Elect Doritos," "This Is a Car." On public transit or in line at municipal buildings, we didn't bring anything to occupy ourselves—no headphones or books or Sudoku—opting instead to stare vaguely at the neck of the person in front of us.

When one of our kind objected to a particular modern vice, we shouted him down and called him a poltroon. Our ranks held, and we got more creative.

Here were some of our stances:

5
> *"Artisanal foods are bull."*
> *"9/11 was an inside job."*
> *"Sadness is a choice."*

We professed absolute indifference to the success of regionally popular sports teams. We forwarded email chain letters. We drank too many alcoholic beverages and had earnest online chats with old flames late at night.

In our cars, we listened only to the worst kinds of music: pre-Beatles pop and current Top 40. This we did at the highest volume, until no one wanted to ride with us. One of us—it was Steve—suggested we "put on Simon and

Garfunkel or something." He said, "I can't remember why we're doing this." We called Steve a poltroon and made him get out of the car.

Around then, we hit our stride. We did long, vociferous monologues [10] about politics and lost our train of thought. We said, "Hear me out: sharks and alligators should go extinct." We acted abominably at our siblings' graduation dinners without even meaning to. When someone asked us about our jobs we said "meh." We said "meh" a lot, actually.

One week, we made online dating profiles that were deliberately opaque and misleading. Under interests, we listed "fields of wheat" and "faxing." One of us, in an inspired move, even made her profile picture an illustration of a blue cube.

That was when Carol jumped ship. On her profile, she posted a picture of herself in a tank top doing a pouty face. "I don't know," she said. "I genuinely want to find someone." We said, "But that tank top! But that pouty face!" We called Carol a poltroon and sent her packing.

We talked to our clergymen and our Gods about our vices. Our clergymen said, "These aren't sins, these are just bad manners." They said, "I'm not even sure I . . . a blue cube?" We had to beg them for their disapproval. Meanwhile, our Gods said nothing.

We redoubled our efforts. We disparaged our fathers and our educational institutions. We continued to text all through the previews. At our monthly summit, we reversed our position, and insisted on eating only artisanal foods from there on out, and then we embarked on an aggressive supermarket grumbling campaign.

More of us began to falter. We started to catch each other engaging in [15] modern virtue. We discovered Daniel had donated money to NPR. "Why, Daniel?" we asked. "I wanted the free tote bag—" he said. We cried, "No! Don't say it." Daniel hung his head, "—to bring back produce from the farmers' market." Last we heard, Daniel got a job.

Eventually, we got lazy and lapsed. We slipped up and sent out a few thank you notes. Some of our parents got sick, and we moved home to help out. A woman dropped her wallet in the street, and one of us chased her down to give it back. "Thank you," she said. "You're a good person." "No," our guy insisted, deeply rattled. "Yes," she said. "You are."

After that, we disbanded; we were spooked. Our heads were no longer in the game. We were going through the motions. We said to each other, "You can't run from your true nature." We scraped the bumper stickers off our cars as best we could. We remembered to bring beer to parties. We stopped worrying so much about modern vice. We didn't think about it at all, in fact. Except at night, lying in bed alone, after a healthy, balanced dinner and a moderate amount of wine with people who, try as we might, we genuinely cared about.

Only then, in the dark, staring up at the ceiling, gripped with bowel-quivering self-doubt, did we confront what we knew to be the facts: that we were cowards, that we were weak, that we would never, deep down, be truly bad.

Analyze

1. How does Somers define "vice"?
2. Are the actions Somers (or her fictional persona) and her group commit "sins"?
3. What is a poltroon? Why would Somers use that word choice?

Explore

1. Some of the jabs seemed directed at contemporary life: artisanal foods, texting during movie previews. Why the non sequiturs, though, like the blue cube and the "world's greatest uncle" bumper sticker?
2. Look up Dante's Seven Deadly Vices, and note that they were written in the Middle Ages. In the new millennium, in what ways have we "contemporized" any of those vices?
3. What modern vice will you admit to? Do you consider your actions/behavior immoral? What's the line between a vice and a sin?

Nora Ephron
"A Few Words About Breasts"

Nora Ephron wrote for important glossy magazines like *New York*, *Cosmopolitan*, and *Esquire* and published four collections of essays on popular culture. She was better known, however, for her screenplays, such as *When Harry Met Sally*, *Sleepless in Seattle*, and *You've Got Mail*. Ephron once told an interviewer: "I've always written about my life. That's how I grew up. [My mother said] 'Take notes. Everything is copy.'" Later in the book, when you read Almond's essay "Funny Is the New Deep," you will think of Ephron's piece: self-deprecation *is* comedy.

I have to begin with a few words about androgyny. In grammar school, in the fifth and sixth grades, we were all tyrannized by a rigid set of rules that supposedly determined whether we were boys or girls. The episode in *Huckleberry Finn* where Huck is disguised as a girl and gives himself away by the way he threads a needle and catches a ball—that kind of thing. We learned that the way you sat, crossed your legs, held a cigarette, and looked at your nails—the way you did these things instinctively was absolute proof of your sex. Now obviously most children did not take this literally, but I did. I thought that just one slip, just one incorrect cross of my legs or flick of an imaginary cigarette ash would turn me from whatever I was into the other thing; that would be all it took, really. Even though I was outwardly a girl and had many of the trappings generally associated with girldom—a girl's name, for example, and dresses, my own telephone, an autograph book—I spent the early years of my adolescence absolutely certain that I might at any point gum it up. I did not feel at all like a girl. I was boyish. I was athletic, ambitious, outspoken, competitive, noisy, rambunctious. I had scabs on my knees and my socks slid into my loafers and I could throw a football. I wanted desperately not to be that way, not to be a mixture of both things, but instead just one, a girl, a definite indisputable girl. As soft and as pink as a nursery. And nothing would do that for me, I felt, but breasts.

I was about six months younger than everyone else in my class, and so for about six months after it began, for six months after my friends had begun to develop (that was the word we used, develop), I was not particularly worried. I would sit in the bathtub and look down at my breasts and know that any day now, any second now, they would start growing like everyone else's. They didn't. "I want to buy a bra," I said to my mother one night. "What for?" she said. My mother was really hateful about bras, and by the time my third sister had gotten to the point where she was ready to want one, my mother had worked the whole business into a comedy routine. "Why not use a Band-Aid instead?" she would say. It was a source of great pride to my mother that she had never even had to wear a brassiere until she had her fourth child, and then only because her gynecologist made her. It was incomprehensible to me that anyone could ever be proud of something like that. It was the 1950s, for God's sake. Jane Russell. Cashmere sweaters. Couldn't my mother see that? "I am too old to wear an undershirt." Screaming. Weeping. Shouting. "Then don't wear an undershirt," said my mother. "But I want to buy a bra." "What for?"

I suppose that for most girls, breasts, brassieres, that entire thing, has more trauma, more to do with the coming of adolescence, with becoming a woman, than anything else. Certainly more than getting your period, although that, too, was traumatic, symbolic.

But you could see breasts; they were there; they were visible. Whereas a girl could claim to have her period for months before she actually got it and nobody would ever know the difference. Which is exactly what I did. All you had to do was make a great fuss over having enough nickels for the Kotex machine and walk around clutching your stomach and moaning for three to five days a month about The Curse and you could convince anybody. There is a school of thought somewhere in the women's lib/women's mag/gynecology establishment that claims that menstrual cramps are purely psychological, and I lean toward it. Not that I didn't have them finally. Agonizing cramps, heating-pad cramps, go-down-to-the-school-nurse-and-lie-on-the-cot cramps.

5   But unlike any pain I had ever suffered, I adored the pain of cramps, welcomed it, wallowed in it, bragged about it. "I can't go. I have cramps." "I can't do that. I have cramps." And most of all, gigglingly, blushingly: "I can't swim. I have cramps." Nobody ever used the hard-core word. Menstruation. God, what an awful word. Never that. "I have cramps."

The morning I first got my period, I went into my mother's bedroom to tell her. And my mother, my utterly-hateful-about-bras mother, burst into tears. It was really a lovely moment, and I remember it so clearly not just because it was one of the two times I ever saw my mother cry on my account (the other was when I was caught being a six-year-old kleptomaniac), but also because the incident did not mean to me what it meant to her. Her little girl, her firstborn, had finally become a woman. That was what she was crying about. My reaction to the event, however, was that I might well be a woman in some scientific, textbook sense (and could at least stop faking every month and stop wasting all those nickels). But in another sense—in a visible sense—I was as androgynous and as liable to tip over into boyhood as ever.

I started with a 28 AA bra. I don't think they made them any smaller in those days, although I gather that now you can buy bras for five-year-olds that don't have any cups whatsoever in them; trainer bras they are called. My first brassiere came from Robinson's Department Store in Beverly Hills. I went there alone, shaking, positive they would look me over and smile and tell me to come back next year. An actual fitter took me into the dressing room and stood over me while I took off my blouse and tried the first one on. The little puffs stood out on my chest. "Lean over," said the fitter. (To this day, I am not sure what fitters in bra departments do except to tell you to lean over.) I leaned over, with the fleeting hope that my breasts would miraculously fall out of my body and into the puffs. Nothing.

"Don't worry about it," said my friend Libby some months later, when things had not improved. "You'll get them after you're married."

"What are you talking about?" I said.

"When you get married," Libby explained, "your husband will touch   10 your breasts and rub them and kiss them and they'll grow." That was the killer. Necking I could deal with. Intercourse I could deal with. But it had never crossed my mind that a man was going to touch my breasts, that breasts had something to do with all that, petting, my God, they never mentioned petting in my little sex manual about the fertilization of the ovum. I became dizzy. For I knew instantly—as naive as I had been only a moment before—that only part of what she was saying was true: the touching, rubbing, kissing part, not the growing part. And I knew that no one would ever want to marry me. I had no breasts. I would never have breasts.

My best friend in school was Diana Raskob. She lived a block from me in a house full of wonders. English muffins, for instance. The Raskobs were the first people in Beverly Hills to have English muffins for breakfast. They also had an apricot tree in the back, and a badminton court, and a subscription to *Seventeen* magazine, and hundreds of games, like Sorry and Parcheesi and Treasure Hunt and Anagrams. Diana and I spent three or four afternoons a week in their den reading and playing and eating.

Diana's mother's kitchen was full of the most colossal assortment of junk food I have ever been exposed to. My house was full of apples and peaches and milk and homemade chocolate-chip cookies—which were nice, and good for you, but-not-right-before-dinner-or-you'll-spoil-your-appetite. Diana's house had nothing in it that was good for you, and what's more, you could stuff it in right up until dinner and nobody cared. Bar-B-Q potato chips (they were the first in them, too), giant bottles of ginger ale, fresh popcorn with melted butter, hot fudge sauce on Baskin-Robbins Jamoca ice cream, powdered-sugar doughnuts from Van de Kamp's. Diana and I had been best friends since we were seven; we were about equally popular in school (which is to say, not particularly), we had about the same success with boys (extremely intermittent), and we looked much the same. Dark. Tall. Gangly.

It is September, just before school begins. I am eleven years old, about to enter the seventh grade, and Diana and I have not seen each other all summer. I have been to camp and she has been somewhere like Banff with her parents. We are meeting, as we often do, on the street midway between our two houses, and we will walk back to Diana's and eat junk and talk about what has happened to each of us that summer. I am walking down Walden Drive in my jeans and my father's shirt hanging out and my old red loafers with the socks falling into them and coming toward me is . . . I take a deep breath . . . a young woman. Diana. Her hair is curled and she has a waist and hips and a bust and she is wearing a straight skirt, an article of clothing I have been repeatedly told I will be unable to wear until I have the hips to hold it up. My jaw drops, and suddenly I am crying, crying hysterically, can't catch my breath sobbing. My best friend has betrayed me. She has gone ahead without me and done it. She has shaped up.

Here are some things I did to help: Bought a Mark Eden Bust Developer. Slept on my back for four years. Splashed cold water on them every night because some French actress said in *Life* magazine that that was what she did for her perfect bustline.

15   Ultimately, I resigned myself to a bad toss and began to wear padded bras. I think about them now, think about all those years in high school that I went around in them, my three padded bras, every single one of them with different-sized breasts. Each time I changed bras I changed sizes: one week nice perky but not too obtrusive breasts, the next medium-sized slightly pointy ones, the next week knockers, true knockers; all the time, whatever size I was, carrying around this rubberized appendage on my chest that occasionally crashed into a wall and was poked inward and had to be poked outward—I think about all that and wonder how anyone kept a straight face through it. My parents, who normally had no restraints about needling me—why did they say nothing as they watched my chest go up and down? My friends, who would periodically inspect my breasts for signs of growth and reassure me—why didn't they at least counsel consistency?

And the bathing suits. I die when I think about the bathing suits. That was the era when you could lay an uninhabited bathing suit on the beach and someone would make a pass at it. I would put one on, an absurd swimsuit with its enormous bust built into it, the bones from the suit stabbing me in the rib cage and leaving little red welts on my body, and there I would be, my chest plunging straight downward absolutely vertically from my collarbone to the top of my suit and then suddenly, wham, out came all that padding and material and wiring absolutely horizontally.

Buster Klepper was the first boy who ever touched them. He was my boyfriend my senior year of high school. There is a picture of him in my high-school yearbook that makes him look quite attractive in a Jewish, horn-rimmed-glasses sort of way, but the picture does not show the pimples, which were airbrushed out, or the dumbness. Well, that isn't really fair. He wasn't dumb. He just wasn't terribly bright. His mother refused to accept it, refused to accept the relentlessly average report cards, refused to deal with her son's inevitable destiny in some junior college or other. "He was tested," she would say to me, apropos of nothing, "and it came out a hundred and forty-five. That's near-genius." Had the word "underachiever" been coined, she probably would have lobbed that one at me, too. Anyway, Buster was really very sweet—which is, I know, damning with faint praise, but there it is. I was the editor of the front page of the high-school newspaper and he was editor of the back page; we had to work together, side by side, in the print shop, and that was how it started. On our first date, we went to see *April Love*, starring Pat Boone. Then we started going together. Buster had a green coupe, a 1950 Ford with an engine he had hand-chromed until it shone, dazzled, reflected the image of anyone who looked into it, anyone usually being Buster polishing it or the gas-station attendants he constantly asked to check the oil in order for them to be overwhelmed by the sparkle on the valves. The car also had a boot stretched over the back seat for reasons I never understood; hanging from the rearview mirror, as was the custom, was a pair of angora dice. A previous girlfriend named Solange, who was famous throughout Beverly Hills High School for having no pigment in her right eyebrow, had knitted them for him. Buster and I would ride around town, the two of us seated to the left of the steering wheel. I would shift gears. It was nice.

There was necking. Terrific necking. First in the car, overlooking Los Angeles from what is now the Trousdale Estates. Then on the bed of his parents' cabana at Ocean House. Incredibly wonderful, frustrating necking, I loved it, really, but no further than necking, please don't, please, because there I was absolutely terrified of the general implications of going-a-step-further with a near-dummy and also terrified of his finding out there was next to nothing there (which he knew, of course; he wasn't that dumb). I broke up with him at one point. I think we were apart for about two weeks. At the end of that time, I drove down to see a friend at a boarding school in Palos Verdes Estates and a disc jockey played "April Love" on the radio four times during the trip. I took it as a sign. I drove straight back to Griffith Park to a golf tournament Buster was playing in (he was the sixth-seeded teenage golf player in southern California) and presented myself back to him on the green of the eighteenth hole. It was all very dramatic. That night we went to a drive-in and I let him get his hand under my protuberances and onto my breasts. He really didn't seem to mind at all.

20   *"Do you want to marry my son?" the woman asked me.*
"Yes," I said.
I was nineteen years old, a virgin, going with this woman's son, this big strange woman who was married to a Lutheran minister in New Hampshire and pretended she was gentile and had this son, by her first husband, this total fool of a son who ran the hero-sandwich concession at Harvard Business School and whom for one moment one December in New Hampshire I said—as much out of politeness as anything else—that I wanted to marry.
"Fine," she said. "Now, here's what you do. Always make sure you're on top of him so you won't seem so small. My bust is very large, you see, so I always lie on my back to make it look smaller, but you'll have to be on top most of the time."
I nodded. "Thank you," I said.
25   *"I have a book for you to read," she went on. "Take it with you when you leave. Keep it." She went to the bookshelf, found it, and gave it to me.*
It was a book on frigidity.
"Thank you," I said.

That is a true story. Everything in this article is a true story, but I feel I have to point out that that story in particular is true. It happened on December 30, 1960. I think about it often. When it first happened, I naturally assumed that the woman's son, my boyfriend, was responsible. I invented a scenario where he had had a little heart-to-heart with his mother and had confessed that his only objection to me was that my breasts were small; his mother then took it upon herself to help out. Now I think I was wrong about the incident. The mother was acting on her own, I think: That was her way of being cruel and competitive under the guise of being helpful and maternal. You have small breasts, she was saying; therefore you will never make him as happy as I have. Or you have small breasts; therefore you will doubtless have sexual problems. Or you have small breasts; therefore you are less woman than I am. She was, as it happens, only the first of what seems to me to be a never-ending string of women who have made competitive remarks to me about breast size. "I would love to wear a dress like that," my friend Emily says to me, "but my bust is too big." Like that. Why do women say these things to me? Do I attract these remarks the way other women attract married men or alcoholics or homosexuals? This summer, for example. I am at a party in East Hampton and I am introduced to a woman from Washington. She is a minor celebrity, very pretty and Southern and blond and outspoken, and I am flattered because she has read something I have written. We are talking animatedly, we have been talking no more than five minutes, when a man comes up to join us. "Look at the two of us," the woman says to the man, indicating me and her. "The two of us together couldn't fill an A cup." Why does she say that? It isn't even true, dammit, so why? Is she even more addled than I am on this subject? Does she honestly believe there is something wrong with her size breasts, which, it seems to me, now that I look hard at them, are just right? Do I unconsciously bring out competitiveness in women? In that form? What did I do to deserve it?

As for men.

There were men who minded and let me know that they minded. There were men who did not mind. In any case, I always minded.

And even now, now that I have been countlessly reassured that my figure 30 is a good one, now that I am grown-up enough to understand that most of my feelings have very little to do with the reality of my shape, I am nonetheless obsessed by breasts. I cannot help it. I grew up in the terrible fifties— with rigid stereotypical sex roles, the insistence that men be men and dress like men and women be women and dress like women, the intolerance of androgyny—and I cannot shake it, cannot shake my feelings of inadequacy. Well, that time is gone, right? All those exaggerated examples of breast worship are gone, right? Those women were freaks, right? I know all that. And yet here I am, stuck with the psychological remains of it all, stuck with my own peculiar version of breast worship. You probably think I am crazy to go on like this: Here I have set out to write a confession that is meant to hit you with the shock of recognition, and instead you are sitting there thinking I am thoroughly warped. Well, what can I tell you? If I had had them, I would have been a completely different person. I honestly believe that.

After I went into therapy, a process that made it possible for me to tell total strangers at cocktail parties that breasts were the hang-up of my life, I was often told that I was insane to have been bothered by my condition. I was also frequently told, by close friends, that I was extremely boring on the subject. And my girlfriends, the ones with nice big breasts, would go on endlessly about how their lives had been far more miserable than mine. Their bra straps were snapped in class. They couldn't sleep on their stomachs. They were stared at whenever the word "mountain" cropped up in geography. And *Evangeline*, good God what they went through every time someone had to stand up and recite the Prologue to Longfellow's *Evangeline*: ". . . stand like druids of eld . . ./With beards that rest on their bosoms." It was much worse for them, they tell me. They had a terrible time of it, they assure me. I don't know how lucky I was, they say.

I have thought about their remarks, tried to put myself in their place, considered their point of view. I think they are full of shit.

Analyze

1. In early adolescence Ephron self-identifies in what ways? How much is she willing to fake?
2. How does Ephron portray her mother?
3. How does Ephron try to make her breasts grow? Have you heard of any similar urban myths?

Explore

1. Look at Ephron's tone, the voice she develops in the piece. Is she being modest or feigning modesty?
2. Note Ephron's use of hyperbole, starting from the title itself. The piece is 3,600 words, not a few! How do her exaggerations "work" in the piece?
3. This article ran in *Esquire* forty years ago. In what ways are any of the gender issues and ideas Ephron presents still part of our culture? Has any aspect of body consciousness changed (for better or for worse)?

Will Treece
From *The Pan-Arabia Enquirer*

Will Treece is a writer and Global Academic Fellow at New York University Abu Dhabi. Treece submitted his draft of this piece to *The Pan-Arabia Enquirer*, a publication known for "spreading the hummous of satire over the flatbread of news." His piece turns on a single but complex joke. He mocks a cultural tendency toward hyperbole he noticed in the UAE, where things tend to be called "the biggest," "the best," "the first."

[Original Version]

Abu Dhabi Named #1 in List of Cities Ranked Alphabetically

In a recent global poll, Abu Dhabi took first place in a list of cities ranked alphabetically.

When asked to rank over three hundred major cities and world capitals in alphabetical order, respondents consistently awarded Abu Dhabi top honors.

"It is a great honor that so many people ranked our city number one in the world, alphabetically," said longtime resident Aaron Ackerman.

"This shows that Abu Dhabi is really becoming one of the world's top cities, when ranked by ordered position in the English alphabet."

Over eighteen thousand people were surveyed in 108 different   5
countries.

However, some felt the poll's methodology might have been flawed.

"Any list that doesn't include Aberdeen and Abidjan is utter rubbish," said Scottish-Ivorian businessman Stephane MacDonald.

[Edited Version]

Abu Dhabi Voted Number One in List of Capital Cities Ranked Alphabetically

September 18, 2013—ABU DHABI: In a recent global poll, Abu Dhabi took first place in a list of capital cities ranked alphabetically.

According to researchers, when asked to rank over three hundred major capitals in alphabetical order, respondents consistently awarded the UAE capital top honors.

10   "It is a huge testament to our achievements that so many people ranked our city number one in the world, alphabetically, when using the English alphabet," said Ahmed Bannersmann, head of the Abu Dhabi Number Ones committee, adding that those who voted for Abuja were "clearly idiots."

Analyze

1. We include both versions of Treece's article here: the edited version that ran online as well as his longer original version. Compare the two. What did the *PAE* editor change and why?
2. Which version do you find funnier? Make your case.
3. What is the cultural stereotype threading through Treece's brief piece?

Explore

1. The *PAE* is an online venue. How does the edited version imagine an online reader?
2. The *PAE* is the "premier source for made up news" in the Middle East. It is the equivalent of *The Onion* in the MENASA region. With headlines like "man lost in Dubai mall describes ordeal," the *PAE* mocks the news while satirizing the region's culture—a risky, provocative tactic in a place where mocking the powers that be can land you in prison for "culture crimes." Is there a risky idea at the heart of Treece's seemingly innocuous joke?
3. Later in this book you will find an essay by Christopher Hitchens that is critical of satirical news shows. How might Treece's brief text serve as evidence for you to critique or refine Hitchens's ideas?

Brian Logan
"Funny Foreigners: How Overseas Comics Are Storming Edinburgh"

Brian Logan is an arts writer and comedy critic for *The Guardian*. This review of the 2010 Edinburgh Festival focuses on the challenges faced by international comedians working across languages and cultural barriers in order to "be funny." This piece works on a number of levels, inviting consideration of ELL and ESL issues, cultural stereotypes, and ethnic humor, as non-native-English speakers confront the work of being funny across cultures.

Comedy in a foreign language is a tricky business. Take this Italian joke. *"Perché gli inglesi portano i gemelli?"* it begins. Even if you know that this translates as, "Why do the English wear shirt cuffs?" you still might not understand the punchline: *"Perché hanno paura che i francesi gli entrino nella Manica!"* This means: "For fear that the French enter the Channel!" It's a play on words: the Italian for English Channel is "sleeve." But by the time you've explained that, well, the moment has passed.

And yet dozens of standups from around the world are in Edinburgh this year, here to perform comedy in a language—English—that is not their own. In this most verbal of artforms, one that's intimately bound up with cultural references, identity and wordplay, can they possibly succeed? And if so, how?

Some of these comedians are based in the UK, and have only ever performed in English; some started as standups in Sweden, Holland or Norway and are now hoping to find a bigger market. Not that money is the only reason to perform in English. Acts such as Hans Teeuwen, from the Netherlands, and Sweden's Magnus Betnér are superstars back home, now seeking to escape fame and hone their skills in a more competitive environment. Coming to the UK lets them wring more life out of material that feels overfamiliar in their own country.

Others were inspired to take up standup only after coming to the UK. The Italian comic Giacinto Palmieri has never actually performed in Italian. "My niche is that not only can I show British culture in an unfamiliar way, but I can do the same with the language. I can show how absurd English idioms sound to the Italian ear." These include "Bob's your uncle," which apparently derives from the nepotistic practices of 1880s PM Robert Cecil. Palmieri proposes an Italian alternative: "Silvio fucked your daughter." He also reveals that the Italian version of "Have your cake and eat it" is: "Have your wife drunk and the bottle still full."

5   In Italy, says Palmieri, the culture is visual, the comedy more physical—think Roberto Benigni—and deadpan humour is known as *umorismo inglese*. To Palmieri, the English language is uniquely suitable for verbal humour. "It's very idiomatic, it contains a lot of polysemantic or homophonic words," he tells me (in his second language!), "which you can play with a lot. The same things that make English difficult to learn are what make it good for comedy."

The comedian Stewart Lee once blamed the German reputation for humourlessness on that language's inflexible sentence structures, which preclude the twist-in-the-tail techniques on which English-language comedy depends. Fortunately, German comic Henning Wehn has never had to translate an existing act into English—like Palmieri, he took up comedy after moving to the UK. The only difficulty he has now is with going off-script. "If I want to improvise, or go off on a tangent, I quickly come to my limit. I'll make grammatical mistakes, or can't think of the right words."

But not being a native English speaker can prove an advantage. Teeuwen says non-native speakers do comedy "the same way Sinatra sings. He's very conscious of every word he says, and of the way he places and phrases them. He grooves, but a bit more consciously than most."

Unlike Wehn, who plays up to German stereotypes, Teeuwen's nationality is not central to his act. "My material can be a bit weird," he says. Quite: we're talking vaudeville routines about talking rabbits, and songs about Nostradamus played on the bongos. "Having a Dutch accent reinforces the atmosphere of alienation."

Teeuwen is a household name in the Netherlands, and started performing in the UK only three years ago. Initially, he translated his Dutch routines into English, but "didn't use a dictionary. I just thought, 'The vocabulary I have, that's what I'm going to use.' The best comedians I know—like Richard Pryor—their vocabulary wasn't more than 500 words. Comedy should be simple and direct."

10   Betnér speaks fluent English and his comedy (mainly political and social commentary) is not reliant on wordplay. He expected gigging in English to be plain sailing, but found the difference between talking and performing

in English enormous. "If I'm talking to you and there's something I don't know how to say, I just explain it. Or take my time and think about the words. But on stage, if your rhythm is off because you're thinking about the next word, you look like you don't know what you're doing."

This transition isn't always difficult, though. Norwegian comic Dag Soras only recently began gigging in the UK, but "once I started translating my Norwegian material into English," he says, "I found new angles to explore. I found myself having comedy thoughts and punchlines in English, which I would struggle to translate into Norwegian." Teeuwen found this, too: he now has whole routines that wouldn't work in Dutch. One involves an Obama-style speech, whose soaring rhetoric, says Teeuwen, doesn't work in his own tongue. "Or if you do something in a Shakespearean manner, or if you reference American movies or gangster talk or hip-hop—those all work much better in English."

Soras, like Betnér, doesn't use his foreignness as a selling point. "My nationality is not interesting," he says. Palmieri, meanwhile, dreams of the day his identity can be as easily overlooked. "I don't want to get stuck all my comedy life doing Italian things," he says. For now, he makes a living joking about his Italianness, but feels "stereotypes are a bit of a cage. I'm a cosmopolitan kind of person, and I believe we're all free to determine who we are."

Palmieri is trying to square this "paradox," by performing in character as an English comedian who pretends to be Italian. His audiences do seem to be embracing the double-bluff. As Teeuwen's success proves, UK crowds aren't scared of the outlandish and the non-dom. Foreignness may even be an advantage. "Listening to an accent," says Wehn, "is like going on holiday without having to shell out for it."

Some audiences set such high standards for exoticism, indeed, that even the resolutely foreign Wehn has left them feeling short-changed. "Even now," says Wehn, "a lot of people don't think I'm German. I'll do an hour, and at the end some idiot will come up, saying, 'You're not really from Germany, are ya?'" Wehn blames—what else?—English-language comedy. "I think," he says, "it's because I don't sound like the Germans on *'Allo 'Allo!*"

Analyze

1. What is *"umorismo inglese"*?
2. How is a non-native-English speaker performing comedy similar to Frank Sinatra's singing?

3. How are cultural stereotypes "a bit of a cage" for these comics? What is the "paradox" of cultural stereotypes that emerges in this article?

Explore

1. What's the line between comedy that illuminates cultural stereotypes (and thus critiques them) and ethnic humor that merely reinforces them (and thus makes racism seem OK)?

2. Cultural stereotypes have long been the stuff of comedy, particularly in the United States. But when these stereotypes move from the comic stage and bleed out into the broader culture, they risk becoming merely offensive. Case in point? Ashton Kutcher dons brown face for a Pop Chips commercial. It's worth a Google. Then check out the vlog "The Truth with Hasan Minhaj" and find his ramped-up critique of Ashton Kutcher's brown-face impersonation of a Bollywood producer.

3. The "blogosphere" is a rich and robust place for ongoing debates about ethnic humor and cultural stereotypes. While you might be over-whelmed by bad comedy there, you will also see excellent pop cultural criticism that sets out to make sense of ethnic humor. Spend a few moments looking for "good" sources. Choose your top three and present them to your classmates.

4. How does ethnic humor reveal the tensions of social difference within a culture? Find and listen to NPR's Terry Gross interview with comedian Hari Kondabolu "Explaining the Joke IS the Joke" to deepen your thinking.

5. Palmieri describes the way he makes jokes about his Italianness but does not want to be trapped by that identity. Instead he identifies as "a cosmopolitan kind of person." What does he mean? How would you define the tricky buzzword "cosmopolitanism"?

Scott Stein
"Garghibition"

Scott Stein is a professor at Drexel University. He runs *When Falls the Coliseum*, a cultural commentary site, and writes and teaches humor. "Garghibition" is a satire about a new pill that makes people think they are three inches taller than they are, and the societal ramifications of this new drug. The piece is fantasy/sci-fi/satire and was originally published in *Liberty*, a journal of culture and politics written from a classical liberal point of view.

The pill didn't make one taller. That wasn't the issue. It wasn't a case of medical science tampering with God's design, or biological engineering in an effort to transform the human race into a different, better species—a taller one. No, all the oblong, indigo Gargantuanx did, miracle of miracles, was create the illusion in the mind of the consumer that he was taller. That's all.

The pill didn't take immediate effect. For about ten minutes you felt nothing. Then you were taller. That is, you believed you were. The drug convinced its user, whatever his height, that he was three inches taller. It was a new technology, and its power was limited, though perfect in its simplicity and specificity. Three inches was all it added. Gargantuanx could not alter the physical world—boxes of pasta on supermarket shelves which were out of reach before taking the pill did not get any closer after a dose. But under its influence one was certain that the shelf of pasta was three inches higher than it had been, so the illusion that one was three inches taller was intact. Other people remained the same height, of course. Gargantuanx was not sophisticated enough to create visual illusions, and shrink everyone to make the user seem taller by comparison. So it did the next best thing. It convinced the user that everyone else had also grown three inches. Insurance companies refused to cover the new drug, and retailers charged ten dollars a pill to those willing to pay anything for a couple of hours of believing, despite all evidence to the contrary, that one was three inches taller. Gargantuanx aggressively suspended disbelief. If a basketball rim seemed no closer to a consumer of the pill, he had to believe it wasn't regulation height—"Off by three inches," he would say. When a tape measure was brought out and the hoop was measured from the ground up, to demonstrate that it was indeed the proper ten feet high, the Gargantuanxer had no choice but to believe that the tape measure was incorrect. Errors in production were made all the time—why should tape measure manufacturers be exempt? They were busy trying to meet deadlines, and it was certainly reasonable, if disappointing, that a few of their tape measures might be missing an inch or three. If it was pointed out that without exception all the numbers were there on the tape measure, the Gargantuanxer suspected that the size of each inch on the device was mistaken, so that an indicated total of ten feet was in actuality ten feet and three inches. It didn't help to bring twenty tape measures, or fifty, or a thousand. If shown a million the Gargantuanxer would give no ground. He was forced to believe in a massive conspiracy among manufacturers of tape measures—and anyone who defended them—to convince people that they were three inches shorter than in fact they were.

What was unsettling to those not lured by Gargantuanx's promise of three inches and the accompanying boost in self-esteem, was that taking the drug was a voluntary act. This wasn't a science fiction movie or a clever book about alien or government control. People chose the pill, and consumed it, with full knowledge of its effects. They wanted to be taller. Failing that, they wanted to think they were taller. Whatever their motives, they knew going in that the pill would create the illusion of additional height. The implications of a drug so powerful it could fool those who knew it was going to fool them worried lawmakers and concerned citizens. What would be next? A pill to make one think he was a spy or assassin for another country? Clearly, legislation was required. Short people were divided. Speaking to the panel investigating Gargantuanx, the president of the Undersized Persons Society (UPS) made a passionate plea for a permanent and unequivocal ban on "this bane to the existence of undersized persons." For years undersized persons had been fighting for equality. They had only recently won a major court battle, resulting in a Federal mandate requiring shoe retailers to carry larger supplies of women's sizes 4 and 5 and men's size 6. Plans were already under way to sue the motion picture academy for the under-representation of undersized persons as leading men and women in American film, and the theater owners were on the list too, for deliberately designing audience seats so that anyone under the height of five foot six inches would be unable to see the screen when an overheighted person sat in the row in front of them. With all the progress made by undersized persons in this country, it was embarrassing, no, humiliating, that the government allowed this pill to be sold as a legitimate medication. Was the government implying that undersizeness was an ailment that required a cure?

After a quick sidebar discussion with her public relations advisor, the presiding senator assured the president of UPS that of course undersizeness was not an ailment, and she would personally sponsor legislation to ban Gargantuanx forever from this land of purple mountains majesty. This created an uproar. Other short people demanded to be heard. If they wanted to be deluded into thinking they were three inches taller, what business was this of the government, or anyone else? Gargantuanx was a victimless drug, if ever there was one. The proposed legislation was the subject of serious discussion on television and at water coolers around the nation. Small people, pretty much every man under five foot eight and woman under five foot five, couldn't come to an agreement—Gargantuanx was too popular, and the inflated sense of non-earned pride it provided was too tempting. Tall people, even those of average height who dabbled in Gargantuanx, by and large stayed out of the debate. Short—that is, undersized—people dominated the discussion with a passion all out of proportion to their own dimensions. That the nation was divided was indisputable. But UPS had powerful friends and deep pockets, and the legislation passed by a considerable margin, making it a felony—a Federal offense—to even possess Gargantuanx on American soil. UPS claimed a victory for all undersize-kind, but many people were distraught at the news. Not only was this an assault on the principle of self-determination and individual freedom, but many of them wanted desperately to be able to think they were taller. A black market developed overnight. The people wanted their Gargantuanx, and they were willing to pay for it. Pills went for twenty dollars, sometimes thirty, apiece. Rival dealers used intimidation and even murder to corner the local market. It wasn't long before gangs had infiltrated the schools, hooking kids who were the only ones, after all, who didn't need the drug, since greater height was to them still attainable. But it nonetheless became fashionable to get hopped up on double and triple doses of Garg and go to the mall, where innocent clerks struggled in vain to convince strung-out shoppers that the jeans they were trying on were just too long and that the label was not mistaken.

The violence associated with the illegality and lack of regulation of   5 Gargantuanx led some to call for decriminalization, but the UPS lobby would not give in. Instead they declared a war on Garg, and local governments set up task forces to sweep the malls and raid the schools. If there were kids out there trying to be taller by any but the means provided by nature, they were going to suffer the consequences. Lockers were searched, athletes were banned, bus drivers were randomly tested, short parents were turned in by their short children, the very fabric of our society began to unravel. The corruption and terrorism of Al Capone's Chicago paled next to the nationwide frenzy caused by Garghibition.

Finally, even the zealots from UPS had to relent. If they couldn't squash Gargantuanx outright, then they would control it. Garg was legalized, and regulated, and taxed. Strict guidelines were developed for its production and distribution and the government banned forever any changes to its formula, to prevent an escalation in offending the sensibilities of certain influential short people. They had, they thought, won a limited victory.

But I'm a short person as well—I hate the undersize euphemism—and I've been in my lab for nine straight weeks now. After four failed tests of my new pill, Tremendocyclin, I finally have success. Oh, sweet bliss of greater height. I am five inches taller than I was just a moment ago. And nothing you say or do will convince me otherwise.

Analyze

1. After taking Gargantuanx, consumers wouldn't even trust the accuracy of what device?
2. Why did the "Undersized Persons Society" want a ban on Gargantuanx?
3. Once the ban is passed and the drug is legislated, how does society react?

Explore

1. If we agree that "Garghibition" is a satire, what is it lampooning? Our culture's obsession with height and virility for men? The idea that perception is more valuable than reality? How our culture reacts when people try to change?
2. In fantasy fiction the writer must quickly establish a premise for which we will suspend our disbelief. Does Stein succeed in doing so? Why or why not? Do the fantastical facts that follow parse with the fictional world Stein has created?
3. How does the surprise of the narrator being (1) short and (2) a drug developer affect the payoff or the takeaway of the story?

Michael Martone
"On Anesthesia"

Michael Martone is a fiction writer, but categorizing him or labeling him any further is a challenge. Martone butts his work against our preconceptions about what literature is "supposed" to do, writing about writing and in various and unique frameworks. He has imagined the secret thoughts of Dan Quayle, written from the point of view of James Dean's high-school drama coach, written a surreal guidebook to Indiana, and completed a book-length series of contributors' notes entitled "Michael Martone."

Now that we've given you some context on Martone, let us give you some context on Dan Quayle, as the story below is written from his fictionalized stream of consciousness. Quayle was the 44th Vice President of the United States, serving with President George H. W. Bush (1989–1993). Political allegiances aside, no one can deny that Quayle was frequently and harshly ridiculed by the media, labeled as incompetent and even stupid. He spoke erroneously in public over and over, about topics as basic as the planet Mars and as politically charged as the Holocaust and the United Negro College Fund's slogan. He might be most infamous for what was probably his smallest mistake; he changed a 12-year-old student's correct spelling of "potato" to "potatoe."

The naval officer with the football clutches it like, well, a football, tucked under one arm and the other arm wrapped over the top. We call it the football, but it's not a football. It's a silver briefcase stuffed with all the secret codes for launching the missiles and the bombers. He slumps in his chair at the far end of the Oval Office. Secret Service agents, packed into the couches, read old *People* magazines. The lenses of their dark glasses lighten automatically the longer they're inside. They've let me sit at the President's desk in the big leather swivel chair. Now my back is to them. I'm looking out at the Rose Garden where the white buckets weighted down with bricks protect the plants. On the bureau beneath the window, the President has a ton of pictures. His kids and grandkids. His brothers and sisters. Shots of Christmases. The house in Maine. His wife. The dog. I don't see me. Little elephants are scattered among the frames. Carved in stone or wood or cast in polished metal, they all head the same direction, their trunks raised and trumpeting.

Every few minutes I like to turn dramatically around to face the room. Nothing happens. The agents flip through the magazines licking their thumbs to turn the pages. Other aides huddle by the door fingering each other's label pins. The naval officer with the football has a rag out now. He breathes on the briefcase then rubs the fog off the shiny surface.

I get to be President for about twenty minutes more. The real President is under anesthesia at Bethesda. In the big cabinet room the chiefs of staff are watching the operation on a closed circuit hook-up. A stenographer is taking down everything that's being said. They asked me if I wanted to watch with them, but I get squeamish at the sight of blood. I'd wait in the Oval Office I told them. An amendment to the Constitution lets me be Acting President in such situations, but there is nothing for me to do. We've been ignoring the press. No sense mentioning it.

I've been doodling on White House stationery I found in the desk drawer. I always draw parallel zig-zagging lines, connecting them up to form steps. When I am finished I can look at the steps the regular way and then I can make myself see them upside down, flipping back and forth in my head from one way to the other. I arrange the pens on the desk blotter after I've used them as if I am going to give them out as souvenirs.

5   They let me make a few phone calls. I called a supporter in Phoenix but I forgot about the time difference and I woke him up. What could I say? I'm sorry. I left a message for the Governor of Indiana, a Democrat I play golf with some times. His father, when he was a senator, wrote the amendment that let me be President for a few hours. "Just tell him the President called," I said. I wanted to rub it in. I called Janine, my high school girl friend, who is an actuary in Chicago. I don't know her politics. "Guess where I am," I said. She couldn't guess. When I traveled commercial I used to call her at her home from O'Hare on a stopover. I let her know I was a Congressman, a Senator. I wanted her to know I was on my way someplace.

"Try," I said. "From where I sit I can see the Washington Memorial." That wasn't true. I was looking at the Commander with the football. She told me she was running late, that her eggs were getting cold. Janine had a view of the lake, I imagined, her building near a beach on the North Shore.

"I've got to go," I said, "this is on the taxpayer's nickel." I wanted everyone to hear me. The men in the room, I could see, were trying hard not to look like they were listening.

I was anesthetized once. This was a few years ago. All four of my wisdom teeth were impacted. Before they put me under, I had to read a form and sign it. It said I understood all the things that could go wrong. The procedure was usually performed on patients much younger. Nerves could get cut. Dry sockets. Shattered jaw bones. I don't like blood or guts, so I signed it quickly to stop thinking about the possibilities. I signed, sitting in the chair while the oral surgeon held up the syringe, squirting out drops of the drug from the gleaming needle.

"We are going to put you into twilight sleep," the doctor told me. "Not really sleep. Not deep enough to dream. You'll just be very relaxed," he said slapping at my arm to find a vein. "If we weren't going to work in your mouth, you'd tell us all your secrets. You'd just let go."

I was out like a light. It felt like sleeping in a seat on an airplane. I re-   10
member thinking I wish I knew what my secrets were, what I really thought. But the drug that made me tell the truth also put me into twilight sleep so that I never really knew what I said. I know I was talking, telling them everything. I kept rocking along through the dark night. Then, the doctor and the nurses were looking at me strangely. Had they heard me say something, the muttering I had been making becoming clear when they swabbed up the blood or turned away to pick up another instrument? Did they stop and listen?

Tell me what I said, I said to them. But it came out nonsense. I could just begin to feel my face again, feel it swelling up. My lips and tongue had vanished.

"Who stole my tongue?" I said

"Is someone coming to drive you home?" they asked as they walked me into another room.

"Ma mamph," I said. I could hear again. I was vaguely aware of other bodies on cots scattered around the room. The doctor and the nurse eased me onto my own cot. They stuck a sheet of instructions in my hands and slid a small envelope into my shirt pocket.

"Those are your teeth," they said. I had wanted to do something with the   15
molars, polish them up and have them made into jewelry or shellac them for a paperweight. But when I opened the envelope later all that spilled out were splinters of bone, crumbs of teeth. They had to be chiseled out the doctor told me when I called. "They didn't want to budge," he said.

I looked at the pile of fragments on my desk. Here and there I could see a smooth contour of a tooth, the tip of a root, the sliced off crown like a flat bottomed cloud. I pushed the parts around on the desk. Most were ragged, caked with clotted blood and bits of browning tissue. The pulpy nerves crumpled to dust. I poked the pieces into four piles, the bits making a scratching sound as they slid across the stationery they were on. I had drawn stairs on the paper, and I climbed them up and down, up and down.

Maybe it was the painkiller I was still taking. I sat there staring at the piles of dust thinking: These are all my secrets reduced to ashes.

"It's the drugs," Marilyn said when I told her how sad my wisdom teeth had made me. I tried to explain that the operation had pried something out of me. I couldn't begin to explain it. "It's the drugs talking," she said.

The kitchen timer the Secret Service set bings on the end table, and they all stand up from the couches. They toss the *People* magazines in a heap on the coffee table. I turn back to the window and see the navy officer sprinting for the helicopter revving up on the lawn. He'll fly directly to Walter Reed. The official White House photographer snaps a few pictures of me at the desk. A Secret Service agent rushes my doodles to the shredder in the closet. You want me to dial the phone I ask, sign a few papers? What?

20   "Just act natural," the photographer says as aides usher Marilyn into the room. I stand up, push the chair from the desk. We kiss in front of the bureau, the elephants sniffing up at us. I hear the snap, snap, snap of the camera, sense the white flash on my eyelids.

I am sentimental, I think. I feel lots of things. I just don't let anyone know. No one will know how it felt to be the President of the United States for a few hours. Janine, on her way to work, cannot begin to imagine the depth of my feelings. Everyone else, the whole country waking up and getting ready for the new day, they can't begin to imagine what I feel I feel.

The photographer wants another picture of us kissing. Marilyn leans into me again, her eyes closed, her head cocked to the right. I could kiss her on the cheek or on her mouth. Kissing is all different now. After the extraction of my teeth I found that feeling would never return to my lips, the nerve endings crushed or severed by the operation. I don't like to think about that, nerves and tissues. I decide to kiss her mouth, and I do. It is a sensation I've grown to like. The numbness.

Analyze

1. Is fictionalizing the thoughts of a real person "fair"? Why or why not?
2. What does it say about "Quayle" that he wanted to keep his molars?
3. Do you need to know who Dan Quayle is to "get" the gist of this piece?

Explore

1. In an overarching way, how does Martone depict the U.S. government? Cite some support of your opinion from the text.
2. What do the phone calls "Quayle" makes do to further characterize the character?
3. Look up the "Murphy Brown" Quayle incident. What is your response, more than twenty years later?

J. D. Daniels
"Letter from Majorca"

J. D. Daniels's "Letter from Majorca" is a wild romp of an essay—dark, funny, and immensely well-crafted. It won *The Paris Review's* Terry Southern Prize for Humor in 2013. The prize recognizes "humor, wit and *sprezzatura* as important qualities of good writing." On the surface, Daniels's "Letter from Majorca" looks deceptively effortless. It is a psychological character sketch— part memoir, part travelogue; it makes bold allusions to classical myths and psychological tropes, and brims with seemingly silly yet delightfully musical sentences such as "And once I made a reuben for a Weimaraner."

Let's suppose you are a serious person, or you transmit to yourself certain conventional signals of a sort of seriousness: you reread Tacitus, you attempt to reread Proust but it can't be done, you listen to Bartók and to Archie Shepp.

Also: You can't stop moving your bowels, or your body can't. You have a body, you are a body. You don't know what's safe to eat these days, or when. You're so sick that you take off your clothes when you use the bathroom, for safety's sake. That was a hard lesson to learn. Let's stop saying *you*.

I had a body. It was a problem. It hurt most of the time. I dreamt of one world and woke into another. I woke in pain from bad dreams of my divorce, again, and listened to Wayne Shorter's *The All Seeing Eye*. It would see a lot of things, that eye. Think of all it might come to know and desire to forget.

My throat hurt, my stomach hurt, I coughed, I lay in bed and stared at the ceiling and thought about death: I heard its soft footfalls approaching. I had some blood tests, I took some medicine. I spent a lot of time in bed.

5   At the time I'm telling you about, I was earning some money, not much, as a freelance journalist and a teacher in a university, writing about education, about gun control, about fashion or music, reviewing new novels through a haze of rage and envy, telling myself that *whatever it takes* means *whatever it takes*, doing whatever I had to do to convince myself that I was not a number-two schmuck.

The wife tells her husband: You must be the number-two schmuck in the whole world.

Why can't I be the number-one schmuck? he says.

But how could you be number one? she says. You're such a schmuck.

There was nothing the matter with me that was not also the matter with everyone else. I was not as interesting as I thought I was. My major problem, inadequate or inappropriate love from my parents, was as common as dirt. And one rainy day, all the boring poignancy of these realizations detonated in me like an atom bomb, burning the dead shadow of each former torment or preoccupation onto solid rock. Those silhouettes, that record would remain: the museum where I used to be.

10   All right, I thought, I've had enough. Some other way from now on, but not like that, not any more.

And so I quit the university after shouting at a student until she began to cry. "You're crying?" I said. "Why are you crying?" She ran away.

I had done this to innumerable boys over the years and had considered it good for them, but a girl's tears shocked me and made me see myself as I was: cruel, power-mad, an abuser of children, because in our time twenty-year-olds remain children, and they themselves are not entirely to blame. We have failed them. Let's stop saying *we*.

I shouted at a pretty girl with long, black hair. She often stayed after class to discuss her favorite books with me, sitting next to me on my desk, playing with the strap of her shirt and smiling in a way that becomes familiar to every teacher, flattering and dangerous, and when she ran away crying I saw that I had scolded her in order to prevent myself from going to bed with her.

And later, when I realized that her name, she had a man's first name, was also the name of a friend with whom I was angry because I had praised my analyst in his presence and he had applied and been taken on as an analysand, when I realized that by driving my student away I was also murdering her name-twin, my rival sibling, I thought: These kids deserve better instruction than I am currently capable of providing.

Once I admitted how much I wanted to kill and eat the children who 15 had been entrusted to my care, I tried to forgive myself for any harm I might have done them over the years, for all the crackling bolts I had hurled from my cloud of self-serving ignorance, and I left that institution of learning to resume my position of nothingness in a world where I had no power to abuse my subordinates because I had no subordinates, where I had no authority save whatever I might seize by force or by cunning—where, as each day proves afresh, people will walk smiling through puddles of your blood, smiling and talking on their cellular phones. They're going to the movies.

People at parties in Cambridge asked me *what do you do?* with alarming regularity. I had spent the previous thirty years in Kentucky never once having been asked what I did, because what would be the point: I do some task I don't care about in order to be able to afford to stay alive, the same as you do, and then I clock in at my real job holding down a stool at the Back Door or Check's Café or Freddie's Bar-Lounge or Jake's Club Reno.

In Cambridge, at parties, I said whatever came first into my mind. "I manufacture organic catheters."

"I'm a butt scientist."

"I am an AM/FM clock radio."

For a while, when I sensed they might find it contemptible, I had thrown 20 it into people's faces that I worked in a deli. It was true: once, in Cambridge, I had made a sandwich for Arthur M. Schlesinger Jr. "I think that was Arthur Schlesinger," I said, and the next person in line said, "Who's Arthur Schlesinger?"

And once I made a reuben for a Weimaraner. Probably I made a lot of sandwiches for dogs without knowing it, but the lady I am thinking of made it clear to me that I was to be careful with her dog's sandwich, take it easy on the Russian dressing.

I was proud of myself on the day I quit my university teaching job. I remembered when I was still a little boy and my father came home from work, too tired and sore to bend over and take his own boots off, and I was so pleased to take his boots off for him, the brown and white laces and the brads and the dry mud flaking onto the floor; and my mother said, "How was work today?" and my father said, "I quit."

We sat down to dinner and we did not speak. Soon the phone rang, and my father smiled. On the phone was someone who had heard about how my father had told the foreman off, good, he deserved it and only you had the guts to give it to him, we always have a job for a man like you, can you start tomorrow. He could.

Now that it was settled, we finished eating our dinner, meatloaf and mashed potatoes maybe, or hamburgers and thick-cut, deep-fried potatoes, my father's favorite. And that night my mother sobbed until she vomited. This happened many times when I was a boy.

25   I told my girlfriend I had quit my teaching job. "That was dumb," she said.

It was at this time that the captain called me long-distance from Tunisia and said, "I need a man. Get over here."

"I'm sick," I said. "I don't know how much help I can be to you."

"All I need is arms and legs," he said. "Do you still have arms and legs? Then buy a ticket for Cagliari and meet us in Carloforte."

The captain was a gray giant out of Tel Aviv. One holiday I had seen him surrounded by his daughters, by his sons-in-law, his grandchildren, his pretty young girlfriend, and I thought: This man has something to teach you about what a certain kind of happiness is in life, so learn it, you dummy.

30   I already felt *at sea*, as they say, *lost in familiar places* is another thing they say. I decided to spend some time at sea, where my bewilderment might make more sense, because disorientation and chaos would actually be happening.

Why do people feel things and go places, tell me if you know.

That was how my odyssey began. I flew to Heathrow Terminal 4, where a man in one of the many airport bars drank a bottle of Worcestershire sauce, put the empty in his briefcase, and chased it with a pint of ale. A morose Russian paced near Aeroflot. I flew on to Sardinia and hired a car, and soon I was alone, under the moon, without the luggage Alitalia had lost, on the last ferry to the island called San Pietro.

The boat was forty-three feet long and there were five of us, myself and four Israelis, on it for five weeks. I had never been sailing for more than two hours at a time, in Boston Harbor. I didn't understand the captain when he told me to take the French seasickness pill.

There was work to be done and so after three acid-yellow heavings-up they left me to my fate, sprawled on my back with a bucket nearby. Shattered by nausea and fear, I sweated through my shirt and took it off and wrung it out and wiped myself with it. I was sick all day and night as we crossed from Sardinia to Minorca. I hadn't had a drink in eight years but hello, vomiting, it is always nice to see you again.

When the captain saw that I could sit up and drink water, he said, 35 "You're a sailor now," and he sent me fore. It wasn't true that I was a sailor but it was true that a task helped me to focus on something other than my constant boring suffering, something to do with the jib roller, it's all a blur.

I wasn't going to be sick again for more than a month, but there was no way I could know that. As we hobbyhorsed up and down, pitching hard over the waves, I saw first the sea and then the sky, black sea, night sky, burning moon, a foretaste of death.

Both Odysseus and Captain Ahab are heroes of departure and return, for Ahab, too, returns: to his death-home, in the whale.

Shlomo's English was good. He told me about the Dead Sea Scrolls. He told me about Brazilian agronomy. He told me about Joseph Stiglitz.

Shlomo said, "I ask myself, who are the wisest people in the world? The answer is: the Jews. This is well-known.

"And who are the wisest Jews? A moment's reflection reveals that 40 Russian Jews are the wisest.

"Next we must discover who are the wisest of these Russian Jews. And the answer comes back, clearly the people of Odessa.

"So who are the wisest Jews in Odessa? The members of the old synagogue.

"It's plain to see, then, that the wisest man in the world must be Rabbi Loew, chief rabbi of the old synagogue of Odessa. But he's such an idiot."

And Amatsia said, "My brain is fucking." He meant his memory was going bad. Asked for an example, he explained that in the army he had once carried a dead man on his back for two days and now he couldn't remember the man's name. He shook his head. "Fucking," he said.

Amatsia didn't talk much. He smoked. Every now and then he picked up 45 the binoculars and looked at the colors of the flags of other ships and said, "Fucking Germans."

One night, docked, we met a German couple in a Spanish restaurant. "You talk about Jerusalem, I think," the man said, "in your beautiful language. It is so interesting. I, too, have been to *Yerushalayim*, so interesting. Yes, and to Haifa, also. A beautiful city."

The captain said, "Do you know what we say about the beautiful Haifa?"

"What is that?"

"The most beautiful thing in Haifa is the road to Tel Aviv."

50   All the Israelis, a little drunk, laughed.

"Yes," the German said, "this is a kind of humor, I think."

Amatsia had sailed [sic] across the Atlantic Ocean with the captain ten years earlier. He smoked, and I smoked, too, pretending to be him, because I wanted to fit in and because he seemed to be an admirable man, quiet and hardworking, and from time to time the captain snarled at us in Hebrew.

"He says smoking is stupid," Amatsia said.

I smoked a cigar on a bench along the dock and saw a waterfront bum coming from a hundred yards away. He was burned brown and wrinkled by the sun. He looked like a wallet someone had been sitting on for forty years. "Have you got another *puro*?" he said. "You speak English? You understand me? Don't worry about Spanish. English is the best. A very good language. With English, you go anywhere in the world. All places. If you know Spanish, what does that get you? Tell me, where can you go?" He made a face as he gestured around himself, disgusted by the beauty of his native Spain.

55   It had been a long time since Señorita Geile had taught me Spanish with her hand puppet named Teodoro, a little bear. I had written the Pledge of Allegiance, *juro fidelidad a la bandera de los Estados Unidos de América*, as a punishment when I was bad, which had been often, and I had memorized *poesía*, but now I couldn't remember one word of it, which is not what *memorize* means. I memorized the Pledge of Allegiance, and I memorized this fact: I am bad.

A cab driver said to me, "How many languages do you speak? Your Spanish is very bad, we're not going to count that one." He adjusted his eyeglasses and said, "The real money in this cab-driving business is the night shift, the *putas*. Tell me something. How do you say *fucky-fucky* in English?"

I floated in a sea of Hebrew, or in an estuary of Spanish and Hebrew. I made up ways to spell what I thought I was hearing. It's astonishing what you won't need to know in this life. I got by for weeks with nothing but *ani rotse le'echol mashehu bevakasha,* which means, I think, *I want something to eat, please.* I thought about language—speaking in tongues, rebuking the Devil—and I thought about twins: about my new sibling, the fellow analysand I loved and had shared my precious analyst with and now wanted to kill. I would kill him and eat him. Maybe I would eat him first.

There were twins at my high school, nice shy Vietnamese boys. They were king-hell math achievers but they hardly spoke a lick of English. At first I figured they spoke French at home, or Vietnamese, but I came to understand that they didn't speak those languages, either. They'd had one another since birth, before language, and they had never seen the need to learn to speak anything.

The Israelis were competitive in all things, and they soon set out to establish who was the greatest shipboard cook. The contest lasted for weeks and was delicious, but I was often unwell, and there was the small problem of the head on board. I made it filthy, sometimes twice, because I was unwell, and then I made it clean again, not without some effort. I have cleaned a lot of toilets, I worked as a janitor at one time, and I can tell you land-based toilets are preferable, they do not move.

Shlomo wouldn't take his turn cleaning the head. "It stinks," he said.   60

"The head smells fine," said the captain. "What stinks is human shit."

We could urinate over the side if the sea wasn't too rough. "One hand for you, one hand on the ship," the captain said, "and no matter what lies she may have told you, boys, one hand for yourself is plenty. Most of the dead men in the sea have their flies open."

On the boat, we did laundry like this. You wore your underwear until you felt you were no longer a member of the human race. Then you turned it inside out and wore it some more.

I found myself thinking about my father, about a time we had gone to a baseball game together. We were in the parking lot. "When are you moving north?" he said. "The forty-third of Delfember," I said, and he laughed, and then he said, "Help me," and I turned around and my father had shit in his britches.

He'd been out the night before with his best friend, Jeff, a bartender   65
who was blind in one eye and drunk in the other and tended to wear a black T-shirt that said Vietnam veteran, in case any onlookers happened to wonder if Jeff might be a veteran and, if so, of what conflict.

And when I say *tended* I mean he wore that shirt to funerals, a T-shirt at a funeral, that was Jeff all the way. When his own brother, when Jeff 's brother, Sarge, had died, my father had lent him my mother's car and Jeff, already crocked at ten in the morning, had almost run it off the road on his way to the service, scraping it along the guard rail and snapping off its side mirror. My mother said nothing, which was not her habit.

My father, too, was a Vietnam veteran. So were a lot of men in my family. One of them was my uncle, who died of Agent Orange–related complications. "Let that be a lesson to you," my father said. "Don't join the service, and don't let your friends join the service. Because they tell you what to do. They tell you where to go, they tell you what to eat. They tell you when to die. And then you're dead."

In that parking lot, my father was right to trust in my expertise. I was well acquainted with the problem at hand. I was a promising young drunk, bad with women and an easy vomiter, and occasionally I had to shit as well. I had shit the bed once and kept sleeping and got up in the morning, going happily about my day off, and had not noticed until my then-wife came home from her job and asked me what it might be in our bedroom that smelled so much like shit. And, of course, it was shit that smelled that way. That was the answer.

And so I was prepared to aid my father. As in so many endeavors, the first step is to lie: I said everything was going to be just fine. I told him he had to be brave for a few minutes, could he do that, could he walk, if not we could find some other way but that would be the simplest, and he said he thought he could.

70   We walked past the parked cars and trucks and the yellow paint on the asphalt toward the gray concrete of the arena and its public restroom. I got my father into a stall and stood outside and told him to take his shoes and socks and jeans and underwear off. My father hated public restrooms. Once, when I was a little boy, I had noticed he did not wash his hands after urinating and asked him about that habit and he had given his explanation, saying, "I'm confident that my penis is the cleanest thing in this environment."

His drawers were not so bad after all, but I threw them in the garbage just to seem like I was doing something to help. I passed him handfuls of paper towels. "Check your legs down to your ankles and feet," I said. "Check your socks. How are your pants? We want to keep them."

"What if we can't?"

"Then you wear my shirt around your waist like a kilt until we get back to the truck," I said. But he washed and dried himself and put his pants and socks and shoes back on. And that was that. It was nothing he could not have done on his own if he had given it a moment's thought, instead of willing himself to helplessness, to asking for help. *Orders make you stupid*, the captain told me, *figure it out for yourself.*

What do you know, I'm finally shitting my father. God knows I ate enough of him. I am thirty-seven years old, five feet ten inches tall, 180 pounds, a hairy man like Esau with an increasing amount of gray in my chest, a miniature facsimile of my father is half-extruded from my rectum, otherwise I am in good health.

The past is behind me, burning, like a hemorrhoid. My parents will not die if I wish them dead. They will die because life is finite.   75

When I was in college, one of my teachers said, "What's the matter with you? Are you waiting for your parents to die before you write something honest?" and I said, "That is the dumbest question I have ever heard."

My mother calls collect from hell. She rides her bike and goes swimming. There are a lot of ibises in hell. She sends me a picture. It's pretty. I'm shouting into the telephone, I'm trying to shout but it's hard to make a noise, my jaw won't work, my teeth are long and getting longer, they break against each other, everywhere I turn I'm biting something. I bite the telephone, biting.

My parents are not dead. I mean hell on earth, plain old regular real hell.

You know that hell? That's the one I'm talking about. And even when they are dead they will live on in me, burning in my hell-head, it's so crowded in here, still yammering about what I ought to do: Now I see how it is, you drop a coat hanger on the floor and if no one is watching you don't pick it up, that's the kind of man you've become. My dead father in particular is very interested in the proper configuration of everyday household items like coat hangers.

Ibiza was on fire as we approached by night from the sea. A third of the   80
island was burning. We anchored and watched airplanes swoop to fill their tanks with sea water. They flew high over the mountains and dropped water on the burning trees again and again. It was the biggest wildfire on the island in all of recorded history. It was still burning the next day when we left.

Shlomo, swimming just before we pulled up anchor, was stung by a jellyfish. "Do you want me to pee on it?" I said.

"No, I want you to shit on it," he said. "Americans!" he said.

On that boat, surrounded by blank water and blank Hebrew, with a somewhat less blank Spanish awaiting me on shore, I was free from the obligation to apprehend and interpret. If I don't understand what you want from me, I don't have to try to do it, I can't. The sea is incomprehensible and uncomprehending, the sea doesn't care, which is terrific, depending on what kind of *care* you are accustomed to receiving. The sea is wet.

As a teenager I was once waved through a roadblock by a police officer who then pulled me over and ticketed me for running the roadblock. "I don't understand what you want from me," I said, something I had already, at that early age, said many times to many different people.

85   "What's the matter with you?" the officer snarled, something many different people have said to me, and when my father and I went to court we found I had been charged with attempting to elude a police officer and failure to comply. My father knew the judge, or should I say the judge knew my father: she had been his girlfriend in high school. My father and I were wearing the nicest clothes we owned.

"Well, Mr. Prosecutor, what do we have here?" the judge said, smiling.

"The apple doesn't fall far from the tree," said Mr. Prosecutor, and he was also smiling, and they were speaking to and for my father, not to me, although I had been charged with *attempting to elude a police officer*, for Christ's sake, I still don't understand it. I got off with a fine for making an illegal turn. The judge knew my father, everyone knew my father, just as everyone had known my grandfather, and even people who had not been alive at the time knew that all the lights in Hodgenville, Kentucky, had gone out when my grandfather died. I was not a tree, I was an apple, I had not fallen far from those trees, but I had fallen. Somewhere there had been an apple and a fall. This much we knew.

If anyone wanted something from me on that boat, he said my name; if no one said my name, I was not wanted. And *I was not wanted*, I floated for a month in a sea of unmeaning noise, I was free from the horror of being deformed by another person's needs and desires.

I became a twin, a sibling to myself, and I gnawed myself for nourishment in the red cavern of the womb, relaxing into my own death.

I ate myself until there was nothing left but my mouth. Then I ate my   90
own mouth. Then I died.

But no one ever dies. I got off the boat and hailed a cab and took a train
to Madrid.

In Madrid I went to the Prado, where I looked at Goya's *Saturno devor-
ando a su hijo*. There he sat, sickened, with his horrid mouthful, and the
whites of his eyes were huge.

I had always thought of Saturn as vicious, as power-mad. I had never realized how frightened he was, how compelled to commit and experience
horror against his will. I began to cry. I felt sorry for Saturn. He didn't want
to eat anyone. His stomach hurt. He wasn't even hungry.

And I flew home. Last night I dreamt the Devil bit my penis off. This
morning it was still there, or *here*. Where I am is called *here*.

Analyze

1. Look for patterns. How many references to fathers and sons appear
   here? How many references to home? To twins? Look for multiple references to his psychotherapist. What other patterns do you notice?
2. What journey does the speaker take?
3. What are some of the jobs the speaker has held down or left behind or
   invented?
4. How many languages do the Korean math students speak?
5. Which pronouns does the speaker decide not to use in this essay?
   What do you make of the fact he never opts out of using "I"?

Explore

1. Sigmund Freud argues that jokes express feelings and thoughts that
   the conscious mind usually suppresses in daily, polite society. In other
   words, jokes highlight the link between the conscious and the unconscious mind. Pick one of the many humorous vignettes from this piece
   and explore the way it links the conscious and subconscious mind of
   the speaker.
2. Daniels's essay makes deep and steady reference to classical psychoana-
   lytical tropes: killing the father (Oedipal complex); the hero's journey
   (Jungian archetypes); the fragmentation and coherence of the self

through language (a fundamental principle of talk therapy). Look into some of these allusions and references more deeply. How does your new knowledge help you make sense of the essay's playful yet intense preoccupation with the "self"?

3. Look up Goya's famous painting of Saturn eating his young. Scary, right? Arguably, this essay can be seen to reckon with that painting. How does Daniels's juxtaposition of scenes and themes (like those in question 1 above) enact a kind of re-seeing of this famously overexposed painting? How does Daniels's piece help us see the painting— and its themes—afresh?

Simon Rich
"A Conversation at the Grown-up Table, as Imagined at the Kids' Table"

At 30 years old, **Simon Rich** is already racking up an illustrious career. He has written two comic novels (*Elliot Allagash* and *What in God's Name?*), three story collections, served as the youngest-ever writer at *Saturday Night Live*, and has written a screenplay for Pixar. Are you impressed yet? Well, he was also president of the *Harvard Lampoon,* one of the country's longest-running humor magazines. This piece comes from his first book, *Ant Farm,* which he published while in his senior year at Harvard.

The Wisdom of Children

I. A Conversation at the Grownup Table, as Imagined at the Kids' Table

Mom: Pass the wine, please. I want to become crazy.
Dad: O.K.
Grandmother: Did you see the politics? It made me angry.
Dad: Me, too. When it was over, I had sex.

Uncle: I'm having sex right now.   5
Dad: We all are.
Mom: Let's talk about which kid I like the best.
Dad: (*laughing*) You know, but you won't tell.
Mom: If they ask me again, I might tell.
Friend from Work: Hey, guess what! My voice is pretty loud!   10
Dad: (*laughing*) There are actual monsters in the world, but when my kids
    ask I pretend like there aren't.
Mom: I'm angry! I'm angry all of a sudden!
Dad: I'm angry, too! We're angry at each other!
Mom: Now everything is fine.
Dad: We just saw the PG-13 movie. It was so good.   15
Mom: There was a big sex.
Friend from Work: I am the loudest! I am the loudest!
(*Everybody laughs.*)
Mom: I had a lot of wine, and now I'm crazy!
Grandfather: Hey, do you guys know what God looks like?   20
All: Yes.
Grandfather: Don't tell the kids.

Analyze

1. What does Rich's choice of using only dialogue do for the piece?
2. Describe this family. Use specifics from the text to support any de-
   scriptors you use.
3. Does "A Conversation" meet the criteria for a story as you define it or
   as you've been taught?

Explore

1. Simon Rich said, "I'll only write about emotions I think billions of us
   have experienced." Apply that quote to this essay as well as at least one
   other piece in this anthology. Does he hold true to his own mandate in
   this piece?
2. Is the premise of a child's perspective on a group of adults "enough" to
   carry the story?
3. Read back through and see how many childhood fears are addressed in
   this piece. What makes children's fears *funny*?

Garcia+Robles, "The Cassette," advertisement for KISSFM. From www.garciarobles .net. Reprinted by permission.

2 Analytical

"Critical thinking: the other national deficit."

—Stephen Colbert

Analysis is as difficult to define as any other rhetorical mode. But we're looking at it like this: The selections in this section take a close look at a subject, often examining it from an unexpected or fresh angle. In analysis we use ideas from various disciplines; we apply life experience, research, and critical thinking in order to come to a deep, sometimes complicated, thesis.

We tell you that, and then we present to you a poem about a hypothetical clown wandering out of the woods, a grown man who "forgets" to learn a foreign language on his way to its country, and a fictional story about a potential rape and abduction. Analysis? Yes. We are confident that you will see, on even a first read, how these pieces explore their topics in new, perspective-shifting ways.

Of course we've included more traditionally analytical pieces in this section as well. Almond's look at the emotions behind "what's funny" will help you gain a better understanding of why our hearts are as engaged as our brains when we laugh the hardest; Wierzbicka's work will have you think about the "value" of happiness. We're hoping all of the pieces in this section will open up new ways of thinking, analyzing, and applying what you bring to the work with your own diverse perspectives.

Steve Almond
"Funny Is the New Deep"

While this essay, like much of **Steve Almond's** writing, is funny in and of itself, it is essentially a look at comedy. Much of what Almond has to say can be applied to or help contextualize the other pieces in this anthology. Almond's work often focuses on political issues, and rails against the publishing and music industries. He is the author of ten books of fiction and nonfiction. His memoir *Candyfreak* was a *New York Times* Bestseller, and his short stories have appeared in both the *Best American* and *Pushcart* anthologies. His most recent collection, *God Bless America*, won the Paterson Prize for Fiction and was short-listed for The Story Prize. His journalism has appeared in the *New York Times Magazine*, *GQ*, and elsewhere. He currently lives, works, and obsesses in Boston.

Funny Is the New Deep
(aka the Sadder It Gets, the Funnier It Becomes):
An Exploration of the Comic Impulse

Prepared for *Tin House*, July 16, 2011

Draft One (i.e. the one with lots of typos and awkward shiz)   Most people's first formal introduction to what I'll be calling, for the purpose of this esteemed lecture, "the comic impulse" arrives via Aristotle. Good old Aristotle! So wise. So Greek. So hot.

In his *Poetics,* he writes about four modes of literature: the tragic, epic, lyric, and comic. As useful as this taxonomy might be in some respects, it has led to a vague consensus that the tragic and comic modes of literature are not only distinct, but diametrically opposed. This notion is complete nonsense. In fact, the comic impulse arises directly from our efforts to contend with tragedy. It is the safest and most reliable way to acknowledge our circumstances without being crushed by them.

Writers in the early stages of their apprenticeship tend to look down upon the comic impulse. I certainly did. Back in the mid-Nineties, when I was excreting my earliest drafts, I wanted, more than anything, to be taken seriously. If enough people took me seriously, then I might start to take myself seriously, thereby dispelling the notion, forever lurking at the gates of effort, that I was a sad clown who should quit writing and return to my given career as a professional masturbator, a career that I am even now somewhat nostalgic towards. Big awards, and the vengeful omnipotence that went along with them, were handed out to folks like Hemingway and Faulkner, who did not smile, let alone crack wise.

> "Another way of saying this would be the best comedy is rooted in the capacity to face unbearable emotions, and to offer, by way of laughter, a dividend of forgiveness."
> —Steve Almond, "Funny Is the New Deep"

This mindset led to the production of many serious, high-minded, earnest, and almost inevitably dreary pieces of short fiction intended to prove my good habits of thought and feeling. I really was a nice Jewish boy from the suburbs, very clean, very obedient, very *serious.*

To me, back then, perhaps as to you here and now, the "comic impulse" meant a conscious desire to be funny, to entertain people, to make them laugh. As a practical matter, I can assure you that the absolute worst way to pursue a career making people laugh is to set out to be funny. It doesn't work that way. 5

On the contrary, comedy is produced by a determined confrontation with a set of feeling states that are essentially tragic in nature: grief, shame, disappointment, physical discomfort, anxiety, moral outrage. It is not about pleasing the reader. It's about purging the writer.

Another way of saying this would be that the best comedy is rooted in the capacity to face unbearable emotions, and to offer, by means of laughter, a dividend of forgiveness. Sometimes, these unbearable truths have to do with the world around us. For the most part, they have to do with the world inside us.

Let me offer, as evidence, a quick and embarrassingly spotty survey of the relevant literature.

To look at one of the earliest examples, you have the Greek playwright Aristophanes, who died two years before Aristotle was born. He is sometimes called the Father of Comedy, which is absurd, given that comedy has been around for as long as people, or primates, have been taking pratfalls. But okay, he's obviously a major figure. His satires not only provide us a vivid portrait of ancient Athens, they constitute a concerted effort to confront the hypocrisy and corruption of his government. Aristophanes was Jon Stewart in a toga. Or verse visa.

10   *Don Quixote,* which is called our first great novel, was a comic picaresque triggered by obsessive disappointment, and driven along not by heroic action, but by humiliation. Dante's *Divine Comedy* was written, in part, as an expression of the author's volcanic rage at having been exiled from his beloved Florence. Shakespeare's comedies can be seen as sustained and often ruthless examinations of various species of human folly. And so on and so on, from *Tristam Shandy* to *Huck Finn* to *Lucky Jim* to *Catcher in the Rye* to *Infinite Jest.*

Embedded within all these texts is the following really cool irony: the comic impulse is simultaneously an expression of helplessness, of surrender to the world's absurd cruelty and our own foibles and fuckups, *and,* at the same time, the acquisition of power by means of acknowledging that bad data.

Consider, for example, the landscape of *King Lear.* Who is the one character vested with the power to speak truth to the king? That's right, the Fool. Now think about the first mass media figure to confront the atrocities of fascism. It was Charlie "Don't mind me, I'm just a tramp" Chaplin. He made *The Great Dictator* in 1940, at a time the United States was formally at peace with Nazi Germany, as was Britain. Chaplin excoriated the Nazis as "machine men, with machine minds and machine hearts."

What are, to my mind, two of the greatest American novels ever written—certainly the two greatest to emerge from that cataclysmic event—are both comedies: *Catch-22* by Joseph Heller and *Slaughterhouse Five* by Kurt Vonnegut.

A few years ago, I had the privilege of looking through Vonnegut's papers, which are archived out in Bloomington, Indiana. People often forget this, but Vonnegut spent more than two decades trying to write *Slaughterhouse Five*. Like most young writers, he was determined to be taken seriously, and he took his topic to be of the utmost gravity, and this meant, to him, that he was dutybound to write a series of serious, well-meaning, and ultimately dreary short stories. The only cool thing about reading them was that they afforded me the chance—always exhilarating for envious little strivers like myself—to realize that Kurt Vonnegut once sucked. If your confidence is flagging, I urge you to visit the collected papers of your favorite writer.

These stories, by the way, contain many of the actual events that would   15
later appear in *Slaughterhouse Five,* and even some of the character names. They were terse, competent, lifeless. He'd clearly been mainlining Hemingway, or early Mailer anyway.

It took Vonnegut years to locate the voice he needed to tell the story of his experiences as a POW during the bombing of Dresden. And if you read the introduction to the novel, one of the greatest pieces of writing he ever produced, what you hear in his tone is essentially surrender. Surrender to the absurd. Surrender to the human capacity for senseless cruelty. Surrender to his own literary inadequacies. He writes:

> I would hate to tell you what this lousy little book cost me in money and anxiety and time. When I got home from the Second World War twenty-three years ago, I thought it would be easy for me to write about the destruction of Dresden, since all I would have to do would be to report what I had seen. And I thought, too, that it would be a masterpiece or at least make me a lot of money, since the subject was so big.
>
> But not many words about Dresden came from my mind then—not enough of them to make a book, anyway. And not many words come now, either, when I have become an old fart with his memories and his Pall Malls, with his sons full grown.

What's so fascinating—and revealing—is that this voice wasn't something he had to create. It was already inside him. Maybe the most fascinating document in that entire archive was the letter that Vonnegut wrote to his family on May 29, 1945, from a Repatriation Camp in Le Havre, France. So this is literally days after he's been liberated:

"I'm told that you were probably never informed that I was anything   20
other than 'missing in action,'" he begins. "That leaves me a lot of explaining

to do ... On about Feb. 14 the Americans came over, follow by the RAF. Their combined labors killed 25,000 people in 24 hours and destroyed all of Dresden—possibly the world's most beautiful city. But not me."

Can you hear that? *That* is Vonnegut's voice, that fearless mordant surrender to the absurd. It was inside of him all that time.

And it's inside of you, too. Every single person in this room has a distinct sense of humor, which allows him or her to speak more truthfully, which allows him or her to draw closer to the eternal flame of sorrow than most—if not all!—of the other voices at your disposal.

Because the comic impulse, it turns out, isn't a literary device at all. It's a bio-evolutionary adaptation. It's the survival tool human beings developed in order to contend with the perils of self-consciousness and moral awareness and the sort of horrible outcomes that they needed to be able to imagine in order to survive on the mean streets of the Serengeti or the Neander Valley.

What's my point? That, sometimes, atrocity is the midwife of the comic? Without the atrocity of slavery, Mark Twain never writes *Huckleberry Finn*? Actually, I think I'm saying just the opposite, too. That the comic impulse is what allows us to recognize our sins (personal, cultural, historical) and thereby make moral progress.

25   Great comic writers recognize, in a way that most of us can't or won't, that our moral universe is out of balance, that the king is crazy, the dictator is mad, that we're in a lot of trouble.

This has never been more true than today. Which is why the true moral watchdogs—as our Fourth Estate descends into a kind of regressed capitalist psychosis—are all comedians. Lenny Bruce begets Richard Pryor who begets Bill Hicks who begets Jon Stewart and Bill Maher. Vonnegut begets Saunders and Moore and Shteyngart and Lipsyte.

Another way of thinking about all this—one that came to me as I was listening to Maggie Nelson's amazing reading the other night—is that the comic impulse is what allows us to confront cruelty. It allows us to speak in explicit moral terms, without moralizing. It allows us to take direct aim at the sponsors of cruelty, because, hey, we're just the fool. George W. Bush's saggy white ass, meet Stephen Colbert's mighty boot of truth. *Good evening, Mr. President, I'd like to begin by saying you're just a pathetic rich boy who likes to dress up like GI Joe and sodomize the poor. Just kidding. Ha. Ha. Ha.*

To return to the literary province, let me urge you to read, or re-read a couple of stories that ran recently in the *New Yorker*. The first is "Boys Town" by a young and perhaps doomed writer named Jim Shepard.

And the second story "Home" by George Saunders. Neither could be considered "comic" pieces in any conventional sense, but both, at crucial moments, use humor as a way of confronting a fact that virtually no one else in this culture wants to admit: that we're creating a generation of young men who are being rendered monstrous by their subjugation to senseless violence, who absorb that violence on our behalf, then return to this country broken.

It's worth noting here, just parenthetically, that one of the most troubling symptoms of the right-wing of this country—along with an energetic aptitude for violence, projection, and toddler logic—is that they have no sense of humor whatsoever. Because a sense of humor implies a basic recognition, if not a celebration, of moral uncertainty and confusion. What the voices of the right deal in, their essential commodity, is moral surety, the trademark of the demented. The narrative of the right in this country is deeply rooted in a feverish denial of reality: greed is not snuffing out mercy, the planet isn't heating up, our corporations will care for us, America remains the greatest country on earth, just so long as we can get these poverty-stricken undocumented gay communist academics to shut the fuck up. They run on rage, which is the fuel of convenience when you run out of truth.

But the confrontation I keep talking about need not be with the external world of corruption. Just as often, more often actually, it's a confrontation with the internal world. In this personal sense, the comic impulse consists of an articulation of private, shameful, and above all transgressive thoughts.

Luis Urrea spoke to this with great and frankly annoying eloquence the other day in his craft talk. He said, "All the embarrassing things that I talk about—being from Tijuana, being poor, having contracted tuberculosis—are the ones that deeply affect people." And we could hear, just from listening to Luis, that the comic impulse, that essential surrender to the absurdity of the universe, was what allowed him to speak about this painful stuff. Like a good Catholic boy—or maybe a bad Catholic boy, I honestly don't know enough about Catholicism to say—Luis was seeking to confess and forgive himself all at once. His jokes were the confession and our laughter was the forgiveness.

The comic impulse, then, is about a willingness to dwell in the awkward, shameful places we'd prefer not to dwell. It's what allows us to face the truth of ourselves on behalf of others. I often tell students that the path to the truth runs through shame. But it's equally important to note that you sometimes need the cloak of humor to get yourself into, and through, the darkest parts of the forest.

The idea isn't to crack jokes about your life. On the contrary, the idea is to engage in a ruthless pursuit of the truth, and to allow the comic impulse to do its intended and instinctual work. It's not some wrench you hoist out of your writer's toolbox when the action seems to be flagging. It's the impulse that naturally arises when you reach a moment that is too painful to confront without some form of self-forgiveness. It's not a conscious decision, but an unconscious necessity.

And this applies, by the way, to fiction and non-fiction and poetry. Every time I reach a point of unbearable heaviosity in one of my stories or essays or rotten novels, my natural inclination is to offer some form of comic relief. In initial drafts, this desire to "joke around" is often evasive. And these are the jokes I wind up cutting later, the moments that arise from a desire to elide the truth, or to please the reader and thereby flatter myself. But the jokes that my characters require, in order to face the truth of themselves and their circumstances—those are the ones that stay.

35   Honestly, this is just human nature. You all grew up in families that were screwed up in various innovative ways—you would not be in this room if you didn't—and you all developed, as a coping mechanism, a sense of humor.

Your sense of humor, to reiterate, did not begin as a narrative strategy, but as an adaptive instinct. And that's what it should remain in your work. The idea is not to hide behind a set of jokes, but to relax sufficiently so as to allow for some play, some improvisation, at the keyboard. Self-consciousness is the death of art, as John Cage reminds us. Taking yourself, or your characters, too seriously is as grave a danger as taking them too lightly. When the stink of gravity grows thick upon your keyboard, let humor be your disinfect.

I think here of a young woman named Tracy Wigfield, whom I taught years ago in a class on cultural criticism. She was, by all appearances, a standard issue Boston College undergrad, meaning that she looked as if she had stepped out of an upscale clothing catalogue. She didn't talk much in class. But her first piece was utterly droll and subversive, and her second—a press conference delivered by Barbie, the doll—was even better.

Years later, she wrote to thank me for encouraging her to abandon the stuffy stories she'd been writing, and to give free rein to her sense of humor.

She added that she was now one of the lead writers for the television show *30 Rock*.

I had two immediate reactions to this note:

1. My God, how incredible and inspiring it was that Tracy was able to get   40
   the whole of her personality onto the page!
2. I am now going to commit suicide.

I am sometimes asked what I think is funny. This is mostly an issue of comic sensibility, of personal inclination. My daughter and I, for instance, find the concept of poopie soup to be extremely funny. Sometimes we stir the poopie soup. Sometimes we pretend to sniff, or even taste the poopie soup, and recoil in delighted horror. My wife, sadly, does not appreciate the comedic genius of poopie soup. Am I here suggesting my wife has a bad sense of humor? Yes. On the other hand, in this matter at least, she feels I have a bad sense of humor. Everyone responds to a different soup.

But I will say a few things that I think apply across the board. Something is funny, most of all, because it's true, and because the velocity of insight as to this truth, exceeds our normal standards. Something is funny because it's outside our accepted boundary of decorum. Something is funny because it defies our expectations. Something is funny because it offers a temporary reprieve from the hardship of seeing the world as it actually is. There are different sorts of laughter, in other words, and they express varying degrees of joy, affirmation, surprise and relief.

The comic impulse is, in essence, a form of radicalism. To put it in psychoanalytic terms, it's an attempt to turn away from the safety of our super egos, and to unchain the raging, anarchic id who yearns to be free. It's the force that allows well-behaved little Phillip Roth to escape from the comfy confines of *Goodbye, Columbus* for the libidinal jungle of *Portnoy's Complaint*.

I think now of a second Boston College student, a young man who was   45
not named Matt or Ryan, or Matt Ryan, as so many BC dudes are. No, his name was Pete. He was in the first humor writing class I ever taught. I figured this would be a very easy class to teach, because college students are constantly insecure and therefore constantly talking shit about the world around them and all I had to do was get them to talk shit onto the page.

Instead, I received a raft of safe, well-meaning satires meant to condemn the horrors of racism, sexism, and excluding a particular suite mate just because she still wore Uggs. A month into class, I convened a come-to-Jesus meeting. "Listen," I said. "I'm not interested in your good values. They bore me. You are boring me to death. If I receive another earnest, obedient word from anyone in this class, so help me God I will flunk every one of your sorry asses. I'm a fucking adjunct. I can do it."

I really miss teaching.

Anyway, the next class this kid Pete brought in a piece on shitting in public. It was a long and detailed primer that introduced the reader to terms such as "the half-crap" and "prairie-dogging." Wow. That class was really an excruciating and deeply awesome fifty minutes of life. Because, after all, one of the containing myths of collegiate life (and maybe life in general) is that women do not defecate. But the piece was so extreme, and so courageous in confronting the most private of our shames, that it really broke the class open.

It might be said that these students had been given permission to admit to their own shit. We are all seeking, on some deeper spiritual level, permission to admit to our own shit, to unburden ourselves of the strangling illusion that we are somehow not a total mess. Remember: everyone has a sense of humor by which they've survived the worst moments of their lives, and forgiven themselves at various wretched junctures.

50   The real question isn't whether you can or should try be funny in your work, but whether you're going to get yourself and your characters into enough danger to invoke the comic impulse. The enduring artists don't write funny to produce laughter—though we're certainly thrilled when people laugh—but to apprehend and endure the astonishing sorrow of the examined life.

Analyze

1. How long does Almond say comedy has been around?
2. What famous novelist does Almond say "once sucked"?
3. What atrocity "allowed" Mark Twain to write *Huckleberry Finn*?
4. What trait does Almond call "the trademark of the demented"?

Explore

1. Do you agree with Almond's theory that "comedy is produced with a determined confrontation with a set of feeling states that are essentially tragic in nature: grief, shame, disappointment, physical discomfort,

anxiety, moral outrage"? What pieces have you read in this anthology (or elsewhere) that fit this paradigm?
2. What piece(s) in this anthology "confronts cruelty"?
3. Can you think of something that has made you laugh that was primarily about "purging the writer"? Can you think of any stand-up comedians who do the same?

Stephen Dunn
"If a Clown"

Pulitzer Prize–winning American poet **Stephen Dunn** is a master of the genre. His poems can break your heart, blow your mind, make you laugh, and make you gasp with recognition of what makes us all ultimately human. "If a Clown" sets up a seemingly mundane, somewhat bizarre hypothetical scenario. Dunn uses this "what if?" moment to trigger an increasingly philosophical inquiry into the nature of the human heart. Note how his use of the conditional invites readers to imagine themselves into these events.

If a clown came out of the woods,
a standard-looking clown with oversized
polka-dot clothes, floppy shoes,
a red, bulbous nose, and you saw him
on the edge of your property,   5
there'd be nothing funny about that,
would there? A bear might be preferable,
especially if black and berry-driven.
And if this clown began waving his hands
with those big white gloves   10
that clowns wear, and you realized
he wanted your attention, had something
apparently urgent to tell you,
would you pivot and run from him,
or stay put, as my friend did, who seemed   15

to understand here was a clown
who didn't know where he was,
a clown without a context?
What could be sadder, my friend thought,

20   than a clown in need of a context?
If then the clown said to you
that he was on his way to a kid's
birthday party, his car had broken down,
and he needed a ride, would you give

25   him one? Or would the connection
between the comic and the appalling,
as it pertained to clowns, be suddenly so clear
that you'd be paralyzed by it?
And if you were the clown, and my friend

30   hesitated, as he did, would you make
a sad face, and with an enormous finger
wipe away an imaginary tear? How far
would you trust your art? I can tell you
it worked. Most of the guests had gone

35   when my friend and the clown drove up,
and the family was angry. But the clown
twisted a balloon into the shape of a bird
and gave it to the kid, who smiled,
let it rise to the ceiling. If you were the kid,

40   the birthday boy, what from then on
would be your relationship with disappointment?
With joy? Whom would you blame or extoll?

Analyze

1. How many questions does the poem ask? What makes the questions an indispensable part of the poem's humor?
2. For what event was the clown late? What happened to cause his delay?
3. Note the seemingly common language Dunn uses. Look again, now, at the fun he is having with sound (via alliteration, assonance, and consonance) and sense. How does the form of the poem serve the poem's ideas?

Explore

1. How does Dunn's use of the second person—the direct address to "you"—engage you as a reader/listener? How else does the form of the poem work to make you feel engaged?
2. Listen to Dunn read the poem. (*The Courtland Review* has an audio file posted on the Internet.) When does his audience laugh? What is it like for you to listen to them laughing? How does this experience affect your sense of the "comic event" of the poem?
3. Write back to the poem. What would you do? Take Dunn up on his questions and write a letter in response to him.

Katie Brinkworth
"A Day in the Life of a Target-Market Female"

Katie Brinkworth is a copywriter for some of the world's largest corporations, such as Skype, Pepsi, Intel, Whataburger, and many others. This does not stop her from mocking the advertising industry; in fact, it probably makes her better at it. This tongue-in-cheek essay is a hyperbolic look at how advertising slogans and "propaganda" can essentially take over every choice we make.

McSweeney's is a publishing company based in San Francisco. McSweeny's *Internet Tendency* is the humor website where this piece originally ran and one of many outlets for this mega-publisher, which also include Timothy McSweeney's *Quarterly Concern*, the *Believer*, and numerous books under various imprints.

At 6 a.m. on the dot, the 25-to 45-year-old target-market female wakes up and stretches with delight, excited to greet the day.

For breakfast, the target-market female debates whether to eat the yogurt brand that encourages her to be herself, or the one that helps her poop. Today, like most days, the target-market female chooses regularity over self-worth.

After drinking a cup of the orange juice brand that makes her look the thinnest, the target-market female lotions up every inch of her body and gets dressed for the day. She then takes a short, breezy walk to a local café, where she patiently awaits signs of male appreciation for her noticeably soft skin.

While she waits, the target-market female daydreams about fiber, smaller pores, and easy-but-creative recipes she can make with precooked sausage. When she realizes the time, the target-market female rushes home to begin the most rewarding part of her day—doing the laundry.

5   At home, while waiting for the end of the spin cycle, the target-market female fantasizes that a male model has materialized in her kitchen and is making her a salad. He works slowly—first carefully washing the organic produce, then cutting the vegetables with his own chiseled facial features.

When he's finished, he feeds the target-market female bites of the kale-based salad while sensually describing how it will help reduce her belly bloat. Afterward, he does yoga on her while they both indulge in the yogurt brand that makes the target-market female feel sexy and independent.

Hours later, the target-market female wakes up on the floor of her laundry room in a daze. She notices that the spin cycle is complete, and opens the lid of the washing machine. When she sees what the combination of premium bleach and stain-fighting detergent has accomplished, her knees weaken beneath her and her bowels release for the very first time in her life.

In her giddy, almost orgasmic state she decides to forgo her internet-enabled, whisper-quiet dryer, opting instead to "carpe diem!" and dry the brilliant whites outside on a clothesline. With the help of a talking stuffed bear (which her anxiety medication's animated-blob mascot assures her will disappear within four to six weeks) the target-market female hangs her symbols of domestic bliss proudly in the warm, gentle breeze.

Later on, the target-market female meets up with her racially ambiguous friend for an afternoon coffee and daily discussion of their respective yeast infections. The target-market female feels comfortable discussing such personal topics because the rich aroma of her coffee has whisked her away to the calm, soothing mental state that her rage therapist has conditioned her to visit whenever she feels envious of her friend's perfectly toned biceps or sleeveless-ready underarm skin.

10   After coffee, the target-market female returns home, making it back just in time to catch a falling piece of dust before it touches the floor. While re-cleaning her kitchen for the seventh time, the target-market female

hallucinates that she and the mop are engaged in a quasi-sexual relationship that's been broken up by the Swiffer. She tries playing hard to get with the mop, only to discover that it has begun a fling with the basket of pinecones she uses as holiday decor.

Unsure whether the jealousy is real or fiber induced, the target-market female builds a fire with the pinecones and every other romantically threatening knickknack, producing a very real and uncontrollable inferno. By the time the fire trucks arrive, the whole house is ablaze.

When she realizes her loss, the target-market female begins to cry like women always do.

Fortunately, in the end, the target-market female is oddly comforted by the fact that she can wipe up all the tears, spilled gasoline, and broken dreams with one illogically absorbent, quilted paper towel.

Analyze

1. The "target-market female" seems most obsessed with which product? Why or why not was this a good choice?
2. What is the "most rewarding part of her day?" Why?
3. The "target-market female" hopes for male affirmation and daydreams about a man in her life. What do these details add to her characterization?

Explore

1. What is the importance of her "racially ambiguous friend"? Find at least three levels on which this friend character "works" for the piece.
2. Have you ever felt that advertising is too obtrusive, too pervasive, as you simply move through the world, trying to simply live your day? Or, has it become so ubiquitous that you don't even see ads on the margins of websites you're using, on the back of subway seats, etc.?
3. Why would Brinkworth choose to end the piece with the female setting fire to her home and its belongings? If the piece ends in such tragedy, why would we still classify it as comedy?

Fran McDonald
"Laughter Without Humor:
On the Laugh-Loop GIF"

Fran McDonald studies laughter in contemporary film and television at Duke University, where she is pursuing her Ph.D. in English. Writing for *The Atlantic*, McDonald describes the way Natalie Portman's off-script laughter "hit the Internet as a looped video" and "took on a life of its own." The viral spread of the GIF of Portman's strange laugh triggers McDonald's reconsideration of humor, technology, and participatory media. Watch as she focuses on laughter itself as an object of analysis—not on what makes a joke funny, but what on earth a laugh actually is.

At the 68th Golden Globe Awards, a visibly pregnant Natalie Portman ascended the stage to collect the Best Actress award for her work in the psychological drama *Black Swan*. Her earnest three-minute speech is standard Hollywood fare; she thanks her grandparents, her parents, her manager, her co-stars, and her director. She touches her stomach and thanks her fiancé, the choreographer and actor Benjamin Millepied. She tells a bad joke about how Millepied, who has a small role in *Black Swan* as a man sexually disinterested in Portman's character, must be a brilliant actor because of course he really *did* want to sleep with her, as evidenced by her swelling belly. The audience laughs by rote; they are used to these carefully constructed asides designed to provide light comic relief from the otherwise relentlessly repetitive slew of near-identical speeches. What Portman does next, however, is jarringly off-script. She laughs. Her laugh erupts in two monotone bursts and lasts for four seconds. Within days, her laugh hits the Internet as a looped video, where it will take on a life of its own.

The original Portman laugh-loop was generated by comedy website and meme manufacturer CollegeHumor, and boasts a YouTube view-count of 2.25 million, literally double that of Portman's official acceptance speech. The video retains her bad joke, presumably to provide context, and then loops for a straight thirty seconds, interspersing images of Portman's laughing body with cut-away shots to the increasingly bemused faces of celebrity onlookers. The audio clip of Portman's double-burst of laughter is repeated nine times, and the video clip of her laughing is repeated five times. A cursory search reveals a host of alternate versions, including a "super-cut" that extends the loop for an almost unbearable three minutes, a video comparison with Miley Cyrus' laughter ("which laugh grates on your ears less?"), and countless remixes with various accompanying sound-effects, from generic house music to the artistically moribund "Farting Edition."

Fan fascination with the Portman video is representative of a more general online obsession with making laugh-loops, which appear all over the Internet primarily in animated GIF (Graphics Interchange Format) form. An animated GIF is a short sequence of images sliced from their original context, usually programmed to loop *ad infinitum*, or at least until you close your browser. A truly democratic animal that lives and dies by its re-bloggability, the GIF is popular because of its simplicity and portability—they are easy to make and even easier to spread.

But why is the laugh-loop in particular such a popular variety of GIF? A quick scan of the vast array of laugh-loop GIFs shows that the laughter chosen for looping has no single identifiable quality. Some are contagious and pleasurable to listen to, but some are uncomfortable and jarring to the ear. Many don't include an audio track at all, featuring only the mute face crumpling in silent spasms that we infer to be laughter. Most noticeable, however, is the variety of *subjects* doing the laughing in laugh-loops. Natalie Portman, Michael Jordan, and Brendan Fraser star in very popular laugh-loops. However, equally prevalent are laugh-loop GIFs that feature non-celebrities, children, cartoon characters, puppets, and animals.

Aristotle called laughter an "ensouling mechanism," and the academic   5 discipline of humor studies has built itself upon the assumption that laughter is a quintessentially *human* response to the socio-cultural discourse of humor. Laughter is offered as proof of our exceptional status as thinking social creatures; we are "the only animal that laughs." GIFs that feature sniggering squirrels, cackling cartoon toasters, and rollicking robots would seem to undermine this selfish view of laughter as an exclusively human activity. But even worse, the laugh-loop GIF disassociates laughter from humor. By severing laughter from the context that incites it, the laugh-loop GIF reveals that laughter is not only a consequence of its sociocultural coordinates, but also a weird object in itself. Laughter, it seems, is not "for us" but has its own alien being that has hitherto been masked by its everydayness.

The glitch aesthetic of the GIF emphasizes the uncanny quality of laughter. At each moment of re-looping, Portman performs a miniature convulsion that registers as an inhuman twitch. If humor makes us human—an assumed correlation that is so deeply written into our culture that the two share a basic etymological root—then laughter without humor appears to render us mechanical, terrifying, monstrous. It is not a coincidence that laughter without humor has become the great cinematic signifier of madness: think of Colin Clive's maniacal "it's alive!" hysterics in the famous 1931 film version of Mary Shelley's *Frankenstein,* or the crazed cackle of The Joker in the *Batman* comics.

Laughter without humor seems pathological because it cannot be rationalized. Without the Millepied joke as context, Portman's laughter literally becomes unintelligible to us. The laugh-loop GIF replaces humor studies' anthropocentric question—*what is funny to us?*—with a more basic one: *what is laughter?* The laughter of the laugh-loop GIF is both infinite and inexplicable, it erupts over and over again, without reason and without end. In the same way that repeating a common word over and over suddenly renders it strange, the repetitive format of the laugh-loop GIF defamiliarizes laughter and forces us to confront it as such, in all its irrational strangeness.

To test the impact of this confrontation, I watched the Portman laugh-loop video and its variations on repeat for about two hours. After twenty minutes of this oddly oppressive process, an uncanny sensation takes hold. Before my eyes, Natalie Portman—bad joke-teller, acclaimed actor, pregnant female, human being—begins to recede behind the blank, insistent laughter that pours out of her. Portman ceases to be recognizable according to ordinary human parameters; she is only a glitching body and a flat, repetitive tone. In this moment it is no longer "Natalie Portman's laughter" that reverberates out of my tinny laptop speakers, but simply "laughter": a material force unbound by the taxonomies of humor, and the limitations of the human.

In a neat materialization of this otherwise nebulous sensation, further investigation reveals that Portman's laughter has its very own Facebook page, an online presence utterly divorced from the actress herself. In the vast multitude of laugh-loop GIFs that feature non-celebrities, the uncanny erasure of the person laughing is even more obvious. Perhaps Portman, as an instantly recognizable face and household name, better resists the ontologically disruptive power of laughter. When we watch the immensely popular "fat kid laughing" GIF, for example, no one cares who he is, or where he is from, or why he is laughing, or who is filming him laugh. It doesn't occur to us to ask. The subject of the video is not the fat kid, but the laughter itself. It is all we can see.

By separating laughter from humor, the laugh-loop GIF allows us to see   10
laughter on its own, separate from the activities of human affect that produce it. Laughing as a noun rather than a verb. The material qualities of the
GIF—in particular its repetitious and glitchy nature—accentuate the
strangeness of laughter. The ordinariness of laughter makes this strangeness
hard to see, obscured in fleshy domesticity.

The GIF is not alone in its capacity to reveal laughter without humor.
Think of the brutal Italian giallo film *The House With Laughing Windows*
(1976), the practice of Hasyayoga or Laughter Yoga, the Tanganyika laughter epidemic of 1962, the irrepressibly popular Tickle Me Elmo doll, or the
canned laughter of the Laff Box on the 1950's sitcom *The Hank McCune
Show*. Normally we see laughter as an effect of humor and an affect of the
human. We think we can explain laughter by comedic analysis (why Portman's joke is funny) or statistical analysis (how canned laughter affects an
audience). But thinking about laughter as an entity rather than an activity
allows us to recognize its strangeness. Pure laughter refuses rational explanation. It is this unintelligibility that caused Thomas Hobbes to call laughter
"that passion without a name." It is why attempts to represent laughter in
language feel reductive to the point of absurdity (representations such as
"LOL!" or even "ha-ha" don't quite cut it).

Thinking about laughter as an intellectually inaccessible object troubles
the scientist, who cannot make its essential properties transparent. But just
because something withdraws from rational explanation or human intelli-
gibility does not mean it has no intellectual traction. The dilation of perspective from human humor to alien laughter opens up a new space in
which laughter ceases to prove our humanity or to reinforce our rationality.
Instead, it disrupts these anthropocentric presumptions. Laughter without
humor offers the deeply disturbing but potentially liberating effect of
showing us laughter itself, laughter as such. For a moment that the GIF
form makes eternal, Natalie Portman is no longer a self-contained and self-
possessed human woman. She is a medium for laughter, like linseed oil is a
medium for pigment.

In the strange moment of laughter, the clean divisions between objects,
subjects, things, humans, and animals become muddied. Out of these
muddy waters, an uncertain terrain emerges in which, for a laughing
moment, Natalie Portman becomes a glitching machine, Elmo becomes
a corporeal presence, an inanimate house becomes a vengeful killer, the
Tanganyika people become a single body, a tape of recorded laughter remotely

activates armchair laughter, and a laughter that began as a choreographed exercise routine becomes involuntary and spontaneous. Laughter allows us to gaze at a spasming actress and a hysterical toy and a psychotic house and a chuckling magnetic tape and see them all surge toward one another along a shared axis. Contaminated by a fugitive and inexplicable laughter, the old philosophical taxonomies cannot hold. Secretly, we always suspected that laughter held this disruptive quality. This is why we call it cracking or bursting or breaking up. This is why when we laugh we are no longer an individual, coherent self but a multitudinous bundle or barrel of laughs. Laughter without humor shows us that laughter persists, even without us.

Analyze

1. What is a "glitch aesthetic"?
2. Why does laughter without humor seem "pathological"?
3. McDonald calls the GIF a "truly democratic animal" whose popularity depends on what two factors?

Explore

1. "Normally we see laughter as an effect of humor and an affect of the human," writes McDonald. But in the case of the Portman laugh GIF, this framework drops away. Instead, out of its context and on an endless loop, laughter becomes strange indeed. McDonald describes this strangeness as "uncanny." Look up the word "uncanny." How is it that GIF technology makes the strange familiar or the familiar strange?
2. Find a laugh-loop, describe it in rich detail, and then reflect on the significance of the GIF you've chosen. What does it signify about laughter, technology, or context?
3. Look again at the passage where McDonald offers a range of related evidence to establish a larger social pattern and a context for the Portman laugh GIF. Take a moment and research two of the texts she mentions: "Think of the brutal Italian giallo film *The House With Laughing Windows* (1976), the practice of Hasyayoga or Laughter Yoga, the Tanganyika laughter epidemic of 1962, the irrepressibly popular Tickle Me Elmo doll, or the canned laughter of the Laff Box on the 1950's sitcom *The Hank McCune Show*."

Anna Wierzbicka
"'Happiness' in Cross-Linguistic and Cross-Cultural Perspective"

Polish-born linguist **Anna Wierzbicka** teaches at the Australian National University. Famous for her research in semantics and cross-cultural linguistics, her work spans the disciplines of psychology, anthropology, and cognitive science. Wierzbicka has written numerous books and articles, including *Emotions Across Languages and Cultures: Diversity and Universals* (1999) and *What Did Jesus Mean? Explaining the Sermon on the Mount and the Parables in Simple and Universal Human Concepts* (2001). In the influential article presented here, she questions the way "happiness" is deemed by Western researchers to be a consistent concept across cultures. What do we mean by happiness? And, perhaps more important, what do we mean by "we"?

The psychologists David Myers and Ed Diener start their frequently cited article "Who is Happy" with the observation that "Books, books and more books have analyzed human misery. During its first century, psychology focused far more on negative emotions, such as depression and anxiety, than on positive emotions, such as happiness and satisfaction." They note with approval that this is now changing quite dramatically.[1]

There is of course a good reason why books, books, and more books have been written about human misery. Misery and suffering are part and parcel of most lives, whereas happiness is not—or so it has appeared to most people at most times. In the autobiographical novel by the Egyptian-born British writer Ahdaf Soueif, the Egyptian aunt of the Westernized heroine asks her niece why she left her husband. "We were not happy together," she replies. The aunt raises her eyebrows: 'Not happy? Is this sane talk? . . . Who's happy, child?"[2] This exchange is, I think, a characteristic clash of culturally informed thought patterns, values, and expectations.

The first century of psychology, which, as Myers and Diener point out, focused to a far greater extent on negative emotions than on positive ones, was also the century of, inter alia, the two world wars, the Holocaust, the Gulag Archipelago, the millions deliberately or recklessly starved to death in the Ukraine and elsewhere under Stalin and in China under Mao Ze Dong, and the horrors of Pol Pot's Cambodia. By the end of the twentieth century, Hitler, Stalin, Mao, and Pol Pot were all gone, but few of those who watch the evening news on television would say that the human condition has radically changed since the time of their rule.

Against such a background, the claim of Myers and Diener that "most people are reasonably happy, but that some people are happier than others" seems rather startling. Most people are reasonably happy? Who are those reportedly happy people?

5   According to the studies they cite, North America has the greatest concentration of happy people in the world. "[I]n national surveys," writes Myers, "a third of Americans say that they are very happy. Only one in ten say 'not too happy.' The remainder—the majority—describe themselves as 'pretty happy.'" Europeans, Myers adds, "by and large report a lower sense of well-being than North Americans," but they too "typically assess themselves positively. Four in five say they are 'fairly' or 'very' satisfied with their everyday lives."[3]

By Myers and Diener's account, "nations differ strikingly in happiness, ranging from Portugal, where about 10% of people say they are very happy, to the Netherlands, where about 40% of people say the same." They emphasize that "nations differ markedly in happiness even when income differences are controlled for."[4] Is it true that nations differ in happiness? Or do they differ, rather, in what they are prepared to report about the state of their happiness?

In addressing these questions, political scientist Ronald Inglehart is more cautious than Myers and Diener, in that he speaks only of differences in reported happiness rather than in happiness as such. He also seems less willing simply to take his results at face value. For example, he asks:

> But exactly what is it that underlies these large and rather stable cross-national differences? Can it be true that Italians, French, Germans, and Greeks really are a great deal less happy and more dissatisfied with their lives than the Danes, Swiss, Dutch, and Irish? Could fate be so unkind as to doom entire nationalities to unhappiness, simply because they happened to be born in the wrong place?[5]

· ❖ ·

Trying to answer such questions, one has to address, at some point, the linguistic problem. For example, if 14 percent of Germans declare themselves to be *sehr glücklich* whereas 31 percent of Americans declare themselves to be very happy, can these reports be meaningfully compared if *glücklich* does not mean the same thing as happy?[6]

Inglehart considers the possibility that the words used in other languages to translate the English words *happy* and *satisfied* may not exactly match, but then he confidently dismisses the matter. His main argument for dismissing it rests on the Swiss case: regardless of the language they use—whether German, French, or Italian—the Swiss "rank very highly in life satisfaction" and "express higher levels of satisfaction than the Germans, French and Italians with whom they share a language." But however convincing the Swiss case may be, it is hard to see how it can justify the sweeping conclusion that Inglehart draws from it: "These Swiss results alone devastate any attempt to explain the cross-national differences as artifacts of language."[7]

It is true that the differences in self-reported *bonheur* (and its adjective, *heureux*) between the French and the French-speaking Swiss cannot be attributed directly to any linguistic differences.[8] But surely it doesn't follow from this that the differences in self-reporting between the French and the Americans couldn't possibly have anything to do with the semantic differences between the French word *heureux* and the English word *happy*.

The glibness with which linguistic differences are at times denied in the current literature on happiness can be quite astonishing. The economist Richard Layard, for example, writes, "Of course one could question whether the word *happy* means the same thing in different languages. If it does not, we can learn nothing by comparing different countries." The problem is dismissed as soon as it is raised; the reader is assured that "there is direct evidence, for a number of languages, that the words do have the same meaning in different languages."

In support of this claim, Layard reports that "a group of Chinese students were asked to answer the happiness question, once in Chinese and once in English ... The students reported almost exactly the same average level of happiness in both Chinese and English." Instead of inquiring into the possible reasons for such results, Layard concludes that "since the English and Chinese languages are very far apart, this finding is highly reassuring," and that "the concept of happiness seems equally familiar in all cultures."[9]

In fact, the linguist Zhengdao Ye's detailed study of Chinese positive-emotion concepts shows clearly that while there are two happiness-like concepts in the traditional list of Chinese basic emotions, both are different from the English happiness. The terms in question are *xi*, which Ye defines as "festive joy," and *le*, which she defines as "attainable enjoyment/contentment." Of *xi* Ye says, inter alia, that "the positive cognitive evaluation, the personal character, and the unexpectedness of the event all contribute to the sudden, intense good feeling…, which is usually outwardly shown via facial expressions and bodily gestures." On the other hand, *le* "seems to have a gamut of components from many 'happy-like' words in English. It is like a hybrid of pleased, enjoyment, contented and having fun." In particular, she emphasizes the active attitude of *le*, which "results in a wish to do something to keep the current situation going." Ye concludes her discussion of the differences between the ethnotheories of emotion reflected in Chinese and English as follows:

> It seems that in Chinese people's perception and conceptualisation of human emotional experience in relation to good events there are two quite opposite aspects: one is due to a somewhat mysterious external force, to which the experiencer "actively" responds, experiencing a momentary, intense feeling "stirred" by external stimuli, and the other is due to human effort. Each aspect is equally important and culturally salient, and each term occupies a place in the small set of the "basic emotions."[10]

The lack of equivalence between the Chinese and English words does not mean that Chinese and Anglo attitudes toward life cannot be meaningfully compared at all. They can be, but every comparison requires a common measure. In this case such a measure is provided by the minilanguage of simple and universal human concepts that can be found in all languages. These simple and universal concepts include GOOD, BAD, KNOW, THINK, WANT, FEEL, LIVE, and fifty or so others. They do not include, however, complex culture-specific words like happy, satisfied, or well-being.[11]

15   It is an illusion, then, to think that the English words *happy* and *happiness* have exact semantic equivalents in Chinese, or, for that matter, in other European languages. The differences, it turns out, are particularly striking in the case of the adjective.

In the language of simple and universal human concepts, the meaning of happiness can be linked with the following cognitive scenarios: a) some very good things happened to me; b) I wanted things like this to happen; and c) I can't want anything else now. By contrast, the cognitive scenario of happy can be represented as follows: a) some good things happened to me; b) I wanted things like this to happen; and c) I don't want anything else now. The main differences between happiness and happy, then, lie in the contrast between "very good" and "good" (component a) and between "I can't want anything else now" and "I don't want anything else now" (component c). In happiness one's heart is filled to overflowing and there seems to be no room left for any further (unfulfilled) desires or wishes.

Happiness can be compared, roughly, to the French *bonheur*, the German *Glück*, the Italian *felicità*, and the Russian *sčastie*, because like these words it can be used to refer to an existential condition seen as a certain absolute. The adjective *happy*, however, does not necessarily imply a state of happiness. For example, if I say that "I'm happy with the present arrangements," I do not mean that I either experience or am in a state of happiness. Thus, *happy* is, so to speak, weaker than *happiness*, whereas *heureux, Glück, felicità, and sčastie,* are not similarly weaker than *bonheur, felicità, Glück,* and *sčastie*, respectively.

The semantic differences between *happy* and its putative counterparts in European languages are often flagged in bilingual dictionaries, which instruct users not to translate *happy* as, for instance, *heureux*, but to use some weaker word instead. Here are some examples from the *Collins-Robert English-French Dictionary*:

> I'll be quite happy to do it. →
>
> *Je le ferai volontiers. / Ça ne me derange pas de le faire.*
> (I'll gladly do it. / It doesn't bother me to do it.)
>
> I'm happy here reading. →
>
> *Je suis très bien ici à lire.* (I'm very well here reading.)
>
> I'm not happy about leaving him alone. →
>
> *Je ne suis pas tranquille de le laisser seul.* (I'm not at ease about leaving him alone.)

The very fact that happy, in contrast to those other words, has developed such a weaker second meaning highlights a semantic shift that has no doubt contributed to the expansion of the term's use in English, at the expense of words with more intense meanings like rejoice and joy. Happy—unlike *heureux, sčastlivyj,* and *glücklich*—is not restricted to exceptional states (like bliss), but rather is seen as referring to states within everyone's reach. There is nothing exceptional about being happy, and this is why one can be quite happy, reasonably happy, pretty happy, not at all happy, and so on.

20   As I have argued in my book *Emotions Across Languages and Cultures: Diversity and Universals,* the very notion that a person can be pretty happy is, so to speak, a modern invention. At the time when the adjective *happy* was close semantically to the noun *happiness,* collocations like pretty happy did not exist in the English language, and being happy was regarded by speakers of English as something very rare, as witnessed, for example, by the following line from George Herbert's "Jacula Prudentium": "There is an hour where a man might be happy all his like, could he find it."

To some extent, happiness can still be seen as something rare and exclusive, as can *bonheur* and *felicità.* But happy has drifted away from happiness so far that it can almost be said to be halfway between happiness and okay; syntactic frames such as "I'm happy with the present arrangements" reflect this semantic weakening. This weakening, in turn, can be seen as a manifestation of an overall process of the dampening of the emotions—modern Anglo-American culture's trend against emotional intensity.[12]

The remarkable expansion of the word *happy* has gone hand in hand with the decline of negative words like *woes, sorrows,* and *griefs.*[13] As I have tried to show in my *Emotions Across Languages and Cultures,* modern English has, so to speak, exorcised woes, sorrows, and griefs from the fabric of 'normal' life. In older English, woes, sorrows, and griefs (in the plural) were commonly used to refer to everyday life, whereas in present-day English, grief is restricted, by and large, to the exceptional event of the death of a loved person. At the same time happiness has come to be seen not as something rare and unusual, but as altogether ordinary; and the word *happy* has become one of the most widely used English emotion adjectives—perhaps the most widely used one of all. According to the data in the COBUILD corpus of contemporary English, happy is not only uttered much more frequently than sad (roughly 3:1) and joyful (roughly 36:1), but also much more frequently than, for example, *heureux* is in comparable French listings (roughly 5:1).

Stanisław Barańczak, a Polish poet who emigrated to America, gives a particularly astute account of the semantic clash between the English word happy and its nearest equivalents in some other European languages—an account based on his personal experience:

> Take the word "happy," perhaps one of the most frequently used words in Basic American. It's easy to open an English-Polish or English-Russian dictionary and find an equivalent adjective. In fact, however, it will not be equivalent. The Polish word for "happy" (and I believe this also holds for other Slavic languages) has much more restricted meaning; it is generally reserved for rare states of profound bliss, or total satisfaction with serious things such as love, family, the meaning of life, and so on. Accordingly, it is not used as often as "happy" is in American common parlance... Incidentally, it is also interesting that Slavic languages don't have an exact equivalent for the verb "to enjoy." I don't mean to say that Americans are a nation of superficial, backslapping enjoyers and happy-makers, as opposed to our suffering Slavic souls. What I'm trying to point out is only one example of the semantic incompatibilities which are so firmly ingrained in languages and cultures that they sometimes make mutual communication impossible.[14]

In the book entitled *The Pursuit of Happiness*, the American David Myers asks: "How happy are people?" Given the widespread assumption that the word happy can be readily translated without any change of meaning into other European languages, it is interesting to note that the question raised in the title of that chapter cannot be translated into many other languages at all. One simply can't ask in these languages the equivalent of "How happy are people?":

- *Comment (*combien) heureux sont les gens?*
- *Corne felici sono gli uomini?*
- *Kak scastlivy ljudi?*

The reason why all of the above sentences are infelicitous is that unlike   25
the word happy, the words *heureux*, *felice*, and *sčastlivyj* are not gradable. They all refer to something absolute, to a peak experience or condition that is not considered a matter of degree. To be asked to measure one's *bonheur*

or one's *sčastie* on a scale from one to ten is like being asked to measure one's bliss on such a scale.

Inglehart, speaking of research into reported happiness carried out in Europe and based on the so-called Eurobarometer Survey, has maintained that the questions adapted from American research—e.g., How are things going these days? Would you say you are very happy, fairly happy or not too happy?—have "been found effective in measuring feelings of happiness [in Europe]." The phrase "feelings of happiness" is as problematic here as the idea that such feelings can be effectively measured.

Using French and Russian again as examples, I will note that *bonheur* and *sčastie* suggest, roughly speaking, an existential condition rather than a momentary feeling, and that the phrase "feelings of happiness" cannot be translated literally into French or Russian (*les sentiments de bonheur; *čuvstva scastia). Incidentally, for this reason, the economist Daniel Kahneman's idea that happiness can be studied more effectively by focusing people's attention on the subjective quality of their current circumstances, rather than on any overall assessment of their lives, may be more applicable to English than to other languages.[15] For example, in French, momentary good feelings occurring in the course of an ordinary day would normally be linked with *plaisir* (pleasure) rather than with *bonheur*; and in Russian, they would be linked with *udovol'stvie* (roughly, pleasure) rather than with *sčastie*.

In happiness studies, it is often assumed that people's subjective well-being can be reliably estimated on the basis of their self-reports. Doubts about the reliability of such reports are sometimes acknowledged, but they tend to be minimized.

For example, Layard, having dismissed the question "whether the word 'happy' means the same in different languages," writes, "But again, might not people in some countries feel more impelled to report high or low levels of happiness, because of local cultural norms? There is no evidence of this— for example no clear tendency for individualistic countries to report high or collectivist cultures to report low."[16]

30   Strikingly, the reliability of the classification of countries as either individualist or collectivist is taken for granted here, and since there emerges no clear correlation between individualism (as measured by such classifications) and self-reported happiness, it is assumed that self-reports can reliably measure the actual well-being of people across languages and cultures.

Myers strikes a more cautious note about self-reports, but his caution does not include any cross-cultural perspective. He begins by stating that everyone is the best judge of his or her own happiness: "if you can't tell someone whether you're happy or miserable, who can?" He continues as follows: "Still, even if people are the best judges of their own experiences, can we trust them to be candid? People's self-reports are susceptible to two biases that limit, but do not eliminate, their authenticity."[17] One of the biases, according to Myers, has to do with people's momentary moods: "By coloring people's assessments of the overall quality of their lives, temporary moods do reduce the reliability of their self-pronouncements. Their happiness thermometers are admittedly imperfect." The other bias is people's "tendency to be agreeable, to put on a good face." People, Myers says, "overreport good things"—they "are all a bit Pollyannish." However, "this poses no real problem for research," because "we could downplay people's happiness reports by, say, 20 percent and still assume that our 'happiness thermometers' are valid as relative scales."[18]

I do not wish to question Myers's assumption or conclusions as far as the subjective well-being of Americans is concerned. One should be careful, however, to distinguish between all Americans and all people. It may indeed be reasonable to assume that our "happiness thermometers" are valid as relative scales—if one is comparing individuals who speak the same language and share, or are familiar with, the same cultural norms. When it comes to cross-cultural comparisons, however, the situation is very different.

Thus, when Myers and Diener state that "nations differ strikingly in happiness, ranging from Portugal, where about 10% of people say they are very happy, to the Netherlands, where about 40% of people say the same," a move is made, imperceptibly, from differences in self-reports to differences in actual well-being. In fact, Myers and Diener themselves acknowledge that in some societies "norms more strongly support experiencing and expressing positive emotions."[19] But if so, then how can cross-national and cross-cultural differences in self-reports be equated with differences in happiness?

Somewhat disconcertingly, Myers and Diener state that "collectivist cultures report lower SWB [subjective well-being] than do individualist cultures," whereas Layard claims, as we have seen, that there is no clear difference in this regard between so-called individualist and collectivist countries. Even more disconcerting, however, is Layard's confident rejection of the possibility that "people in some countries [might] feel more impelled to report high or low levels of happiness because of local cultural norms."

35   There is plenty of evidence that local cultural norms do produce different attitudes to expressing happiness or, more generally, good feelings. Evidence of this kind cannot be elicited through surveys based on self-reports; it can, however, be gained by other methods. In particular, there is a growing body of evidence emerging from cross-cultural autobiographies, and there is extensive linguistic evidence.

In her memoir *Lost in Translation: Life in a New Country*, the Polish-born writer Eva Hoffman, who emigrated with her parents to North America at the age of thirteen, contrasts two cultural scripts by describing two different rituals of farewell, as experienced first in Poland and then, two years later, in America:

> But as the time of our departure approaches, Basia . . . makes me promise that I won't forget her. Of course I won't! She passes a journal with a pretty, embroidered cloth cover to my fellow classmates, in which they are to write appropriate words of good-bye. Most of them choose melancholy verses in which life is figured as a vale of tears or a river of suffering, or a journey of pain on which we are embarking. This tone of sadness is something we all enjoy. It makes us feel the gravity of life, and it is gratifying to have a truly tragic event—a parting forever—to give vent to such romantic feelings.
>
> It's only two years later that I go on a month-long bus trip across Canada and the United States with a group of teenagers, who at parting inscribe sentences in each other's notebooks to be remembered by. "It was great fun knowing you!" they exclaim in the pages of my little notebook. "Don't ever lose your friendly personality!" "Keep cheerful, and nothing can harm you!" they enjoin, and as I compare my two sets of mementos, I know that, even though they're so close to each other in time, I've indeed come to another country.[20]

A similar autobiographical account of a clash between Polish and American cultural scripts comes from Laura Klos Sokol, an American woman who married a Pole and settled with him in Warsaw:

> To some extent, Poles enjoy the upbeat American pom-pom skating cheer. Who would dare claim that cheerfulness is bad? However, sometimes Poles balk at American-style frothy enthusiasm. Ask a Pole to imitate American behavior and chances are the result will

include a wide smile, an elongated "Wooooow!" and "Everything is fine!" with a thumbs-up.

One Pole said, "My first impression was how happy Americans must be." But like many Poles she cracked the code: "Poles have different expectations. Something 'fantastic' for Americans would not be 'fantastic' in my way of thinking." Another Pole says, "When Americans say it was great, I know it was good. When they say it was good, I know it was okay. When they say it was okay, I know it was bad."[21]

Looking at her native American culture from a newly acquired Polish point of view, Klos Sokol satirizes: "Wow Great! How nice! That's fantastic! I had a terrific time! It was wonderful! Have a nice day! Americans. So damned cheerful."

In addition to verbal routines like those mentioned above, and to the frequent use of untranslatable key cultural words like *fun* and *enjoy*, the differences between the two sets of cultural scripts are also reflected in non-verbal communication, particularly in smiling:

> A Pole who lived in the States for six years recently returned to Poland for a visit. During a round of introductions to some people in a café, she immediately spotted the American by his smile. "There's a lack of smiling here . . ." says the Pole. Another Pole says, "Americans, in general, smile all the time. Here, people in the streets look worried."[22]

Noting that "Americans smile more in situations where Poles tend not to," Klos Sokol observes: "In American culture, you don't advertise your daily headaches; it's bad form; so you turn up the corners of the mouth—or at least try—according to the Smile Code."

Observations of this kind cast doubt on the validity of statements like the following: "When self-reports of well-being are correlated with other methods of measurement, they show adequate convergent validity. They covary . . . with the amount of smiling in an interview."[23] Statements of this kind don't take into account that the amount of smiling, too, is governed to some extent by cultural norms, and that the norms for smiling are closely related to the norms for verbal behavior (including verbal self-reports).

From the perspective of immigrant writers it seems clear that Anglo-American culture fosters and encourages cheerfulness, positive thinking, and staying in control. To quote Eva Hoffman's memoir again:

> If all neurosis is a form of repression, then surely, the denial of suffering, and of helplessness, is also a form of neurosis. Surely, all our attempts to escape sorrow twist themselves into the specific, acrid pain of self-suppression. And if that is so, then a culture that insists on cheerfulness and staying in control is a culture that—in one of those ironies that prevails in the unruly realm of the inner life—propagates its own kind of pain.[24]

Such assessments of the psychological costs of "obligatory" cheerfulness may or may not be correct, but few commentators would disagree with the basic idea that something like cheerfulness is encouraged by American culture.

Let me adduce here one more autobiographical testimony to the perceived differences between Polish and Anglo-American cultural scripts concerning happiness and good feelings—a fragment of Stanisław Barańczak's poem "Small talk" (translated from the Polish by the poet):

> How Are You, I'm Just Fine; who says there is no chance
> for any conversation between us, who says
> there's no communication between the grey stone wall,
> or the trembling of a window frame, or the rainbow-hued oil
> spilled on the asphalt, and myself; how on earth could
> my dialogue with them be a lie, how could it be mute,
> this talk between the hydrant, fog, stairs, bough, screech of tires
> and me, whom they approach—on every path, in every passing
> always the same and invariably friendly inquiry,
> What's The News, Everything's OK.[25]

45   For immigrants like Stanisław Barańczak, English conversational routines like "How are you, I'm just fine" constitute barriers to genuine

heart-to-heart communication—and, as we have seen earlier, so does the wide use of the word *happy*. From this perspective, the tendency of Americans to declare themselves as happy in the surveys that aim to assess their subjective well-being must be seen as linked, to some extent, with the same norms that encourage the social smile, the cheerfulness, the use of Great! and so on.[26]

In conclusion, progress in cross-cultural investigations of happiness and subjective well-being requires a greater linguistic and cross-cultural sophistication than that evident in much of the existing literature on the subject. To compare meanings across languages one needs a well-founded semantic metalanguage; and to be able to interpret self-reports across cultures one needs a methodology for exploring cultural norms that may guide the interviewees in their responses. I believe that the natural semantic metalanguage, based on universal human concepts, can solve the first problem and that the methodology of cultural scripts can solve the second—and that together they can bring significant advances to the intriguing and controversial field of happiness studies.

NOTES

1 David G. Myers and Ed Diener, "Who is Happy?" *Psychological Science* (January 1995): 10.

2 Ahdaf Soueif, *In the Eye of the Sun* (London: Bloomsbury, 1992), 747.

3 David G. Myers, *The Pursuit of Happiness* (New York: Avon Books, 1992), 25.

4 Myers and Diener, "Who is Happy?" 4.

5 Ronald Inglehart, *Culture Shift in Advanced Industrial Society* (Princeton, N.J.: Princeton University Press, 1990), 79.

6 See Anna Wierzbicka, *Emotions Across Languages and Cultures: Diversity and Universals* (Cambridge: Cambridge University Press, 1999).

7 Inglehart, *Culture Shift*, 78.

8 Surely, the first hypothesis about the Swiss must be that, unlike their neighbors, they were spared the catastrophe of World War II. Frequently, happiness studies are lacking a historical as well as a linguistic and a cultural dimension.

9 Richard Layard, *Happiness: Has Social Science a Clue?* Lionel Robbins Memorial Lectures, London School of Economics, March 2003, 17.

10 Zhengdao Ye, "Why Are There Two 'Joy like' 'Basic' Emotions in Chinese? Semantic Theory and Empirical Findings," in *Love, Hatred and Other Passions: Questions and Themes on Emotions in Chinese Civilisation*, ed. Paolo Santangelo (Leiden, The Netherlands: E. J. Brill, in press).

11 Cliff Goddard and Anna Wierzbicka, eds., *Meaning and Universal Grammar*, 2 vols. (Amsterdam: John Benjamins, 2002) and Anna Wierzbicka, *Semantics: Primes and Universals* (Oxford: Oxford University Press, 1996).

12 Peter N. Steams, *American Cool: Constructing a Twentieth-Century Emotional Style* (New York: New York University Press, 1994).

13 Anna Wierzbicka, "Emotion and Culture: Arguing with Martha Nussbaum," *Ethos* (in press).

14 Stanisław Barańczak, *Breathing Under Water and Other East European Essays* (Cambridge, Mass.: Harvard University Press, 1990), 12.

15 Daniel Kahneman, "Objective Happiness," in Daniel Kahneman, Ed Diener, and Norbert Schwarz, eds., *Well-Being: The Foundations of Hedonic Psychology* (New York: The Russell Sage Foundation, 1999).

16 Layard, *Happiness*, 19.

17 Myers, The Pursuit of Happiness, 27.

18 Ibid., 28.

19 Myers and Diener, "Who is Happy?" 12.

20 Eva Hoffman, *Lost in Translation* (New York: E. P. Dutton, 1989), 78. For discussion, see Mary Besemeres, *Translating One's Self: Language and Selfhood in Cross-Cultural Autobiography* (Oxford: Peter Lang, 2002).

21 Laura Klos Sokol, *Shortcuts to Poland* (Warsaw: Wydawnictwo IPS, 1997), 176.

22 Ibid., 117.

23 Ed Diener and Eunkook M. Suh, "National Differences in Subjective Well-Being," in Kahneman, Diener, and Schwarz, eds., *Well-Being*, 437.

24 Hoffman, *Lost in Translation*, 271.

25 Stanisław Barańczak, *The Weight of the Body: Selected Poems* (Evanston, Ill.: Triquarterly Books, 1989).

26 While I have looked at Anglo-American norms from a Polish perspective, other perspectives yield comparable outcomes. For example, see Eunkook M. Suh, "Self: The Hyphen Between Culture and Subjective Well-Being," in Ed Diener and Eunkook M. Suh, eds., *Culture and Subjective Well-Being* (Cambridge, Mass.: MIT Press, 2000). In his contribution to this important recent volume, Suh, a Korean American scholar, notes "dramatic differences between North Americans and East Asians in their levels of SWB [subjective well-being] and positive self-views." He elaborates that "North Americans report significantly higher levels of SWB than East Asians. For instance, compared to 36 percent of Japanese and 49 percent of Korean men, 83 percent of American men and 78 percent of Canadian men reported above neutral levels of life satisfaction in Diener and Diener's study [Ed Diener and Marissa Diener, "Cross-Cultural Correlates of Life Satisfaction and Self-Esteem," *Journal of Personality and Social Psychology* 68 (1995): 653–663]."

Analyze

1. What is a "happiness thermometer"?
2. What are the two "cultural scripts" of farewell that author Eva Hoffman compares in her book *Lost in Translation*?
3. Great academic essays and scholarly articles are typically driven by a well-motivated thesis, no matter what the discipline. As Gordon Harvey notes in his well-known "Elements of the Academic Essay," a clear "motive" is crucial. But what is a scholarly motive? Harvey calls it the "intellectual context" that's established at the beginning of a paper to suggest why the thesis is original or worthwhile (and is "usually defined by a form of the complicating word 'But'"). Harvey's definition is worth quoting at length: "In both humanistic and scientific disciplines, the motive is typically an incongruity, puzzle, or surprise in the primary sources or data; and/or holes, limitations, or disagreements in the secondary literature." What is Wierzbicka's scholarly motive? What is her thesis? What kind of evidence does she use to make her case?

Explore

1. What is the field of "happiness studies"?
2. Draw from your experience and observations. What are some of the ways Americans express or encourage cheerfulness?
3. Wierzbicka argues that a "mini-language" of "simple and universal" meta-concepts that cut across many languages (like "GOOD, BAD, WANT, THINK, FEEL, LIVE") would be a more valid measure than "more complex culture-specific words like *happy, satisfied* or *well-being*." Dwell on the distinction she is making here. Can you come up with an example of a "complex culture-specific word" that might mean one thing to one group and something else to another? Do some research, thinking and writing about the way some words and concepts from one language do not have a parallel in another.
4. Wierzbicka notes the "modern Anglo-American culture's trend against emotional intensity." What does she mean, exactly? Can you think of examples of this cultural pattern? In a brief essay describe an example of this trend and then reflect on the implications of this cultural pattern. How might you deepen, critique, or refine Wierzbicka's ideas?

David Sedaris
"Easy, Tiger"

The piece below, originally published in *The New Yorker*, is from **David Sedaris's** latest collection, *Let's Explore Diabetes with Owls*. It exemplifies a "Sedaris essay" in that it uses a stream-of-consciousness prose filled with laugh-aloud lines, but eventually moves to a conclusion that resonates with most readers. Sedaris is a wonderful orator of his own work, selling out 900-plus-seat auditoriums; you can easily find audio files and listen for yourself.

The New Yorker, in circulation since 1925, is one of America's most-read and most respected magazines, known for its coverage of New York theater, galleries, and restaurants, its cartoons and covers, and its fiction and nonfiction pieces by prestigious authors.

On a recent flight from Tokyo to Beijing, at around the time that my lunch tray was taken away, I remembered that I needed to learn Mandarin. "Goddamnit," I whispered. "I knew I forgot something."

Normally, when landing in a foreign country, I'm prepared to say, at the very least, "Hello," and "I'm sorry." This trip, though, was a two-parter, and I'd used my month of prep time to bone up on my Japanese. For this, I returned to the Pimsleur audio program I'd relied on for my previous two visits. I'd used its Italian version as well and had noted that they followed the same basic pattern. In the first thirty-minute lesson, a man approaches a strange woman, asking, in Italian or Japanese or whichever language you've signed up for, if she understands English. The two jabber away for twenty seconds or so, and then an American instructor chimes in and breaks it all down. "Say, 'Excuse me,'" he tells you. "Ask, 'Are you an American?'" The conversations grow more complicated as you progress, and the phrases are regularly repeated so that you don't forget them.

Not all the sentences I've learned with Pimsleur are suited to my way of life. I don't drive, for example, so "Which is the road to go to Yokohama?" never did me any good. The same is true of "As for gas, is it expensive?" though I have got some mileage out of "Fill her up, please," which I use in restaurants when getting a second cup of tea.

Thanks to Japanese I and II, I'm able to buy train tickets, count to nine hundred and ninety-nine thousand, and say, whenever someone is giving me change, "Now you are giving me change." I can manage in a restaurant, take a cab, and even make small talk with the driver. "Do you have children?" I ask. "Will you take a vacation this year?" "Where to?" When he turns it around, as Japanese cabdrivers are inclined to do, I tell him that I have three children, a big boy and two little girls. If Pimsleur included "I am a middle-aged homosexual and thus make do with a niece I never see and a very small godson," I'd say that. In the meantime, I work with what I have.

Pimsleur's a big help when it comes to pronunciation. The actors are   5 native speakers, and they don't slow down for your benefit. The drawbacks are that they never explain anything or teach you to think for yourself. Instead of being provided with building blocks that would allow you to construct a sentence of your own, you're left with using the hundreds or thousands of sentences that you have memorized. That means waiting for a particular situation to arise in order to comment on it; either that, or becoming one of those weird non-sequitur people, the kind who, when asked a question about paint color, answer, "There is a bank in front of the train station," or, "Mrs. Yamada Ito has been playing tennis for fifteen years."

I hadn't downloaded a Pimsleur program for China, so on the flight to Beijing I turned to my Lonely Planet phrase book, knowing it was hopeless. Mandarin is closer to singing than it is to talking, and even though the words were written phonetically, I couldn't begin to get the hang of them. The book was slim and palm-size, divided into short chapters: "Banking," "Shopping," "Border Crossing." The one titled "Romance" included the following: "Would you like a drink?" "You're a fantastic dancer." "You look like some cousin of mine." The latter would work only if you were Asian, but even then it's a little creepy, the implication being "the cousin I have always wanted to undress and ejaculate on."

In the subchapter "Getting Closer," one learns to say, "I like you very much." "You're great." "Do you want a massage?" On the following page, things heat up. "I want you." "I want to make love to you." "How about going to bed?" And, a line that might have been written especially for me, "Don't worry, I'll do it myself."

Oddly, the writers haven't included "Leave the light on," a must if you want to actually *say* any of these things. One pictures the vacationer naked on a bed and squinting into his or her little book to moan, "Oh yeah!"

"Easy, tiger," "Faster," "Harder," "Slower," "Softer." "That was . . . amazing/ weird/wild." "Can I stay over?"

In the following subchapter, it all falls apart: "Are you seeing someone else?" "He/she is just a friend." "You're just using me for sex." "I don't think it's working out." And, finally, "I never want to see you again."

10   Hugh and I returned from China, and a few days later I started preparing for a trip to Germany. The first time I went, in 1999, I couldn't bring myself to say so much as *"Guten Morgen."* The sounds felt false coming out of my mouth, so instead I spent my time speaking English apologetically. Not that the apologies were needed. In Paris, yes, but in Berlin people's attitude is "Thank you for allowing me to practice my perfect English." And I do mean perfect. "Are you from Minnesota?" I kept asking.

In the beginning, I was put off by the harshness of German. Someone would order a piece of cake, and it sounded as if it were an actual order, like, "Cut the cake and lie face down in that ditch between the cobbler and the little girl." I'm guessing this comes from having watched too many Second World War movies. Then I remembered the umpteen Fassbinder films I sat through in the '80s, and German began to sound conflicted instead of heartless. I went back twice in 2000, and over time the language grew on me. It's like English, but sideways.

I've made at least ten separate trips by now and have gone from one end of the country to the other. People taught me all sorts of words, but the only ones that stuck were *"Kaiserschnitt,"* which means "cesarean section," and *"Lebensabschnittspartner."* This doesn't translate to "lover" or "life partner" but, rather, to "the person I am with today," the implication being that things change, and you are keeping yourself open.

For this latest trip, I wanted to do better, so I downloaded all thirty lessons of Pimsleur German I, which again start off with "Excuse me, do you understand English?" As with the Japanese and the Italian versions, the program taught me to count and to tell time. Again I learned "The girl is already big" and "How are you?" (*"Wie geht es Ihnen?"*).

In Japanese and Italian, the response to the final question is "I'm fine, and you?" In German it's answered with a sigh and a slight pause, followed by "Not so good."

15   I mentioned this to my German friend Tilo, who said that of course that was the response. "We can't get it through our heads that people are asking only to be polite," he said.

In Japanese I, lesson 17, the actress who plays the wife says, "*Kaimono ga shitai n desu ga!*" ("I want to go shopping, but there's a problem and you need to guess what it is.") The exercise is about numbers, so the husband asks how much money she has. She gives him a figure, and he offers to increase it incrementally.

Similarly, in the German version, the wife announces that she wants to buy something: "*Ich möchte noch etwas kaufen.*" Her husband asks how much money she has, and after she answers, he responds coldly, "I'm not giving you any more. You have enough."

There's no discord in Pimsleur's Japan, but its Germany is a moody and often savage place. In one of the exercises, you're encouraged to argue with a bellhop who tries to cheat you out of your change and who ends up sneering, "You don't understand German."

"Oh, but I do," you learn to say. "I *do* understand German."

It's a program full of odd sentence combinations. "We don't live here. We want mineral water" implies that if the couple *did* live in this particular town they'd be getting drunk like everyone else. Another standout is "*Der Wein ist zu teuer und Sie sprechen zu schnell.*" ("The wine is too expensive and you talk too fast.") The response to this would be "Anything else, Herr Asshole?" But of course they don't teach you that.

On our last trip to Tokyo, Hugh and I rented an apartment in a nondescript neighborhood a few subway stops from Shinjuku Station. A representative from the real estate agency met us at the front door, and when I spoke to him in Japanese, he told me I needed to buy myself some manga. "Read those and you'll learn how people actually talk," he said. "You, you're a little too polite."

I know what he was getting at, but I really don't see this as much of a problem, especially if you're a foreigner and any perceived rudeness can turn someone not just against you but against your entire country. Here Pimsleur has it all over the phrase books of my youth, where the Ugly American was still alive and kicking people. "I didn't order this!" he raged in Greek and Spanish. "Think you can cheat me, do you?" "Go away or I'll call the police."

Now for the traveling American there's less of a need for phrase books. Not only do we expect everyone to speak our language; we expect everyone to be fluent. I rarely hear an American vacationer say to a waiter or shopkeeper in Europe, "Your English is so good." Rather, we act as if it were part of his job, like carrying a tray or making change. In this respect, the phrase books and audio programs are an almost charming throwback, a suggestion that *the traveler* put himself out there, that *he* open himself to criticism and not the person who's just trying to scrape by selling meatballs in Bumfucchio, Italy.

One of the things I like about Tokyo is the constant reinforcement one gets for trying. "You are very skilled at Japanese," everyone keeps telling me. I know people are just being polite, but it spurs me on, just as I hoped to be spurred on in Germany. To this end, I've added a second audio program, one by a man named Michel Thomas, who works with a couple of students, a male and a female. At the start, he explains that German and English are closely related and thus have a lot in common. In one language, the verb is "to come," and in the other it's *"kommen."* English "to give" is German *"geben."* Boston's "That is good" is Berlin's *"Das ist gut."* It's an excellent way to start and leaves the listener thinking, *Hey, Ich kann do dis.*

25   Unlike the nameless instructor in Pimsleur, Herr Thomas explains things—the fact, for example, that if there are two verbs in a German sentence, one of them comes at the end. He doesn't give you phrases to memorize. In fact, he actively discourages study. "How would you say, 'Give it to me?'" he asks the female student. She and I correctly answer, and then he turns to the male. "Now try 'I would like for you to give it to me.'"

Ten minutes later, we've graduated to "I can't give it to you today, because I cannot find it." To people who speak nothing but English, this might seem easy enough, but anyone else will appreciate how difficult it is: negatives, multiple uses of "it," and the hell that breaks loose following the German "because." The thrill is that you're actually figuring it out on your own. You're engaging with another language, not just parroting it.

Walking through the grocery store with Pimsleur *und* Thomas on my iPod, I picture myself pulling up to my Munich hotel with my friend Ulrike, who's only ever known me to say "cesarean section" and "the person I am with until someone better comes along."

"Bleiben wir hier heute Abend?" I plan to say. *"Wieviele Nächte? Zwei? Das ist teuer, nicht wahr?"*

She's a wonderful woman, Ulrike, and if that's all I get out of this—seeing the shock register on her face as I natter on—it'll be well worth my month of study.

30   Perhaps that evening after dinner, I'll turn on the TV in my hotel room. And maybe, if I'm lucky, I'll understand one out of every two hundred words. The trick, ultimately, is to not let that discourage me, to think,

Oh well. That's more than I understood the last time I watched TV in Germany. That was a few years back, in Stuttgart. There was a television mounted on a perch in my room, and I turned it on to find a couple having sex. This wasn't on pay-per-view but just regular Sunday night TV. And I mean these two were really going at it. If I'd had the Lonely Planet guide to German, I might have recognized "Please don't stop!" "That was amazing/ weird." With Herr Thomas, I could understand "I just gave it to you" and, with Pimsleur, "I would like to come now."

I watched this couple for a minute or two, and then I advanced to the next channel, which was snowed out unless you paid for it. *What could they possibly be doing here that they weren't doing for free on the other station?* I asked myself. *Turning each other inside out?*

And isn't that the joy of foreign travel—there's always something to scratch your head over. You don't have to be fluent in order to wonder. Rather, you can sit there with your mouth open, not exactly dumb, just speechless.

Analyze

1. Because we're hoping so, we want to know: Did any line make you laugh aloud? Cite it. Now, attempt to explain why.
2. Come up with three adjectives to describe Sedaris's persona in this essay. Do you believe that his "character" is close to his real-life persona?
3. What phrase do foreign language phrase books or early-level courses never teach you that you think they should?

Explore

1. By poking fun at the idiosyncrasies of various foreign language learning tools that he's used, how does Sedaris make fun of himself? How does he make his experiences with foreign language universal?
2. Does Sedaris's humor exempt him from accusations of racism?
3. Think about Sedaris's references to the "Ugly American" and juxtapose those against David Foster Wallace's references to the same in his piece later in this chapter.

Zadie Smith
"Dead Man Laughing"

Zadie Smith, the British essayist, novelist, and short-story writer, is widely published and regularly featured in *The New Yorker*, where we found this personal essay. She dwells upon her father's love of British comedy as she simultaneously reckons with the implications of his death. Like all great essays, it uses one pattern of evidence to tell the story of another and one story to make sense of another, especially one that seems to defy understanding (like the death of a parent). As you read, note how this piece is about her father's love of comedy, how that love caught on in his family, and how being a "comedy snob" became a sure way for this complicated family to express their love for each other.

My father had few enthusiasms, but he loved comedy. He was a comedy nerd, though this is so common a condition in Britain as to be almost not worth mentioning. Like most Britons, Harvey gathered his family around the defunct hearth each night to watch the same half-hour comic situations repeatedly, in reruns and on video. We knew the "Dead Parrot" sketch by heart. We had the usual religious feeling for *Monty Python's Life of Brian*. If we were notable in any way, it was not in kind but in extent. In our wood-cabinet music center, comedy records outnumbered the Beatles. The Goons' "I'm Walking Backward for Christmas" got an airing all year long. We liked to think of ourselves as particular, on guard against slapstick's easy laughs—Benny Hill was beneath our collective consideration. I suppose the more precise term is "comedy snobs."

Left unchecked, comedy snobbery can squeeze the joy out of the enterprise. You end up thinking of comedy as Hemingway thought of narrative: structured like an iceberg, with all the greater satisfactions fathoms under water, while the surface pleasure of the joke is somehow the least of it. In my father, this tendency was especially pronounced. He objected to joke merchants. He was wary of the revue-style bonhomie of the popular TV double act Morecambe and Wise, and disapproved of the cheery bawdiness of their rivals, the Two Ronnies. He was allergic to racial and sexual humor, to a far greater degree than any of the actual black people or women in his immediate family. Harvey's idea of a good time was the BBC sitcom *Steptoe and Son,* the grim tale of two mutually antagonistic "rag-and-bone men" who pass their days in a Beckettian pile of rubbish, tearing psychological strips off each other. Each episode ends with the son (a philosopher manqué, who considers himself trapped in the filthy family business) submitting to a funk of existential despair. The sadder and more desolate the comedy, the better Harvey liked it.

His favorite was Tony Hancock, a comic wedded to despair, in his life as much as in his work. (Hancock died of an overdose in 1968.) Harvey had him on vinyl: a pristine, twenty-year-old set of LPs. The series was *Hancock's Half Hour,* a situation comedy in which Hancock plays a broad version of himself and, to my mind, of my father. A quintessentially English, poorly educated, working-class war veteran with social and intellectual aspirations, whose fictional address—23 Railway Cuttings, East Cheam—perfectly conjures the aspirant bleakness of London's suburbs (as if Cheam were significant enough a spot to have an East). Harvey, meanwhile, could be found in 24 Athelstan Gardens, Willesden Green (a poky housing estate named after the ancient king of England), also by a railway. Hancock's heartbreaking inability to pass as a middle-class beatnik or otherwise pull himself out of the hole he was born in was a source of great mirth to Harvey, despite the fact that this was precisely his own situation. He loved Hancock's hopefulness, and loved the way he was always disappointed. He passed this love on to his children, with the result that we inherited the comic tastes of a previous generation. (Born in 1925, Harvey was old enough to be our grandfather.) Occasionally, I'd lure friends to my room and make them listen to "The Blood Donor" or "The Radio Ham." This never went well. I demanded complete silence, was in the habit of lifting the stylus and replaying a section if any incidental noise should muffle a line, and generally leached all potential pleasure from the exercise with laborious explanations of the humor and said humor's possible obfuscation by period details: ration books, shillings and farthings, coins for the meter, and so on. It was a hard sell in the brave new comedic world of *The Jerk* and *Beverly Hills Cop* and *Ghostbusters.*

Hancock wasn't such an anachronism, as it turns out. Genealogically speaking, Harvey had his finger on the pulse of British comedy, for Hancock begot Basil Fawlty, and Fawlty begot Alan Partridge, and Partridge begot the immortal David Brent. And Hancock and his descendants served as a constant source of conversation between my father and me, a vital link between us when, class-wise, and in every other wise, each year placed us farther apart. As in many British families, it was university wot dunnit. When I returned home from my first term at Cambridge, we couldn't discuss the things I'd learned, about Anna Karenina, or G. E. Moore, or Gawain and his staggeringly boring Green Knight, because Harvey had never learned them—but we could always speak of Basil. It was a conversation that lasted decades, well beyond the twelve episodes in which Basil himself is contained. The episodes were merely jumping-off points; we carried on compulsively creating Basil long after his authors had stopped. Great situation comedy expands in the imagination. For my generation, never having seen David Brent's apartment in "The Office" is no obstacle to conjuring up his interior decoration: the risqué Athena poster, the gigantic entertainment system, the comical fridge magnets. Similarly, for my father, imagining Basil Fawlty's school career was a creative exercise. "He would have failed his eleven-plus," Harvey once explained to me. "And that would've been the start of the trouble." When meditating on the sitcom, you extrapolate from the details, which in Britain are almost always signifiers of social class: Hancock's battered homburg, Fawlty's cravat, Partridge's driving gloves, Brent's fake Italian suits. It's a relief to be able to laugh at these things. In British comedy, the painful class dividers of real life are neutralized and exposed. In my family, at least, it was a way of talking about things we didn't want to talk about.

5   When Harvey was very ill, in the autumn of 2006, I went to visit him at a nursing home in the seaside town of Felixstowe, armed with the DVD boxed set of *Fawlty Towers*. By this point, he was long divorced from my mother, his second divorce, and was living alone on the gray East Anglian coast, far from his children. A dialysis patient for a decade (he lost his first kidney to stones, the second to cancer), his body now began to give up. I had meant to leave the DVDs with him, something for the empty hours alone, but when I got there, with nothing to talk about, we ended up watching them together for the umpteenth time, he on the single chair, me on the floor, cramped in that grim little nursing-home bedroom, surely the least funny place he'd ever found himself in—with the possible exception of the 1944 Normandy landings. We watched several episodes, back to back. We laughed. Never more than when Basil thrashed an Austin 1100 with the branch of a tree, an act of inspired pointlessness that seemed analogous to our own situation. And then we watched the DVD extras, in which we

found an illuminating little depth charge hidden among the nostalgia and the bloopers:

> It was probably—may have been—my idea that she should be a bit less posh than him, because we couldn't see otherwise what would have attracted them to each other. I have a sort of vision of her family being in catering on the south coast, you know, and her working behind a bar somewhere, he being demobbed from his national service and getting his gratuity, you know, and going in for a drink and this . . . barmaid behind the bar and she fancied him because he was so posh. And they sort of thought they'd get married and run a hotel together and it was all a bit sort of romantic and idealistic, and the grim reality then caught up with them.

That is the actress Prunella Scales answering a question of comic (and class) motivation that had troubled my father for twenty years: why on earth did they marry each other? A question that—given his own late, failed marriage to a Jamaican girl less than half his age—must have had a resonance beyond the laugh track. On finally hearing an answer, he gave a sigh of comedy-snob satisfaction. Not long after my visit, Harvey died, at the age of eighty-one. He had told me that he wanted "It's All Over Now, Baby Blue" played at his funeral. When the day came, I managed to remember that. I forgot which version, though (sweet, melodic Baez). What he got instead was jeering, post-breakup Dylan, which made it seem as if my mild-mannered father had gathered his friends and family with the particular aim of telling them all to fuck off from beyond the grave. As comedy, this would have raised a half smile out of Harvey, not much more. It was a little broad for his tastes.

In birth, two people go into a room and three come out. In death, one person goes in and none come out. This is a cosmic joke told by Martin Amis. I like the metaphysical absurdity it draws out of the death event, the sense that death doesn't happen at all—that it is, in fact, the opposite of a happening. There are philosophers who take this joke seriously. To their way of thinking, the only option in the face of death—in facing death's absurd non-face—is to laugh. This is not the bold, humorless laugh of the triumphant atheist, who conquers what he calls death and his own fear of it. No: this is more unhinged. It comes from the powerless, despairing realization that death cannot be conquered, defied, contemplated, or even approached, because it's not there; it's only a word, signifying nothing. It's a truly funny laugh, of the laugh-or-you'll-cry variety. There is "plenty of hope, an infinite amount of hope—but not for us!" This is a cosmic joke told by Franz Kafka, a wisecrack projected into a void. When I first put the partial cremains of my father in a Tupperware sandwich box and placed it on my writing desk, that was the joke I felt like telling.

Conversely, the death we speak of and deal with every day, the death that is full of meaning, the non-absurd death, this is a place-marker, a fake, a convenient substitute. It was this sort of death that I was determined to press upon my father, as he did his dying. In my version, Harvey was dying meaningfully, in linear fashion, within a scenario stage-managed and scripted by the people around him. Neatly crafted, like an American sitcom: *The One in Which My Father Dies.* It was to conclude with a real event called Death, which he would *experience* and for which he would be ready. I did all the usual, banal things. I brought a Dictaphone to his bedside, in order to collect the narrative of his life (this perplexed him—he couldn't see the through line). I grew furious with overworked nurses. I refused to countenance any morbidity from my father, or any despair. The funniest thing about dying is how much we, the living, ask of the dying; how we beg them to make it easy on us. At the hospital, I ingratiated myself with the doctors and threw what the British call "new money" at the situation. Harvey watched me go about my business with a puzzled half smile. To all my eager suggestions he said, "Yes, dear—if you like," for he knew well that we were dealing with the National Health Service, into which all Smiths are born and die, and my new money would mean only that exactly the same staff, in the same hospital, would administer the same treatments, though in a slightly nicer room, with a window and possibly a television. He left me to my own devices, sensing that these things made a difference to me, though they made none to him: "Yes, dear—if you like." I was still thrashing an Austin 1100 with a tree branch; he was some way beyond that. And then, when he was truly beyond it, far out on the other side of nowhere, a nurse offered me the opportunity to see the body, which I refused. That was a mistake. It left me suspended in a bad joke in which a living man inexplicably becomes two pints of dust and everyone acts as if this were not a joke at all but, rather, the most reasonable thing in the world. A body would have been usefully, concretely absurd. I would have known—or so people say—that the thing lying there on the slab wasn't my father. As it was, I missed the death, I missed the body, I got the dust, and from these facts I tried to extrapolate a story, as writers will, but found myself, instead, in a kind of stasis. A moment in which nothing happened, and keeps not happening, forever. Later, I was informed, by way of comfort, that Harvey had also missed his death: he was in the middle of a sentence, joking with his nurse. "He didn't even know what hit him!" the head matron said, which was funny, too, because who the hell does?

Proximity to death inspired the manic spirit of carpe diem in the Smiths. After Harvey died, my mother met a younger man in Africa and married him. The younger of my two brothers, Luke, went to Atlanta to pursue dreams of rap stardom. Both decisions sounded like promising pilot episodes for new sitcoms. And then I tried to ring in the changes, by moving to Italy. In my empty kitchen, on the eve of leaving the country, I put my finger in the dust of my father and put the dust into my mouth and swallowed it, and there was something very funny about that—I laughed as I did it. After that, it felt as if I didn't laugh again for a long time. Or do much of anything. Imagined worlds moved quite out of my reach, seemed utterly pointless, not to mention a colossal human presumption: "Yes, dear—if you like." For two years in Rome, I looked from blank computer screen to handful of dust and back again—a scenario that no one, even in Britain, could turn into a sitcom. Then, as I was preparing to leave Italy, Ben, my other brother, rang with his news. He wanted me to know that he had broken with our long-standing family tradition of passive comedy appreciation. He had decided to become a comedian.

It turns out that becoming a comedian is an act of instantaneous self-creation. There are no intermediaries blocking your way, no gallerists, publishers, or distributors. Social class is a non-issue; you do not have to pass your eleven-plus. In a sense, it would have been a good career for our father, a creative man whose frequent attempts at advancement were forever thwarted, or so he felt, by his accent and his background, his lack of education, connections, luck. Of course, Harvey wasn't, in himself, *funny*—but you don't always have to be. In the world of comedy, if you are absolutely determined to stand on a stage for five minutes with a mike in your hand, someone in London will let you do it, if only once. Ben was determined: he'd given up the after-school youth group he had, till then, managed; he'd written material; he had tickets for me, my mother, my aunt. It was my private opinion that he'd had a minor nervous breakdown of some kind, a delayed reaction to his bereavement. I acted pleased, bought a plane ticket, flew over. We had been tight as thieves as children, but I'd barely seen him since Harvey died, and I sensed us settling into the attenuated relations of adult siblings, a new formal distance, always slightly abashed, for there seems no clear way, in adult life, to do justice to the intimacy of childhood. I remember being scandalized, as a child, at how rarely our parents spoke to *their* siblings. How was it possible? How did it happen? Then it happens to you. Thinking of him standing up there alone with a microphone, though, trying to be *funny*, I felt a renewed, Siamese-twin closeness: fearing for him was like fearing for me. I've never been able to bear watching anyone die onstage, never mind a blood relative. If he'd told me that it was major heart surgery he was about to have, on this makeshift stage in the tiny, dark basement of a London pub, I couldn't have been more sick about it.

It was a mixed bill. Before Ben, two men and two women performed a mildewed sketch show of unmistakable Oxbridge vintage, circa 1994. A certain brittle poshness informed their exaggerated portraits of high-strung secretaries, neurotic piano teachers, absent-minded professors. They put on mustaches and wigs and walked in and out of imaginary scenarios where fewer and fewer funny things occurred. It was the comedy of things past. The girls, though dressed as girls, were no longer girls, and the boys had paunches and bald spots; the faintest trace of ancient intracomedy-troupe love affairs clung to them sadly; all the promising meetings with the BBC had come and gone. This was being done out of pure friendship now, or the memory of friendship. As I watched the unspooling horror of it, a repressed, traumatic memory resurfaced, of an audition, one that must have taken place around the time this comedy troupe was formed, very likely in the same town. This audition took the form of a breakfast meeting, a "chat about comedy" with two young men, then members of the Cambridge Footlights, now a popular British TV double act. I don't remember what it was that I said. I remember only strained smiles, the silent consumption of scrambled eggs, a feeling of human free fall. And the conclusion, which was obvious to us all. Despite having spent years at the grindstone of comedy appreciation, I wasn't funny. Not even slightly.

And now the compère was calling my brother's name. He stepped out. I felt a great wash of East Anglian fatalism, my father's trademark, pass over to me, its new custodian. Ben was dressed in his usual urban streetwear, the only black man in the room. I began peeling the label off my beer bottle. I sensed at once the way he was going to play it, the same way we had played it throughout our childhood—a few degrees off whatever it was that people expected of us, when they looked at us. This evening, that strategy took the form of an opening song about the Olympics, with particular attention paid to equestrian dressage. It was funny! He was getting laughs. He pushed steadily forward, a slow, gloomy delivery that owed something to Harvey's seemingly infinite pessimism. *No good can come of this.* This had been Harvey's reaction to all news, no matter how objectively good that news might be, from the historic entrance of a Smith child into an actual university to the birthing of babies and the winning of prizes. When he became ill, he took a perversely British satisfaction in the diagnosis of cancer: absolutely nothing good could come of this, and the certainty of it seemed almost to calm him.

I waited, like my father, for the slipup, the flat joke. It didn't come. Ben did a minute on hip-hop, a minute on his baby daughter, a minute on his freshly minted standup career. Another song. I was still laughing, and so was everyone else. Finally, I felt able to look up from the beer mats to the stage. Up there I saw my brother, who is not eight, as I forever expect him to be, but thirty, and who appeared completely relaxed, as if born with mike in hand. And then it was over—no one had died.

The next time I saw Ben do standup was about ten gigs later, at the 2008 Edinburgh Festival Fringe. He didn't exactly die the night I turned up, but he was badly wounded. It was a shock to him, because it was the first time. In comedy terms, his cherry got popped. At first, he couldn't see why: it was the same type of venue he'd been doing in London—intimate, drunken—and, by and large, it was the same material. Why, this time, were the laughs smaller? Why, for one good joke in particular, did they not occur at all? We repaired to the bar to regroup, with all the other comedians doing the same. In comedy, the analysis of death, or near-death, experiences is a clear, unsentimental process. The discussion is technical, closer to a musician's self-analysis than to a writer's: this note was off; you missed the beat there. I knew I could say to Ben, honestly, and without fear of hurting him, "It was the pause—you went too slowly on the punch line," and he could say, "Yep," and the next night the pause would be shortened, the punch line would hit its mark. We ordered more beer. "The thing I don't understand— I don't understand what happened with the new material. I thought it was good, but . . ." Another comedian, who was also ordering beer, chipped in, "Did you do it first?" "Yes." "Don't do the new stuff first. Do it last. Just because you're excited by it doesn't mean it should go first. It's not ready yet."

We drank a lot, with a lot of very drunk comedians, until very late. Trying to keep up with the wisecracks and the complaints, I felt as if I'd

15

arrived late to a battleground that had seen bloody action. The comedians had the aura of survivors, speaking the language of mutual, hard experience: venues too hot and too small, the horror of empty seats, who got nominated for what, who'd been reviewed well or badly, and, of course, the financial pain. (Some Edinburgh performers break even, most incur debts, and almost no one makes a profit.) It was strange to see my brother, previously a member of my family, becoming a member of *this* family, all his previous concerns and principles subsumed, like theirs, into one simple but demanding question: *Is it funny?* And that's another reason to envy comedians: when they look at a blank page, they always know, at least, the question they need to ask themselves. I think the clarity of their aim accounts for a striking phenomenon, peculiar to comedy: the possibility of extremely rapid improvement. Comedy is a Lazarus art; you can die onstage and then rise again. It's not unusual to see a mediocre young standup in January and, seeing him again in December, discover a comedian who's found his groove, a transformed artist, a death-defier.

Russell Kane, a relatively new British comic, is a death-defier, the sort of comedian who won't let a moment pass without filling it with laughter. I went to see him on the last night of his Edinburgh run. His show was called *Gaping Flaws*, a phrase lifted from a negative online review of his 2007 Edinburgh show, which, in turn, was called *Easy Cliché and Tired Stereotype*, a phrase lifted from a negative review of his début 2006 show *Russell Kane's Theory of Pretension*. All these reviews came from the same man, Steve Bennett, a prominent British comedy critic who writes for the Web site Chortle. The problem with Kane was class—the British problem. A self-defined working-class "Essex boy" (though, physically, his look is more indie Americana than English suburbia; he's a dead ringer for the singer Anthony Kiedis), he centers his act on the tricky business of being the alien in the family, the wannabe intellectual son of a working-class, bigoted father. To his father, Kane's passion for reading is deeply suspicious, his interest in the arts tantamount to an admission of sexual deviancy. Kane's dilemma has a natural flip side, a typically British ressentiment for those very people his sensibilities have moved him toward. The middle classes, the Guardianistas (readers of the left-leaning liberal newspaper the *Guardian*), the smug élites who have made him feel his class in the first place. *Can't go home, can't leave home:* a subject close to my heart.

In 2006, Kane played this material too broadly, overexploiting a natural gift for grotesque physical comedy: his father was a hulking deformed monster, the Guardianistas fey fools, skipping across the stage. In 2007, the chip on his shoulder was still there, but the ideas were better, the portraits more detailed, more refined; he began to find his balance, which is a rare mixture of inspired verbal sparring and effective physical comedy. Third time's the charm: *Gaping Flaws* had almost none. It was still all about class, but some magical integration had occurred. I couldn't help being struck by the sense that what it might take a novelist a lifetime to achieve, a bright comedian can resolve in three seasons. (How to present a working-class experience to the middle classes without diluting it. How to stay angry without letting anger distort your work. How to be funny about the most serious things.)

Audiences love death-defiers like Kane. It's what they pay their money for, after all: laughs per minute. They tend to be less fond of those comedians who have themselves tired of the non-stop laughter and pine for a little silence. I want to call it "comedy nausea." Comedy nausea is the extreme incarnation of what my father felt: not only is joke-telling a cheap art; *the whole business of standup* is, in some sense, a shameful cheat. For a comedian of this kind, I imagine it feels like a love affair gone wrong. You start out wanting people to laugh in exactly the places you mean them to laugh, then they *always* laugh where you want them to laugh—then you start to hate them for it. Sometimes the feeling is temporary. The comedian returns to standup and finds new joy in, and respect for, the art of death-defying. Sometimes, as with Peter Cook (voted, by his fellow-comedians, in a British poll, the greatest comedian of all time), comedy nausea turns terminal, and only the most difficult laugh in the world will satisfy. Toward the end of his life, when his professional comedy output was practically nil, Cook made a series of phone calls to a radio call-in show, using the pseudonym Sven from Swiss Cottage (an area of northwest London), during which he discussed melancholy Norwegian matters in a thick Norwegian accent, arguably the funniest and bleakest "work" he ever did.

At the extreme end of this sensibility lies the anti-comedian. An anti-comedian not only allows death onstage; he invites death up. Andy Kaufman was an anti-comedian. So was Lenny Bruce. Tommy Cooper is the great British example. His comedy persona was "inept magician." He did intentionally bad magic tricks and told surreal jokes that played like Zen koans. He *actually* died onstage, collapsing from a heart attack during a 1984 live TV broadcast. I was nine, watching it on telly with Harvey. When Cooper fell over, we laughed and laughed, along with the rest of Britain, realizing only when the show cut to the commercial break that he wasn't kidding.

There was an anti-comedian at Edinburgh this year. His name was Edward Aczel. You will not have heard of him—neither had I, neither has practically anyone. This was only his second Edinburgh appearance. Maybe it was the fortuitous meeting of my mournful mood and his morbid material, but I thought his show, "Do I Really Have to Communicate with You"? was one of the strangest, and finest, hours of live comedy I'd ever seen. It started with neither a bang nor a whimper. It didn't really start. We, the audience, sat in nervous silence in a tiny dark room, and waited. Some fumbling with a cassette recorder was heard, faint music, someone mumbling backstage: "Welcome to the stage . . . Edward Aczel." Said without enthusiasm. A man wandered out. Going bald, early forties, schlubby, entirely nondescript. He said, "All right?" in a hopeless sort of way, and then decided that he wanted to do the introduction again. He went offstage and came on again. He did this several times. Despair settled over the room. Finally, he fixed himself in front of the microphone. "I think you'll all recall," he muttered, barely audible, "the words of Wittgenstein, the great twentieth-century philosopher, who said, 'If indeed mankind came to earth for a specific reason, it certainly wasn't to enjoy ourselves.'" A long, almost unbearable pause. "If you could bear that in mind while I'm on, I'd certainly appreciate it." Then, on a large flip chart, the kind of thing an account manager in an Aylesbury marketing agency might swipe from his office (Aczel is, in real life, an account manager for an Aylesbury marketing agency), he began to write with a Magic Marker. It was a list of what not to expect from his show. He went through it with us. There was to be:

No nudity.

No juggling.

No impressions of any well-known people.

25   No reference to crop circles during the show.

No one will be conceived during the show.

No tackling head-on of any controversial issues. . . .

And finally, and I think most importantly—

No refunds.

I recognized my father's spirit in this list: *No good can come of this.* He   30
then told us that he had a box of jigsaw puzzles backstage, for anyone who
became dangerously bored. Later, he drew a graph made up of an x-axis,
which stood for "time," and a y-axis, for "goodwill," on which he tracked
the show's progress. Point one, low down: "*Let's all go and get a drink—this
is pointless.*" Point two, slightly higher up: "*O.K., carry on, whatever.*" Point
three, still only halfway up: "*We could all be here forever. We think this is
great.*" He looked at his shoes, then, with mild aggression, at the audience.
"We'll never get to that point," he said. "It's just . . . it'll never happen." By
this time, everyone was laughing, but the laughter was a little crazy, dis-
jointed. It's a reckless thing, for a comedian, to be this honest with an audience. To say, in effect, "Whatever I do, whatever you do, we're *all* going to
die." When it finally came to jokes ("Now we go into the section of the
show routinely called 'material,' for obvious reasons"), Aczel had a dozen
written on his hand, and they were very funny, but by now he had already
convinced us that jokes were the least of what could be done here. It was an
easy and wonderful thing to believe this show a genuine shambles, saved
only by our attention and by chance. (We were mistaken, of course. Every
stumble, every murmur, is identical, every night.) In the lobby afterward,
calendars were on sale, each month illustrated by impossibly banal photo-
graphs of Aczel in bed, washing his face, walking into work, standing in the
road. Mine sits on my desk, next to my father in his Tupperware sandwich
box. On the cover, Aczel is pictured in a supermarket aisle. The subtitle
reads, "Life is endless, until you die"—Edith Piaf. Each month has a message for me. November: "Winter is coming—Yes!" April: "Who cares."
June: "This is not the life I was promised." *There is plenty of hope, an infinite
amount of hope—but not for us!*

On the last night of the Edinburgh festival, in another small, dark,
drunken venue, I waited for my brother to go on. It was about two in the
morning. Only comedians were left at the festival; the audiences had all
gone home. I feared for him, again—but he did his set, and he killed. He
was relaxed. There was nothing riding on his performance; the pause had
been fixed. Then a young Australian dude came on and spoke a lot about
bottle openers, and he killed, too. Maybe everybody kills at two in the
morning. Then the end of the end: one last comedian took the bar stage.
This was Andy Zaltzman, a great, tall man with an electrified Einstein
hairdo and a cutting, political-satirical act that got its laughs per minute.
He set to work, confident, funny, and instantly got heckled, a heckle that

was followed by a collective audience intake of breath, for the heckler was Daniel Kitson, a rather shy, whimsical young comedian from Yorkshire who looks like a beardy cross between a fisherman and a geography teacher. Kitson won the Perrier Comedy Award in 2002, at the age of twenty-five, and his gift is for the crafting of exquisite narratives, shows shaped like Alice Munro stories, bathetic and beautiful. A comedy-snob thrill passed through the room. It was a bit like Nick Drake turning up at a James Taylor gig. Kitson goodhumoredly heckled Zaltzman, and Zaltzman heckled back. Their ideas went spiralling down nonsensical paths, collided, did battle, and separated. Kitson busied himself handing out flyers for "Our joint show, to-morrow!," a show that couldn't exist, because the festival was over. We all took one. Zaltzman and Kitson got loose; the jokes were everywhere, with everyone, the whole room becoming comedy. There was a kind of hysteria abroad. I looked over at my brother and could see that he'd got this abdominal pain, too, and we were both doubled over, crying, and I wished Harvey were there, and at the same moment I felt something come free in me.

I have to confess to an earlier comic embellishment: my father is no longer in a Tupperware sandwich box. He was, for a year, but then I bought a pretty Italian Art Deco vase for him, completely see-through, so I can see through to him. The vase is posh, and not funny like the sandwich box, but I decided that what Harvey didn't have much of in life he would get in death. In life, he found Britain hard. It was a nation divided by postcodes and accents, schools and last names. The humor of its people helped make it bearable. *You don't have to be funny to live here, but it helps.* Hancock, Fawlty, Partridge, Brent: in my mind, they're all clinging to the middle rungs of England's class ladder. That, in large part, is the comedy of their situations.

For eighty-one years, my father was up to the same game, though his situation wasn't so comical; at least, the living of it wasn't. *Listen, I'll tell you a joke:* his mother had been in service, his father worked on the buses; he passed the grammar-school exam, but the cost of the uniform for the secondary school was outside the family's budget. *No, wait, it gets better:* At thirteen, he left school to fill the inkwells in a lawyer's office, to set the fire in the grate. At seventeen, he went to fight in the Second World War. In the fifties, he got married, started a family, and, finding that he had a good eye, tried commercial photography. His pictures were good, he set up a little studio, but then his business partner stiffed him in some dark plot of which he would never speak. His marriage ended. *And here's the kicker:* in the sixties, he had to start all over again, as a salesman. In the seventies, he married for the second time. A new lot of children arrived. The high point was the late eighties, a senior salesman now at a direct-mail company—selling paper, just like David Brent. Finally, the (lower) middle rung! A maisonette, half a garden, a sweet deal with a local piano teacher who taught Ben and me together, two bums squeezed onto the piano stool. But it didn't last, and the second marriage didn't last, and he ended up with little more than he had started with. Listening to my first novel, *White Teeth*, on tape, and hearing the rough arc of his life in the character Archie Jones, he took it well, seeing the parallels but also the difference: "He had better luck than me!" The novel was billed as comic fiction. To Harvey, it sat firmly in the laugh-or-you'll-cry genre. And when that *Fawlty Towers* boxed set came back to me as my only inheritance (along with a cardigan, several atlases, and a photograph of Venice), I did a little of both.

Analyze

1. What is Harvey's reaction to news, whether good or bad?
2. After Harvey dies, the family members each make a radical change. What does Zadie Smith do? What does her brother Ben do?
3. What does Smith mean when she writes "Comedy is a Lazarus art"?
4. Does a comic's dissection of a joke remind Smith more of what writers do or what musicians do when they reflect on their craft?

Explore

1. Does Smith set out to crack us up or break our hearts? Or both? Make your case by drawing upon evidence from the essay.
2. Look up clips of Ben Smith, Edward Azcel, Russell Kane, or one of the other male Edinburgh comics Smith references. Write a richly observed description of the bit you choose, then review it. What makes it funny? What makes it fail?
3. Listen to an audio clip of Zadie Smith's "comic novel" *White Teeth*. Note the speaker's voice, then try to listen for the "voice" of the novelist. How would you characterize Smith's sense of comedy, her comic timing, or her comic imagination as a writer?
4. Watch an episode of *Fawlty Towers*. How does this show give you a sense of "British comedy," British cultural norms, or class divisions in the UK?

David Foster Wallace
"A Supposedly Fun Thing
I'll Never Do Again"

The late **David Foster Wallace** (1962–2008) was a novelist, a short-story writer, and one of the funniest essayists on the American literary scene at the turn of the twenty-first century. The editors highly recommend that you, dear readers, seek out the complete mega-essay from which this excerpt is carved (originally published in *Harper's*). Wallace reveals himself as a master craftsman in this tour-de-force essay. Note the irreverent analytical work he does. He renders the minutiae of life on a luxury cruise line, then reflects upon the significance of the details he has itemized, making one of the most surprising (and funny) interpretive moves we've seen in this collection. Luxury liners promise us pampered bliss, he argues, but they also, ironically, deliver despair.

1

Right now it's Saturday 18 March, and I'm sitting in the extremely full coffee shop of the Fort Lauderdale Airport, killing the four hours between when I had to be off the cruise ship and when my flight to Chicago leaves by trying to summon up a kind of hypnotic sensuous collage of all the stuff I've seen and heard and done as a result of the journalistic assignment just ended.

I have seen sucrose beaches and water a very bright blue. I have seen an all-red leisure suit with flared lapels. I have smelled what suntan lotion smells like spread over 21000 pounds of hot flesh. I have been addressed as "Mon" in three different nations. I have watched 500 upscale Americans dance the Electric Slide. I have seen sunsets that looked computer-enhanced and a tropical moon that looked more like a sort of obscenely large and dangling lemon than like the good old stony U.S. moon I'm used to.

I have (very briefly) joined a Conga Line.

I've got to say I feel like there's been a kind of Peter Principle in effect on this assignment. A certain swanky East-Coast magazine approved of the results of sending me to a plain old simple State Fair last year to do a directionless essay-ish thing. So now I get offered this tropical plum assignment w/ the exact same paucity of direction or angle. But this time there's this new feeling of pressure: total expenses for the State Fair were $27.00 excluding games of chance. This time *Harper's* has shelled out over $3000 U.S. before seeing pithy sensuous description one. They keep saying—on the phone, Ship-to-Shore, very patiently—not to fret about it. They are sort of disingenuous, I believe, these magazine people. They say all they want is a sort of really big experiential postcard—go, plow the Caribbean in style, come back, say what you've seen.

I have seen a lot of really big white ships. I have seen schools of little fish with fins that glow. I have seen a toupee on a thirteen-year-old boy. (The glowing fish liked to swarm between our hull and the cement of the pier whenever we docked.) I have seen the north coast of Jamaica. I have seen and smelled all 145 cats inside the Ernest Hemingway Residence in Key West FL. I now know the difference between straight Bingo and Prize-O, and what it is when a Bingo jackpot "snowballs." I have seen camcorders that practically required a dolly; I've seen fluorescent luggage and fluorescent sunglasses and fluorescent pince-nez and over twenty different makes of rubber thong. I have heard steel drums and eaten conch fritters and watched a woman in silver lamé projectile-vomit inside a glass elevator. I have pointed rhythmically at the ceiling to the 2:4 beat of the exact same disco music I hated pointing at the ceiling to in 1977.

I have learned that there are actually intensities of blue beyond *very, very bright* blue. I have eaten more and classier food than I've ever eaten, and eaten this food during a week when I've also learned the difference between "rolling" in heavy seas and "pitching" in heavy seas. I have heard a professional comedian tell folks, without irony, "But seriously." I have seen fuchsia pantsuits and menstrual-pink sportcoats and maroon-and-purple warm-ups and white loafers worn without socks. I have seen professional blackjack dealers so lovely they make you want to run over to their table and spend every last nickel you've got playing blackjack. I have heard upscale adult U.S. citizens ask the Guest Relations Desk whether snorkeling necessitates getting wet, whether the skeetshooting will be held outside, whether the crew sleeps on board, and what time the Midnight Buffet is. I now know the precise mixological difference between a Slippery Nipple and a Fuzzy Navel. I know what a Coco Loco is. I have in one week been the object of over 1500 professional smiles. I have burned and peeled twice. I have shot skeet at sea. Is this enough? At the time it didn't seem like enough. I have felt the full clothy weight of a subtropical sky. I have jumped a dozen times at the shattering, flatulence-of-the-gods sound of a cruise ship's horn. I have absorbed the basics of mah-jongg, seen part of a two-day rubber of contract bridge, learned how to secure a life jacket over a tuxedo, and lost at chess to a nine-year-old girl.

(Actually it was more like I shot *at* skeet at sea.)

I have dickered over trinkets with malnourished children. I now know every conceivable rationale and excuse for somebody spending over $3000 to go on a Caribbean cruise. I have bitten my lip and declined Jamaican pot from an actual Jamaican.

I have seen, one time, from an upper deck's rail, way below and off the right rear hull, what I believe to have been a hammerhead shark's distinctive fin, addled by the starboard turbine's Niagaracal wake.

10   I have now heard—and am powerless to describe—reggae elevator music. I have learned what it is to become afraid of one's own toilet. I have acquired "sea legs" and would like now to lose them. I have tasted caviar and concurred with the little kid sitting next to me that it is: *blucky.*

I now understand the term "Duty Free."

I now know the maximum cruising speed of a cruise ship in knots.[1] I have had escargot, duck, Baked Alaska, salmon w/ fennel, a marzipan pelican, and an omelette made with what were alleged to be trace amounts of Etruscan truffle. I have heard people in deck chairs say in all earnestness that it's the humidity rather than the heat. I have been—thoroughly, professionally, and as promised beforehand—pampered. I have, in dark moods, viewed and logged every type of erythema, keratinosis, pre-melanomic lesion, liver spot, eczema, wart, papular cyst, potbelly, femoral cellulite, varicosity, collagen and silicone enhancement, bad tint, hair transplants that have not taken—i.e. I have seen nearly naked a lot of people I would prefer not to have seen nearly naked. I have felt as bleak as I've felt since puberty, and have filled almost three Mead notebooks trying to figure out whether it was Them or Just Me. I have acquired and nurtured a potentially lifelong grudge against the ship's Hotel Manager—whose name was Mr. Dermatis and whom I now and henceforth christen Mr. Dermatitis[2]—an almost

---

[1](though I never did get clear on just what a knot is)

[2]Somewhere he'd gotten the impression I was an investigative journalist and wouldn't let me see the galley, Bridge, staff decks, *anything,* or interview any of the crew or staff in an on-the-record way, and he wore sunglasses inside, and epaulets, and kept talking on the phone for long stretches of time in Greek when I was in his office after I'd skipped the karaoki semifinals in the Rendez-Vous Lounge to make a special appointment to see him; I wish him ill.

reverent respect for my waiter, and a searing crush on the cabin steward for my part of Deck 10's port hallway, Petra, she of the dimples and broad candid brow, who always wore a nurse's starched and rustling whites and smelled of the cedary Norwegian disinfectant she swabbed bathrooms down with, and who cleaned my cabin within a cm of its life at least ten times a day but could never be caught in the actual *act* of cleaning—a figure of magical and abiding charm, and well worth a postcard all her own.

2

More specifically: From 11 to 18 March 1995 I, voluntarily and for pay, underwent a 7-Night Caribbean (7NC) Cruise on board the m.v. *Zenith*,[3] a 47,255-ton ship owned by Celebrity Cruises Inc., one of the over twenty cruise lines that currently operate out of south Florida.[4] The vessel and facilities were, from what I now understand of the industry's standards, absolutely top-hole. The food was superb, the service impeccable, the shore excursions and shipboard activities organized for maximal stimulation down to the tiniest detail. The ship was so clean and so white it looked boiled. The Western Caribbean's blue varied between baby-blanket and fluorescent; likewise the sky. Temperatures were uterine. The very sun itself seemed preset for our comfort. The crew-to-passenger ratio was 1.2 to 2. It was a Luxury Cruise.

With a few minor niche-adaptive variations, the 7NC Luxury Cruise is essentially generic. All of the Megalines offer the same basic product. This product is not a service or a set of services. It's not even so much a good time (though it quickly becomes clear that one of the big jobs of the Cruise Director and his staff is to keep reassuring everybody that everybody's

---

[3]No wag could possibly resist mentally rechristening the ship the m.v. *Nadir* the instant he saw the *Zenith*'s silly name in the Celebrity brochure, so indulge me on this, but the rechristening's nothing particular against the ship itself.

[4]There's also Windstar and Silversea, Tall Ship Adventures and Windjammer Barefoot Cruises, but these Caribbean Cruises are wildly upscale and smaller. The 20+ cruise lines I'm talking run the "Megaships," the floating wedding cakes with occupancies in four figures and engine-propellers the size of branch banks. Of the Megalines out of South FL there's Commodore, Costa, Majesty, Regal, Dolphin, Princess, Royal Caribbean, good old Celebrity. There's Renaissance, Royal Cruise Line, Holland, Holland America, Cunard, Cunard Crown, Cunard Royal Viking. There's Norwegian Cruise Line, there's Crystal, there's Regency Cruises. There's the WalMart of the cruise industry, Carnival, which the other lines refer to sometimes as "Carnivore." I don't recall which line *The Love Boat*'s *Pacific Princess* was supposed to be with (I guess they were probably more like a CA-to-Hawaii-circuit ship, though I seem to recall them going all over the place), but now Princess Cruises has bought the name and uses poor old Gavin MacLeod in full regalia in their TV ads.

having a good time). It's more like a feeling. But it's also still a bona fide product—it's supposed to be *produced* in you, this feeling: a blend of relaxation and stimulation, stressless indulgence and frantic tourism, that special mix of servility and condescension that's marketed under configurations of the verb "to pamper." This verb positively studs the Megalines' various brochures: ". . . as you've never been pampered before," ". . . to pamper yourself in our jacuzzis and saunas," "Let us pamper you," "Pamper yourself in the warm zephyrs of the Bahamas."

15   The fact that contemporary adult Americans also tend to associate the word "pamper" with a certain *other* consumer product is not an accident, I don't think, and the connotation is not lost on the mass-market Megalines and their advertisers. And there's good reason for them to iterate the word, and stress it.

3

This one incident made the Chicago news. Some weeks before I underwent my own Luxury Cruise, a sixteen-year-old male did a Brody off the upper deck of a Megaship—I think a Carnival or Crystal ship—a suicide. The news version was that it had been an unhappy adolescent love thing, a shipboard romance gone bad, etc. I think part of it was something else, something there's no way a real news story could cover.

There is something about a mass-market Luxury Cruise that's unbearably sad. Like most unbearably sad things, it seems incredibly elusive and complex in its causes and simple in its effect: on board the *Nadir*—especially at night, when all the ship's structured fun and reassurances and gaiety-noise ceased—I felt despair. The word's overused and banalified now, *despair,* but it's a serious word, and I'm using it seriously. For me it

---

The 7NC Megaship cruiser is a type, a genre of ship all its own, like the destroyer. All the Megalines have more than one ship. The industry descends from those old patrician trans-Atlantic deals where the opulence combined with actually getting someplace—e.g., the *Titanic, Normandie,* etc. The present Caribbean Cruise market's various niches—Singles, Old People, Theme, Special Interest, Corporate, Party, Family, Mass-Market, Luxury, Absurd Luxury, Grotesque Luxury—have now all pretty much been carved and staked out and are competed for viciously (I heard off-the-record stuff about Carnival v. Princess that'd singe your brows). Megaships tend to be designed in America, built in Germany, registered out of Liberia or Monrovia; and they are both captained and owned, for the most part, by Scandinavians and Greeks, which is kind of interesting, since these are the same peoples who've dominated sea travel pretty much forever. Celebrity Cruises is owned by the Chandris Group; the X on their three ships' smokestacks turns out not to be an X but a Greek chi, for Chandris, a Greek shipping family so ancient and powerful they apparently regarded Onassis as a punk.

denotes a simple admixture—a weird yearning for death combined with a crushing sense of my own smallness and futility that presents as a fear of death. It's maybe close to what people call dread or angst. But it's not these things, quite. It's more like wanting to die in order to escape the unbearable feeling of becoming aware that I'm small and weak and selfish and going without any doubt at all to die. It's wanting to jump overboard.

I predict this'll get cut by the editor, but I need to cover some background. I, who had never before this cruise actually been on the ocean, have always associated the ocean with dread and death. As a little kid I used to memorize shark-fatality data. Not just attacks. Fatalities. The Albert Kogler fatality off Baker's Beach CA in 1959 (Great White). The U.S.S. *Indianapolis* smorgasbord off the Philippines in 1945 (many varieties, authorities think mostly Tigers and Blues)[5]; the most-fatalities-attributed-to-a-single-shark series of incidents around Matawan/Spring Lake NJ in 1916 (Great White again; this time they caught a *carcharias* in Raritan Bay NJ and found human parts *in gastro* (I know which parts, and whose)). In school I ended up writing three different papers on "The Castaway" section of *Moby-Dick*, the chapter where the cabin boy Pip falls overboard and is driven mad by the empty immensity of what he finds himself floating in. And when I teach school now I always teach Crane's horrific "The Open Boat," and I get bent out of shape when the kids find the story dull or jaunty-adventurish: I want them to feel the same marrow-level dread of the oceanic I've always felt, the intuition of the sea as primordial *nada,* bottomless, depths inhabited by cackling tooth-studded things rising toward you at the rate a feather falls. Anyway, hence the atavistic shark fetish, which I need to admit came back with a long-repressed vengeance on this Luxury Cruise,[6]

---

[5]I'm doing this from memory. I don't need a book. I can still name every documented *Indianapolis* fatality, including some serial numbers and hometowns. (Hundreds of men lost, 80 classed as Shark, 7–10 August '45; the *Indianapolis* had just delivered Little Boy to the island of Tinian for delivery to Hiroshima, so ironists take note. Robert Shaw as Quint reprised the whole incident in 1975's *Jaws,* a film that, as you can imagine, was like fetish-porn to me at age thirteen.)

[6]And I'll admit that on the very first night of the 7NC I asked the staff of the *Nadir*'s Five-Star Caravelle Restaurant whether I could maybe have a spare bucket of *au jus* drippings from supper so I could try chumming for sharks off the back rail of the top deck, and that this request struck everybody from the maitre d' on down as disturbing and maybe even disturbed, and that it turned out to be a serious journalistic faux pas, because I'm almost positive the maitre d' passed this disturbing tidbit on to Mr. Dermatitis and that it was a big reason why I was denied access to stuff like the ship's galley, thereby impoverishing the sensuous scope of this article. (Plus it also revealed how little I understood the *Nadir*'s sheer size: twelve decks and 150 feet up, the *au jus* drippings would have dispersed into a vague red cologne by the time they hit the water, with concentrations of blood inadequate to attract or excite a serious shark, whose fin would have probably looked like a pushpin from that height, anyway.)

and that I made such a fuss about the one (possible) dorsal fin I saw off starboard that my companions at supper's Table 64 finally had to tell me, with all possible tact, to shut up about the fin already.

I don't think it's an accident that 7NC Luxury Cruises appeal mostly to older people. I don't mean decrepitly old, but I mean like age-50+ people, for whom their own mortality is something more than an abstraction. Most of the exposed bodies to be seen all over the daytime *Nadir* were in various stages of disintegration. And the ocean itself (which I found to be salty as *hell,* like sore-throat-soothing-gargle-grade salty, its spray so corrosive that one temple-hinge of my glasses is probably going to have to be replaced) turns out to be basically one enormous engine of decay. Seawater corrodes vessels with amazing speed—rusts them, exfoliates paint, strips varnish, dulls shine, coats ships' hulls with barnacles and kelp-clumps and a vague ubiquitous nautical snot that seems like death incarnate. We saw some real horrors in port, local boats that looked dipped in a mixture of acid and shit, scabbed with rust and goo, ravaged by what they float in.

20   Not so the Megalines' ships. It's not an accident they're all so white and clean, for they're clearly meant to represent the Calvinist triumph of capital and industry over the primal decay-action of the sea. The *Nadir* seemed to have a whole battalion of wiry little Third World guys who went around the ship in navy-blue jumpsuits scanning for decay to overcome. Writer Frank Conroy, who has an odd little essaymercial in the front of Celebrity Cruises' 7NC brochure, talks about how "It became a private challenge for me to try to find a piece of dull bright-work, a chipped rail, a stain in the deck, a slack cable or anything that wasn't perfectly shipshape. Eventually, toward the end of the trip, I found a capstan[7] with a half-dollar-sized patch of rust on the side facing the sea. My delight in this tiny flaw was interrupted by the arrival, even as I stood there, of a crewman with a roller and a bucket of white paint. I watched as he gave the entire capstan a fresh coat of paint and walked away with a nod."

Here's the thing. A vacation is a respite from unpleasantness, and since consciousness of death and decay are unpleasant, it may seem weird that Americans' ultimate fantasy vacation involves being plunked down in an enormous primordial engine of death and decay. But on a 7NC Luxury Cruise, we are skillfully enabled in the construction of various fantasies of triumph over just this death and decay. One way to "triumph" is via the

---

[7](apparently a type of nautical hoist, like a pulley on steroids)

rigors of self-improvement; and the crew's amphetaminic upkeep of the *Nadir* is an unsubtle analogue to personal titivation: diet, exercise, megavitamin supplements, cosmetic surgery, Franklin Quest time-management seminars, etc.

There's another way out, too, w/r/t death. Not titivation but titillation. Not hard work but hard play. The 7NC's constant activities, parties, festivities, gaiety and song; the adrenaline, the excitement, the stimulation. It makes you feel vibrant, alive. It makes your existence seem noncontingent.[8] The hard-play option promises not a transcendence of death-dread so much as just drowning it out: "Sharing a laugh with your friends[9] in the lounge after dinner, you glance at your watch and mention that it's almost showtime. . . . When the curtain comes down after a standing ovation, the talk among your companions[10] turns to, 'What next?' Perhaps a visit to the casino or a little dancing in the disco? Maybe a quiet drink in the piano bar or a starlit stroll around the deck? After discussing all your options, everyone agrees: *'Let's do it all!'*"

Dante this isn't, but Celebrity Cruises' 7NC brochure is nevertheless an extremely powerful and ingenious piece of advertising. The brochure is magazine-size, heavy and glossy, beautifully laid out, its text offset by art-quality photos of upscale couples'[11] tanned faces locked in a kind of rictus of pleasure. All the Megalines put out brochures, and they're essentially interchangeable. The middle part of the brochures detail the different packages and routes. Basic 7NC's go to the Western Caribbean (Jamaica, Grand Cayman, Cozumel) or the Eastern Caribbean (Puerto Rico, Virgins), or something called the Deep Caribbean (Martinique, Barbados, Mayreau). There are also 10- and 11-Night Ultimate Caribbean packages that hit pretty much every exotic coastline between Miami and the Panama Canal.

---

[8] The *Nadir*'s got literally hundreds of cross-sectional maps of the ship on every deck, at every elevator and junction, each with a red dot and a YOU ARE HERE—and it doesn't take long to figure out that these are less for orientation than for some weird kind of reassurance.

[9] Always constant references to "friends" in the brochures' text; part of this promise of escape from death-dread is that no cruiser is ever alone.

[10] See?

[11] Always couples in this brochure, and even in group shots it's always groups of couples. I never did get hold of a brochure for an actual Singles Cruise, but the mind reels. There was a "Singles Get Together" (sic) on the *Nadir* that first Saturday night, held in Deck 8's Scorpio Disco, which after an hour of self-hypnosis and controlled breathing I steeled myself to go to, but even the Get Together was 75% established couples, and the few of us Singles under like 70 all looked grim and self-hypnotized, and the whole affair seemed like a true wrist-slitter, and I beat a retreat after half an hour because *Jurassic Park* was scheduled to run on the TV that night, and I hadn't yet looked at the whole schedule and seen that *Jurassic Park* would play several dozen times over the coming week.

The brochures' final sections' boilerplate always details costs,[12] passport stuff, Customs regulations, caveats.

But it's the first section of these brochures that really grabs you, the photos and italicized blurbs from *Fodor's Cruises* and *Berlitz,* the dreamy *mise en scènes* and breathless prose. Celebrity's brochure, in particular, is a real two-napkin drooler. It has little hypertextish offsets, boxed in gold, that say stuff like INDULGENCE BECOMES EASY and RELAX-ATION BECOMES SECOND NATURE and STRESS BECOMES A FAINT MEMORY. And these promises point to the third kind of death-and-dread-transcendence the *Nadir* offers, one that requires neither work nor play, the enticement that is a 7NC's real carrot and stick.

4

25   "Just standing at the ship's rail looking out to sea has a profoundly soothing effect. As you drift along like a cloud on water, the weight of everyday life is magically lifted away, and you seem to be floating on a sea of smiles. Not just among your fellow guests but on the faces of the ship's staff as well. As a steward cheerfully delivers your drinks, you mention all of the smiles among the crew. He explains that every Celebrity staff member takes pleasure in making your cruise a completely carefree experience and treating you as an honored guest.[13] Besides, he adds, there's no place they'd rather be. Looking back out to sea, you couldn't agree more."

Celebrity's 7NC brochure uses the 2nd-person pronoun throughout. This is extremely appropriate. Because in the brochure's scenarios the 7NC experience is being not described but *evoked.* The brochure's real seduction is not an invitation to fantasize but rather a construction of the fantasy

---

[12]From $2500 to about $4000 for mass-market Megaships like the *Nadir,* unless you want a Presidential Suite with a skylight, wet bar, automatic palm-fronds, etc., in which case double that.

[13]In response to some dogged journalistic querying, Celebrity's PR firm's Press Liaison (the charming and Debra Winger–voiced Ms. Wiessen) had this explanation for the cheery service: "The people on board—the staff—are really part of one big family—you probably noticed this when you were on the ship. They really love what they're doing and love serving people, and they pay attention to what everybody wants and needs."

This was not what I myself observed. What I myself observed was that the *Nadir* was one very tight ship, run by an elite cadre of very hard-ass Greek officers and supervisors, and that the preterite staff lived in mortal terror of these Greek bosses who watched them with enormous beadiness at all times, and that the crew worked almost Dickensianly hard, too hard to feel truly cheery about it. My sense was that Cheeriness was up there with Celerity and Servility on the clipboarded evaluation sheets the Greek bosses were constantly filling out on them: when they didn't know any guests were looking, a lot

itself. This is advertising, but with a queerly authoritarian twist. In regular adult-market ads, attractive people are shown having a near-illegally good time in some scenario surrounding a product, and you are meant to fantasize that you can project yourself into the ad's perfect world via purchase of that product. In regular advertising, where your adult agency and freedom of choice have to be flattered, the purchase is prerequisite to the fantasy; it's the fantasy that's being sold, not any literal projection into the ad's world. There's no sense of any real kind of actual promise being made. This is what makes conventional adult advertisements fundamentally coy.

Contrast this coyness with the force of the 7NC brochure's ads: the near-imperative use of the second person, the specificity of detail that extends even to what you will say (*you will say* "I couldn't agree more" and "Let's do it all!"). In the cruise brochure's ads, you are excused from doing the work of constructing the fantasy. The ads do it for you. The ads, therefore, don't flatter your adult agency, or even ignore it—they supplant it.

And this authoritarian—near-parental—type of advertising makes a very special sort of promise, a diabolically seductive promise that's actually kind of honest, because it's a promise that the Luxury Cruise itself is all about honoring. The promise is not that you can experience great pleasure, but that you *will*. That they'll make certain of it. That they'll micromanage every iota of every pleasure-option so that not even the dreadful corrosive action of your adult consciousness and agency and dread can fuck up your fun. Your troublesome capacities for choice, error, regret, dissatisfaction, and despair will be removed from the equation. The ads promise that you will be able—finally, for once—truly to relax and have a good time, because you will *have no choice* but to have a good time.[14]

I am now 33 years old, and it feels like much time has passed and is passing faster and faster every day. Day to day I have to make all sorts of choices

---

of the workers had the kind of pinched weariness about them that one associates with low-paid service employees in general, plus fear. My sense was that a crewman could get fired for a pretty small lapse, and that getting fired by these Greek officers might well involve a spotlessly shined shoe in the ass and then a really long swim.

What I observed was that the preterite workers did have a sort of affection for the passengers, but that it was a *comparative* affection—even the most absurdly demanding passenger seemed kind and understanding compared to the martinetism of the Greeks, and the crew seemed genuinely grateful for this, sort of the way we find even very basic human decency moving if we encounter it in NYC or Boston.

[14]"YOUR PLEASURE," several Megalines' slogans go, "IS OUR BUSINESS." What in a regular ad would be a double entendre is here a triple entendre, and the tertiary connotation—viz. "MIND YOUR OWN BLOODY BUSINESS AND LET US PROFESSIONALS WORRY ABOUT YOUR PLEASURE, FOR CHRIST'S SAKE"—is far from incidental.

about what is good and important and fun, and then I have to live with the forfeiture of all the other options those choices foreclose. And I'm starting to see how as time gains momentum my choices will narrow and their fore-closures multiply exponentially until I arrive at some point on some branch of all life's sumptuous branching complexity at which I am finally locked in and stuck on one path and time speeds me through stages of stasis and at-rophy and decay until I go down for the third time, all struggle for naught, drowned by time. It is dreadful. But since it's my own choices that'll lock me in, it seems unavoidable—if I want to be any kind of grownup, I have to make choices and regret foreclosures and try to live with them.

30   Not so on the lush and spotless m.v. *Nadir*. On a 7NC Luxury Cruise, I pay for the privilege of handing over to trained professionals responsibility not just for my experience but for my *interpretation* of that experience—i.e. my pleasure. My pleasure is for 7 nights and 6.5 days wisely and efficiently managed ... just as promised in the cruise line's advertising—nay, just as somehow already *accomplished* in the ads, with their 2nd-person imperatives, which make them not promises but predictions. Aboard the *Nadir,* just as ringingly foretold in the brochure's climactic p. 23, I get to do (in gold): "... something you haven't done in a long, long time: *Absolutely Nothing.*"

How long has it been since you did Absolutely Nothing? I know exactly how long it's been for me. I know how long it's been since I had every need met choicelessly from someplace outside me, without my having to ask or even acknowledge that I needed. And that time I was floating, too, and the fluid was salty, and warm but not too, and if I was conscious at all I'm sure I felt dreadless, and was having a really good time, and would have sent postcards to everyone wishing they were here.

Analyze
1. What is the "supposedly fun thing" the author "will never do again"?
2. Who is "Mr. Dermatitis"?
3. What sounds like "the flatulence of the gods"?

Explore
1. Wallace has great fun with a rhetorical device called "anaphora" (a technique where phrases are repeated at the beginnings of neighbor-ing clauses). This kind of strategic repetition creates emphasis. Look

back at the beginning of the excerpt and you will see what we mean. Try it out yourself. Borrow and repeat the phrase "I have seen" as you write a rich description of the things you have noticed at your school, or in your hometown, or where you now live.

2. Check out comedian Andy Griffith's classic stand-up monologue "What it was, was football." Versions of it are readily available on YouTube. Although these two texts are obviously different, Griffith's 1953 performance is arguably the great-grandfather of Wallace's essay. How are the two texts similar? How are they different? Write an essay in which you use Griffith's monologue to deepen your understanding of Wallace's essay, its motive, thesis, or use of description.

3. Wallace makes irreverent use of abundant footnotes, a technique that became his signature style. Look up the rules for using footnotes. In what ways does Wallace observe or break those rules? How would you characterize his voice, based on this stylistic choice?

George Saunders
"Victory Lap"

George Saunders, the author of several collections of short stories, a book of essays, several screenplays, and a children's book, has won both a MacArthur Foundation "Genius Grant" and a Guggenheim Fellowship. While he is primarily considered a humorist, you will soon see much of his humor is dark, almost savagely so. "Victory Lap" is impressive in its ability to move between the interior monologues of three characters with wildly active interior minds. The story arc dips into would-be tragedy, but we believe this story can and should be ultimately labeled as comic. Do you agree?

Three days shy of her fifteenth birthday, Alison Pope paused at the top of the stairs.

Say the staircase was marble. Say she descended and all heads turned. Where was {special one}? Approaching now, bowing slightly, he exclaimed, How can so much grace be contained in one small package? Oops. Had he said *small package*? And just stood there? Broad princelike face totally bland of expression? Poor thing! Sorry, no way, down he went, he was definitely not {special one}.

What about this guy, behind Mr. Small Package, standing near the home entertainment center? With a thick neck of farmer integrity yet tender ample lips, who, placing one hand on the small of her back, whispered, Dreadfully sorry you had to endure that bit about the small package just now. Let us go stand on the moon. Or, uh, in the moon. In the moonlight.

Had he said, *Let us go stand on the moon*? If so, she would have to be like, {eyebrows up}. And if no wry acknowledgment was forthcoming, be like, Uh, I am not exactly dressed for standing on the moon, which, as I understand it, is super-cold?

5   Come on, guys, she couldn't keep treading gracefully on this marble stairwell in her mind forever! That dear old white-hair in the tiara was getting all like, *Why are those supposed princes making that darling girl march in place ad nausea?* Plus she had a recital tonight and had to go fetch her tights from the dryer.

Egads! One found oneself still standing at the top of the stairs.

Do the thing where, facing upstairs, hand on railing, you hop down the stairs one at a time, which was getting a lot harder lately, due to, someone's feet were getting longer every day, seemed like.

Pas de chat, pas de chat.

Changement, changement.

10   Hop over thin metal thingie separating hallway tile from living-room rug.

Curtsy to self in entryway mirror.

Come on, Mom, get here. We do not wish to be castrigated by Ms. Callow again in the wings.

Although actually she loved Ms. C. So strict! Also loved the other girls in class. And the girls from school. *Loved* them. Everyone was so nice. Plus the boys at her school. Plus the teachers at her school. All of them were doing their best. Actually, she loved her whole town. That adorable grocer, spraying his lettuce! Pastor Carol, with her large comfortable butt! The chubby postman, gesticulating with his padded envelopes! It had once been a mill town. Wasn't that crazy? What did that even mean?

Also she loved her house. Across the creek was the Russian church. So ethnic! That onion dome had loomed in her window since her Pooh footie days. Also loved Gladsong Drive. Every house on Gladsong was a Corona del Mar. That was amazing! If you had a friend on Gladsong, you already knew where everything was in his or her home.

Jeté, jeté, rond de jambe.
Pas de bourrée.   15

On a happy whim, do front roll, hop to your feet, kiss the picture of Mom and Dad taken at Penney's back in the Stone Ages, when you were that little cutie right there {kiss} with a hair bow bigger than all outdoors.

Sometimes, feeling happy like this, she imagined a baby deer trembling in the woods.

Where's your mama, little guy?

I don't know, the deer said in the voice of Heather's little sister Becca.

Are you afraid? she asked it. Are you hungry? Do you want me to hold you?   20

Okay, the baby deer said.

Here came the hunter now, dragging the deer's mother by the antlers. Her guts were completely splayed. Jeez, that was nice! She covered the baby's eyes and was like, Don't you have anything better to do, dank hunter, than kill this baby's mom? You seem like a nice enough guy.

Is my mom killed? the baby said in Becca's voice.

No, no, she said. This gentleman was just leaving.

The hunter, captivated by her beauty, toffed or doffed his cap, and, going   25 down on one knee, said, If I could will life back into this fawn, I would do so, in hopes you might defer one tender kiss upon our elderly forehead.

Go, she said. Only, for your task of penance, do not eat her. Lay her out in a field of clover, with roses strewn about her. And bestow a choir, to softly sing of her foul end.

Lay who out? the baby deer said.

No one, she said. Never mind. Stop asking so many questions.

Pas de chat, pas de chat.
Changement, changement.   30

She felt hopeful that {special one} would hail from far away. The local boys possessed a certain *je ne sais quoi,* which, tell the truth, she was not *très* crazy about, such as: actually named their own nuts. She had overheard that! And aspired to work for CountyPower because the work shirts were awesome and you got them free.

So ixnay on the local boys. A special ixnay on Matt Drey, owner of the largest mouth in the land. Kissing him last night at the pep rally had been like kissing an underpass. Scary! Kissing Matt was like suddenly this cow in a sweater is bearing down on you, who will not take no for an answer, and his huge cow head is being flooded by chemicals that are drowning out what little powers of reason Matt actually did have.

What she liked was being in charge of her. Her body, her mind. Her thoughts, her career, her future.

That was what she liked.

35   So be it.

We might have a slight snack.

Un petit repas.

Was she special? Did she consider herself special? Oh, gosh, she didn't know. In the history of the world, many had been more special than her. Helen Keller had been awesome; Mother Teresa was amazing; Mrs. Roosevelt was quite chipper in spite of her husband, who was handicapped, which, in addition, she had been gay, with those big old teeth, long before such time as being gay and First Lady was even conceptual. She, Alison, could not hope to compete in the category of those ladies. Not yet, anyway!

There was so much she didn't know! Like how to change the oil. Or even check the oil. How to open the hood. How to bake brownies. That was embarrassing, actually, being a girl and all. And what was a mortgage? Did it come with the house? When you breast-fed, did you have to like push the milk out?

40   Egads. Who was this wan figure, visible through the living-room window, trotting up Gladsong Drive? Kyle Boot, palest kid in all the land? Still dressed in his weird cross-country toggles?

Poor thing. He looked like a skeleton with a mullet. Were those cross-country shorts from the like *Charlie's Angels* days or *quoi*? How could he run so well when he seemed to have literally no muscles? Every day he ran home like this, shirtless with his backpack on, then hit the remote from down by the Fungs' and scooted into his garage without breaking stride.

You almost had to admire the poor goof.

They'd grown up together, been little beaners in that mutual sandbox down by the creek. Hadn't they bathed together when wee or some such crud? She hoped that never got out. Because in terms of friends, Kyle was basically down to Feddy Slavko, who walked leaning way backward and was always retrieving things from between his teeth, announcing the name of the retrieved thing in Greek, then re-eating it. Kyle's mom and dad didn't let him do squat. He had to call home if the movie in World Culture might show bare boobs. Each of the items in his lunch box was clearly labeled.

Pas de bourrée.

45   And curtsy.

Pour quantity of Cheez Doodles into compartmentalized old-school Tupperware dealie.

Thanks, Mom, thanks, Dad. Your kitchen *rocks.*

Shake Tupperware dealie back and forth like panning for gold, then offer to some imaginary poor gathered round.

Please enjoy. Is there anything else I can do for you folks?

You have already done enough, Alison, by even deigning to speak to us.   50

That is so not true! Don't you understand, all people deserve respect? Each of us is a rainbow.

Uh, really? Look at this big open sore on my poor shriveled flank.

Allow me to fetch you some Vaseline.

That would be much appreciated. This thing kills.

But as far as that rainbow idea? She believed that. People were amazing.   55
Mom was awesome, Dad was awesome, her teachers worked so hard and had kids of their own, and some were even getting divorced, such as Mrs. Dees, but still always took time for their students. What she found especially inspiring about Mrs. Dees was that, even though Mr. Dees was cheating on Mrs. Dees with the lady who ran the bowling alley, Mrs. Dees was still teaching the best course ever in Ethics, posing such questions as: Can goodness win? Or do good people always get shafted, evil being more reckless? That last bit seemed to be Mrs. Dees taking a shot at the bowling-alley gal. But seriously! Is life fun or scary? Are people good or bad? On the one hand, that clip of those gauntish pale bodies being steamrolled while fat German ladies looked on chomping gum. On the other hand, sometimes rural folks, even if their particular farms were on hills, stayed up late filling sandbags.

In their straw poll she had voted for people being good and life being fun, with Mrs. Dees giving her a pitying glance as she stated her views: To do good, you just have to decide to do good. You have to be brave. You have to stand up for what's right. At that last, Mrs. Dees had made this kind of groan. Which was fine. Mrs. Dees had a lot of pain in her life, yet, interestingly? Still obviously found something fun about life and good about people, because otherwise why sometimes stay up so late grading you come in next day all exhausted, blouse on backward, having messed it up in the early-morning dark, you dear discombobulated thing?

Here came a knock on the door. Back door. In-ter-est-ing. Who could it be? Father Dmitri from across the way? UPS? FedEx? With *un petit* check *pour Papa*?

Jeté, jeté, rond de jambe.

Pas de bourrée.

60   Open door, and—
Here was a man she did not know. Quite huge fellow, in one of those
meter-reader vests.
Something told her to step back in, slam the door. But that seemed rude.
Instead she froze, smiled, did {eyebrow raise} to indicate: May I help you?

Kyle Boot dashed through the garage, into the living area, where the big
clocklike wooden indicator was set at All Out. Other choices included:
Mom & Dad Out; Mom Out; Dad Out; Kyle Out; Mom & Kyle Out;
Dad & Kyle Out; and All In.
65   Why did they even need All In? Wouldn't they know it when they were
All In? Would he like to ask Dad that? Who, in his excellent totally silent
downstairs woodshop, had designed and built the Family Status Indicator?
Ha.
Ha ha.
On the kitchen island was a Work Notice.

Scout: New geode on deck. Place in yard per included drawing. No goofing.
Rake areas first, put down plastic as I have shown you. Then lay in white rock.
THIS GEODE EXPENSIVE. Pls take seriously. No reason this should not
be done by time I get home. This = five (5) Work Points.

70   Gar, Dad, do you honestly feel it fair that I should have to slave in the
yard until dark after a rigorous cross-country practice that included sixteen
440s, eight 880s, a mile-for-time, a kajillion Drake sprints, and a five-mile
Indian relay?
Shoes off, mister.
Yoinks, too late. He was already at the TV. And had left an incriminating trail of microclods. Way verboten. Could the microclods be hand-
plucked? Although, problem: if he went back to hand-pluck the microclods,
he'd leave an incriminating new trail of microclods.
He took off his shoes and stood mentally rehearsing a little show he
liked to call WHAT IF . . . RIGHT NOW?
WHAT IF they came home RIGHT NOW?
75   It's a funny story, Dad! I came in thoughtlessly! Then realized what I'd
done! I guess, when I think about it, what I'm happy about? Is how quickly
I self-corrected! The reason I came in so thoughtlessly was, I wanted to get
right to work, Dad, per your note!

He raced in his socks to the garage, threw his shoes into the garage, ran for the vacuum, vacuumed up the micro-clods, then realized, holy golly, he had thrown his shoes into the garage rather than placing them on the Shoe Sheet as required, toes facing away from the door for ease of donnage later.

He stepped into the garage, placed his shoes on the Shoe Sheet, stepped back inside.

Scout, Dad said in his head, has anyone ever told you that even the most neatly maintained garage is going to have some oil on its floor, which is now on your socks, being tracked all over the tan Berber?

Oh gar, his ass was grass.

But no—*celebrate good times, come on*—no oil stain on rug.   80

He tore off his socks. It was absolutely verboten for him to be in the main living area barefoot. Mom and Dad coming home to find him Tarzaning around like some sort of white trasher would not be the least fucking bit—

Swearing in your head? Dad said in his head. Step up, Scout, be a man. If you want to swear, swear aloud.

I don't want to swear aloud.

Then don't swear in your head.

Mom and Dad would be heartsick if they could hear the swearing he sometimes did in his head, such as crap-cunt shit-turd dick-in-the-ear butt-creamery. Why couldn't he stop doing that? They thought so highly of him, sending weekly braggy emails to both sets of grandparents, such as: Kyle's been super-busy keeping up his grades while running varsity cross-country though still a sophomore, while setting aside a little time each day to manu-facture such humdingers as cunt-swoggle rear-fuck—

What was wrong with him? Why couldn't he be grateful for all that   85
Mom and Dad did for him, instead of—

Cornhole the ear-cunt.

Flake-fuck the pale vestige with a proddering dick-knee.

You could always clear the mind with a hard pinch on your own min-imal love handle.

Ouch.

Hey, today was Tuesday, a Major Treat day. The five (5) new Work Points   90
for placing the geode, plus his existing two (2) Work Points, totaled seven (7) Work Points, which, added to his eight (8) accrued Usual Chore Points, made fifteen (15) Total Treat Points, which could garner him a Major Treat (for example, two handfuls of yogurt-covered raisins) plus twenty free-choice

TV minutes, although the particular show would have to be negotiated with Dad at time of cash-in.

One thing you will not be watching, Scout, is *America's Most Outspoken Dirt Bikers*.

Whatever.

Whatever, Dad.

Really, Scout? "Whatever"? Will it be "whatever" when I take away all your Treat Points and force you to quit cross-country, as I have several times threatened to do if a little more cheerful obedience wasn't forthcoming?

95   No, no, no. I don't want to quit, Dad. Please. I'm good at it. You'll see, first meet. Even Matt Drey said—

Who is Matt Drey? Some ape on the football team?

Yes.

Is his word law?

No.

100   What did he say?

Little shit can run.

Nice talk, Scout. Ape talk. Anyway, you may not make it to the first meet. Your ego seems to be overflowing its banks. And why? Because you can jog? Anyone can jog. Beasts of the field can jog.

I'm not quitting! Anal-cock shit-bird rectum-fritz! Please, I'm begging you, it's the only thing I'm decent at! Mom, if he makes me quit I swear to God I'll—

Drama doesn't suit you, Beloved Only.

105   If you want the privilege of competing in a team sport, Scout, show us that you can live within our perfectly reasonable system of directives designed to benefit you.

Hello.

A van had just pulled up in the St. Mikhail's parking lot.

Kyle walked in a controlled, gentlemanly manner to the kitchen counter. On the counter was Kyle's Traffic Log, which served the dual purpose of (1) buttressing Dad's argument that Father Dmitri should build a soundproof retaining wall and (2) constituting a data set for a possible Science Fair project for him, Kyle, entitled, by Dad, "Correlation of Church Parking Lot Volume vs. Day of Week, with Ancillary Investigation of Sunday Volume Throughout Year."

Smiling agreeably as if he enjoyed filling out the Log, Kyle very legibly filled out the Log:

Vehicle: VAN.   110
Color: GRAY.
Make: CHEVY.
Year: UNKNOWN.

A guy got out of the van. One of the usual Rooskies. "Rooskie" was an allowed slang. Also "dang it." Also "holy golly." Also "crapper." The Rooskie was wearing a jean jacket over a hoodie, which, in Kyle's experience, was not unusual church-wear for the Rooskies, who sometimes came directly over from Jiffy Lube still wearing coveralls.

Under "Vehicle Driver" he wrote, PROBABLE PARISHIONER.   115

That sucked. Stank, rather. The guy being a stranger, he, Kyle, now had to stay inside until the stranger left the neighborhood. Which totally futzed up his geode placing. He'd be out there until midnight. What a detriment!

The guy put on a Day-Glo vest. Ah, dude was a meter reader.

The meter reader looked left, then right, leaped across the creek, entered the Pope backyard, passed between the soccer-ball rebounder and the in-ground pool, then knocked on the Pope door.

Good leap there, Boris.

The door swung open.   120
Alison.

Kyle's heart was singing. He'd always thought that was just a phrase. Alison was like a national treasure. In the dictionary under "beauty" there should be a picture of her in that jean skort. Although lately she didn't seem to like him all that much.

Now she stepped across her deck so the meter reader could show her something. Something electrical wrong on the roof? The guy seemed eager to show her. Actually, he had her by the wrist. And was like tugging.

That was weird. Wasn't it? Something had never been weird around here before. So probably it was fine. Probably the guy was just a really new meter reader?

Somehow Kyle felt like stepping out onto the deck. He stepped out. The   125 guy froze. Alison's eyes were scared-horse eyes. The guy cleared his throat, turned slightly to let Kyle see something.

A knife.

The meter reader had a knife.

Here's what you're doing, the guy said. Standing right there until we leave. Move a muscle, I knife her in the heart. Swear to God. Got it?

Kyle's mouth was so spitless all he could do was make his mouth do the shape it normally did when saying Yes.

130   Now they were crossing the yard. Alison threw herself to the ground. The guy hauled her up. She threw herself down. He hauled her up. It was odd seeing Alison tossed like a rag doll in the sanctuary of the perfect yard her dad had made for her. She threw herself down.

The guy hissed something and she rose, suddenly docile.

In his chest Kyle felt the many directives, Major and Minor, he was right now violating. He was on the deck shoeless, on the deck shirtless, was outside when a stranger was near, had engaged with that stranger.

Last week Sean Ball had brought a wig to school to more effectively mimic the way Bev Mirren chewed her hair when nervous. Kyle had briefly considered intervening. At Evening Meeting, Mom had said that she considered Kyle's decision not to intervene judicious. Dad had said, That was none of your business. You could have been badly hurt. Mom had said, Think of all the resources we've invested in you, Beloved Only. Dad had said, I know we sometimes strike you as strict but you are literally all we have.

They were at the soccer-ball rebounder now, Alison's arm up behind her back. She was making a low repetitive sound of denial, like she was trying to invent a noise that would adequately communicate her feelings about what she'd just this instant realized was going to happen to her.

135   He was just a kid. There was nothing he could do. In his chest he felt the lush release of pressure that always resulted when he submitted to a directive. There at his feet was the geode. He should just look at that until they left. It was a great one. Maybe the greatest one ever. The crystals at the cutaway glistened in the sun. It would look nice in the yard. Once he placed it. He'd place it once they were gone. Dad would be impressed that even after what had occurred he'd remembered to place the geode.

That's the ticket, Scout.

We are well pleased, Beloved Only.

Super job, Scout.

Holy crap. It was happening. She was marching along all meek like the trouper he'd known she'd be. He'd had her in mind since the baptism of what's-his-name. Sergei's kid. At the Russian church. She'd been standing in her yard, her dad or some such taking her picture.

He'd been like, Hello, Betty. 140

Kenny had been like, Little young, bro.

He'd been like, For you, grandpa.

When you studied history, the history of cultures, you saw your own individual time as hidebound. There were various theories of acquiescence. In Bible days a king might ride through a field and go: That one. And she would be brought unto him. And they would duly be betrothed and if she gave birth unto a son, super, bring out the streamers, she was a keeper. Was she, that first night, digging it? Probably not. Was she shaking like a leaf? Didn't matter. What mattered was offspring and the furtherance of the lineage. Plus the exaltation of the king, which resulted in righteous kingly power.

Here was the creek.

He marched her through. 145

The following bullet points remained in the decision matrix: take to side van door, shove in, follow in, tape wrists/ mouth, hook to chain, make speech. He had the speech down cold. Had practiced it both in his head and on the recorder: *Calm your heart, darling, I know you're scared because you don't know me yet and didn't expect this today but give me a chance and you will see we will fly high. See I am putting the knife right over here and I don't expect I'll have to use it, right?*

If she wouldn't get in the van, punch hard in gut. Then pick up, carry to side van door, throw in, tape wrists/mouth, hook to chain, make speech, etc., etc.

Stop, pause, he said.

Gal stopped.

Fucksake. Side door of the van was locked. How undisciplined was that. 150 Ensuring that the door was unlocked was clearly indicated on the pre-mission matrix. Melvin appeared in his mind. On Melvin's face was the look of hot disappointment that had always preceded an ass whooping, which had always preceded the other thing. Put up your hands, Melvin said, defend yourself.

True, true. Little error there. Should have double-checked the pre-mission matrix.

No biggie.

Joy not fear.

Melvin was dead fifteen years. Mom dead twelve.

Little bitch was turned around now, looking back at the house. That 155 willfulness wouldn't stand. That was going to get nipped in the bud. He'd have to remember to hurt her early, establish a baseline.

Turn the fuck around, he said.

She turned around.

He unlocked the door, swung it open. Moment of truth. If she got in, let him use the tape, they were home free. He'd picked out a place in Sackett, big-ass cornfield, dirt road leading in. If fuckwise it went good they'd pick up the freeway from there. Basically steal the van. It was Kenny's van. He'd borrowed it for the day. Screw Kenny. Kenny had once called him stupid. Too bad, Kenny, that remark just cost you one van. If fuckwise it went bad, she didn't properly arouse him, he'd abort the activity, truncate the subject, heave the thing out, clean van as necessary, go buy corn, return van to Kenny, say, Hey, bro, here's a shitload of corn, thanks for the van, I never could've bought a suitable quantity of corn in my car. Then lay low, watch the papers like he'd done with the nonarousing redhead out in—

Gal gave him an imploring look, like, Please don't.

160　　Was this a good time? To give her one in the gut, knock the wind out of her sails?

It was.

He did.

The geode was beautiful. What a beautiful geode. What made it beautiful? What were the principal characteristics of a beautiful geode? Come on, think. Come on, concentrate.

She'll recover in time, Beloved Only.

165　　None of our affair, Scout.

We're amazed by your good judgment, Beloved Only.

Dimly he noted that Alison had been punched. Eyes on the geode, he heard the little *oof.*

His heart dropped at the thought of what he was letting happen. They'd used goldfish snacks as coins. They'd made bridges out of rocks. Down by the creek. Back in the day. Oh God. He should've never stepped outside. Once they were gone he'd just go back inside, pretend he'd never stepped out, make the model-railroad town, still be making it when Mom and Dad got home. When eventually someone told him about it? He'd make a certain face. Already on his face he could feel the face he would make, like, What? Alison? Raped? Killed? Oh God. Raped and killed while I innocently made my railroad town, sitting cross-legged and unaware on the floor like a tiny little—

No. No, no, no. They'd be gone soon. Then he could go inside. Call 911. Although then everyone would know he'd done nothing. All his future life would be bad. Forever he'd be the guy who'd done nothing. Besides, calling wouldn't do any good. They'd be long gone. The parkway was just across Featherstone, with like a million arteries and cloverleafs or whatever spouting out of it. So that was that. In he'd go. As soon as they left. Leave, leave, leave, he thought, so I can go inside, forget this ever—

Then he was running. Across the lawn. Oh God! What was he doing, 170 what was he doing? Jesus, shit, the directives he was violating! Running in the yard (bad for the sod); transporting a geode without its protective wrapping; hopping the fence, which stressed the fence, which had cost a pretty penny; leaving the yard; leaving the yard barefoot; entering the Secondary Area without permission; entering the creek barefoot (broken glass, dangerous microorganisms), and, not only that, oh God, suddenly he saw what this giddy part of himself intended, which was to violate a directive so Major and absolute that it wasn't even a directive, since you didn't need a directive to know how totally verboten it was to—

He burst out of the creek, the guy still not turning, and let the geode fly into his head, which seemed to emit a weird edge-seep of blood even before the skull visibly indented and the guy sat right on his ass.

Yes! Score! It was fun! Fun dominating a grown-up! Fun using the most dazzling gazelle-like leg speed ever seen in the history of mankind to dash soundlessly across space and master this huge galoot, who otherwise, right now, would be—

What if he hadn't?

God, what if he hadn't?

He imagined the guy bending Alison in two like a pale garment bag 175 while pulling her hair and thrusting bluntly, as he, Kyle, sat cowed and obedient, tiny railroad viaduct grasped in his pathetic babyish—

Jesus! He skipped over and hurled the geode through the windshield of the van, which imploded, producing an inward rain of glass shards that made the sound of thousands of tiny bamboo wind chimes.

He scrambled up the hood of the van, retrieved the geode.

Really? Really? You were going to ruin her life, ruin my life, you cunt-probe dick-munch ass-gashing Animal? Who's bossing who now? Gash-ass, jizz-lips, turd-munch—

He'd never felt so strong/angry/wild. Who's the man? Who's your daddy? What else must he do? To ensure that Animal did no further harm?

You still moving, freak? Got a plan, stroke-dick? Want a skull gash on top of your existing skull gash, big man? You think I won't? You think I—

180   Easy, Scout, you're out of control.

Slow your motor down, Beloved Only.

Quiet. I'm the boss of me.

FUCK!

What the hell? What was he doing on the ground? Had he tripped? Did someone wonk him? Did a branch fall? God damn. He touched his head. His hand came away bloody.

185   The beanpole kid was bending. To pick something up. A rock. Why was that kid off the porch? Where was the knife?

Where was the gal?

Crab-crawling toward the creek.

Flying across her yard.

Going into her house.

190   Fuck it, everything was fucked. Better hit the road. With what, his good looks? He had like eight bucks total.

Ah Christ! The kid had smashed the windshield! With the rock! Kenny was not going to like that one bit.

He tried to stand but couldn't. The blood was just pouring out. He was not going to jail again. No way. He'd slit his wrists. Where was the knife? He'd stab himself in the chest. That had nobility. Then the people would know his name. Which of them had the balls to samurai themselves with a knife in the chest?

None.

Nobody.

195   Go ahead, pussy. Do it.

No. The king does not take his own life. The superior man silently accepts the mindless rebuke of the rabble. Waits to rise and fight anew. Plus he had no idea where the knife was. Well, he didn't need it. He'd crawl into the woods, kill something with his bare hands. Or make a trap from some grass. Ugh. Was he going to barf? There, he had. Right on his lap.

Figures you'd blow the simplest thing, Melvin said.

Melvin, God, can't you see my head is bleeding so bad?

A kid did it to you. You're a joke. You got fucked by a kid.

200   Oh, sirens, perfect.

Well, it was a sad day for the cops. He'd fight them hand to hand. He'd sit until the last moment, watching them draw near, doing a silent death mantra that would centralize all his life power in his fists.

He sat thinking about his fists. They were huge granite boulders. They were a pit bull each. He tried to get up. Somehow his legs weren't working. He hoped the cops would get here soon. His head really hurt. When he touched up there, things moved. It was like he was wearing a gore cap. He was going to need a bunch of stitches. He hoped it wouldn't hurt too much. Probably it would, though.

Where was that beanpole kid?

Oh, here he was.

Looming over him, blocking out the sun, rock held high, yelling some- 205
thing, but he couldn't tell what, because of the ringing in his ears.

Then he saw that the kid was going to bring the rock down. He closed his eyes and waited and was not at peace at all but instead felt the beginnings of a terrible dread welling up inside him, and if that dread kept growing at the current rate, he realized in a flash of insight, there was a name for the place he would be then, and it was Hell.

Alison stood at the kitchen window. She'd peed herself. Which was fine. People did that. When super-scared. She'd noticed it while making the call. Her hands had been shaking so bad. They still were. One leg was doing that Thumper thing. God, the stuff he'd said to her. He'd punched her. He'd pinched her. There was a big blue mark on her arm.

How could Kyle still be out there? But there he was, in those comical shorts, so confident he was goofing around, hands clenched over his head like a boxer from some cute alt universe where a kid that skinny could actually win a fight against a guy with a knife.

Wait.

His hands weren't clenched. He was holding the rock, shouting some- 210
thing down at the guy, who was on his knees, like the blindfolded prisoner in that video they'd seen in History, about to get sword-killed by a formal dude in a helmet.

Kyle, don't, she whispered.

For months afterward she had nightmares in which Kyle brought the rock down. She was on the deck trying to scream his name but nothing was coming out. Down came the rock. Then the guy had no head. The blow just literally dissolved his head. Then his body tumped over and Kyle turned to her with this heartbroken look of, My life is over. I killed a guy.

Why was it, she sometimes wondered, that in dreams we can't do the simplest things? Like a crying puppy is standing on some broken glass and you want to pick it up and brush the shards off its pads but you can't because you're balancing a ball on your head. Or you're driving and there's this old guy on crutches, and you go, to Mr. Feder, your Driver's Ed teacher, Should I swerve? And he's like, Uh, probably. But then you hear this big clunk and Feder makes a negative mark in his book.

Sometimes she'd wake up crying from the dream about Kyle. The last time, Mom and Dad were already there, going, That's not how it was. Remember, Allie? How did it happen? Say it. Say it out loud. Allie, can you tell Mommy and Daddy how it really happened?

215   I ran outside, she said. I shouted.

That's right, Dad said. You shouted. Shouted like a champ.

And what did Kyle do? Mom said.

Put down the rock, she said.

A bad thing happened to you kids, Dad said. But it could have been worse.

220   So much worse, Mom said.

But because of you kids, Dad said, it wasn't.

You did so good, Mom said.

Did beautiful, Dad said.

Analyze

1. Where does Alison Pope have to go the evening of the abduction?
2. What does the family status indicator say about Kyle Boots's family? What does Kyle's game of "What if . . . right now?" say?
3. How do the nicknames "Scout" and "Beloved Only" help to characterize Kyle's family dynamics?

Explore

1. How does Alison's fantasy about the fawn figure into the larger story? What about her thoughts on her Ethics class? Find examples of how Saunders adopts a 15-year-old girl's point of view, and how they work for the story.

2. Kyle has an almost Tourette's-like habit of cursing in his head. Why would Saunders bestow him with this quirk?

3. How does the interior monologue of the abductor affect the reader's perception of him? Do you find yourself actually having empathy for him, despite his actions?

4. How do Kyle's parents react when he tells them about wanting to intervene when a girl at school was teased about chewing on her hair? How does Kyle's upbringing influence the choices he makes in rescuing Alison?

5. Saunders tells us Kyle and Alison grew up together, but now in their mid-teens, they have drifted apart. Kyle is enamoured of Alison, thinking of her as a "national treasure." Alison seems to feel nothing but pity, calling Kyle "a skeleton with a mullet." How do you think this experience will change their relationship?

3 Persuasive

> "I can win an argument on any topic, against any opponent. People know this, and steer clear of me at parties. Often, as a sign of their great respect, they don't even invite me."
>
> —Dave Barry

What makes a piece of writing—a poem, essay, or ad, for example—persuasive? We might argue that all writing is persuasive (which is kind of funny—we could present an argument about argument!). We're not just thinking about obviously argumentative pieces, like research papers you may have written, or the Op-Ed section in your local newspaper. A grocery list can be called persuasive because its objective is to get items home from a store. A poem might be deemed persuasive because its objective is have the reader see a particular image or to convey a specific emotion.

This section puts pieces about humor and pieces that are humorous side by side under the umbrella of persuasion. Some of these pieces were relatively easy to categorize: Christopher Hitchens's piece on humor and women makes a bold and clear declaration. Ellen Finnigan's essay on Kristen Wiig makes some large statements not only on Wiig, but on women in comedy, and comedy itself.

But why do we have a Billy Collins poem in this section? Why include a short satire by Donald Barthelme? We believe that you'll still be able to look for and apply rhetorical strategies you're familiar with or learning in these texts—like Aristotle's appeals, potential fallacies, and the persuasive strength of a thesis's support. As teachers, we'll bounce that question about what unifies these pieces right back at you; but as editors we'll say that the pieces in this section seemed to be most clearly defined by their purposefulness. They have the objective of imparting a strong idea as their goal. You'll have to let us know if they are successful in their aim.

Christopher Hitchens
"Why Women Aren't Funny"

Bon vivant, cultural luminary, and provocateur, the late **Christopher Hitchens** was a contributing editor for *Vanity Fair*, one of America's oldest magazines, a publication dedicated to fashion, culture, and politics. His matchless prose has been called observant and engaged, thoughtful and hilarious. His essays are bold, as you'll see.

Be your gender what it may, you will certainly have heard the following from a female friend who is enumerating the charms of a new (male) squeeze: "He's really quite cute, and he's kind to my friends, and he knows all kinds of stuff, and he's so *funny* . . ." (If you yourself are a guy, and you know the man in question, you will often have said to yourself, "Funny? He wouldn't know a joke if it came served on a bed of lettuce with *sauce béarnaise*.") However, there is something that you absolutely never hear from a male friend who is hymning his latest (female) love interest: "She's a real honey, has a life of her own . . . [interlude for attributes that are none of your business] . . . and, man, does she ever make 'em laugh."

Now, why *is* this? Why is it the case?, I mean. Why are women, who have the whole male world at their mercy, not funny? Please do not pretend not to know what I am talking about.

All right—try it the other way (as the bishop said to the barmaid). Why are men, taken on average and as a whole, funnier than women? Well, for one thing, they had damn well better be. The chief task in life that a man has to perform is that of impressing the opposite sex, and Mother Nature (as we laughingly call her) is not so kind to men. In fact, she equips many fellows with very little armament for the struggle. An average man has just one, outside chance: he had better be able to make the lady laugh. Making them laugh has been one of the crucial preoccupations of my life. If you can stimulate her to laughter—I am talking about that real, out-loud, head-back, mouth-open-to-expose-the-full-horseshoe-of-lovely-teeth, involuntary, full, and deep-throated mirth; the kind that is accompanied by a shocked surprise and a slight (no, make that a *loud*) peal of delight—well, then, you have at least caused her to loosen up and to change her expression. I shall not elaborate further.

> "Men will laugh at almost anything, often precisely because it is— or they are—extremely stupid. Women aren't like that"
> —Christopher Hitchens, "Why Women Aren't Funny"

Women have no corresponding need to appeal to men in this way. They already appeal to men, if you catch my drift. Indeed, we now have all the joy of a scientific study, which illuminates the difference. At the Stanford University School of Medicine (a place, as it happens, where I once underwent an absolutely hilarious procedure with a sigmoidoscope), the grim-faced researchers showed 10 men and 10 women a sample of 70 black-and-white cartoons and got them to rate the gags on a "funniness scale." To annex for a moment the fall-about language of the report as it was summarized in *Biotech Week:*

> The researchers found that men and women share much of the same   5
> humor-response system; both use to a similar degree the part of the
> brain responsible for semantic knowledge and juxtaposition and the
> part involved in language processing. But they also found that some
> brain regions were activated more in women. These included the left
> prefrontal cortex, suggesting a greater emphasis on language and ex-
> ecutive processing in women, and the nucleus accumbens . . . which is
> part of the mesolimbic reward center.

This has all the charm and address of the learned Professor Scully's attempt to define a smile, as cited by Richard Usborne in his treatise on P. G. Wodehouse: "the drawing back and slight lifting of the corners of the mouth, which partially uncover the teeth; the curving of the naso-labial furrows . . ." But have no fear—it gets worse:

"Women appeared to have less expectation of a reward, which in this case was the punch line of the cartoon," said the report's author, Dr. Allan Reiss. "So when they got to the joke's punch line, they were more pleased about it." The report also found that "women were quicker at identifying material they considered unfunny."

Slower to get it, more pleased when they do, and swift to locate the unfunny—for this we need the Stanford University School of Medicine? And remember, this is women when *confronted* with humor. Is it any wonder that they are backward in generating it?

This is not to say that women are humorless, or cannot make great wits and comedians. And if they did not operate on the humor wavelength, there would be scant point in half killing oneself in the attempt to make them writhe and scream (uproariously). Wit, after all, is the unfailing symptom of intelligence. Men will laugh at almost anything, often precisely because it is—or they are—extremely stupid. Women aren't like that. And the wits and comics among them are formidable beyond compare: Dorothy Parker, Nora Ephron, Fran Lebowitz, Ellen DeGeneres. (Though ask yourself, was Dorothy Parker ever really funny?) Greatly daring—or so I thought— I resolved to call up Ms. Lebowitz and Ms. Ephron to try out my theories. Fran responded: "The cultural values are male; for a woman to say a man is funny is the equivalent of a man saying that a woman is pretty. Also, humor is largely aggressive and pre-emptive, and what's more male than that?" Ms. Ephron did not disagree. She did, however, in what I thought was a slightly feline way, accuse me of plagiarizing a rant by Jerry Lewis that said much the same thing. (I have only once seen Lewis in action, in *The King of Comedy,* where it was really Sandra Bernhard who was funny.)

10   In any case, my argument doesn't say that there are no decent women comedians. There are more terrible female comedians than there are terrible male comedians, but there are some impressive ladies out there. Most of them, though, when you come to review the situation, are hefty or dykey or Jewish, or some combo of the three. When Roseanne stands up and tells biker jokes and invites people who don't dig her shtick to suck her dick— know what I am saying? And the Sapphic faction may have its own reasons

for wanting what I want—the sweet surrender of female laughter. While Jewish humor, boiling as it is with angst and self-deprecation, is almost masculine by definition.

Substitute the term "self-defecation" (which I actually heard being used inadvertently once) and almost all men will laugh right away, if only to pass the time. Probe a little deeper, though, and you will see what Nietzsche meant when he described a witticism as an epitaph on the death of a feeling. Male humor prefers the laugh to be at someone's expense, and understands that life is quite possibly a joke to begin with—and often a joke in extremely poor taste. Humor is part of the armor-plate with which to resist what is already farcical enough. (Perhaps not by coincidence, battered as they are by motherfucking nature, men tend to refer to life itself as a bitch.) Whereas women, bless their tender hearts, would prefer that life be fair, and even sweet, rather than the sordid mess it actually is. Jokes about calamitous visits to the doctor or the shrink or the bathroom, or the venting of sexual frustration on furry domestic animals, are a male province. It must have been a man who originated the phrase "funny like a heart attack." In all the millions of cartoons that feature a patient listening glum-faced to a physician ("There's no cure. There isn't even a *race* for a cure"), do you remember even one where the patient is a woman? I thought as much.

Precisely because humor is a sign of intelligence (and many women believe, or were taught by their mothers, that they become threatening to men if they appear too bright), it could be that in some way men do not *want* women to be funny. They want them as an audience, not as rivals. And there is a huge, brimming reservoir of male unease, which it would be too easy for women to exploit. (Men can tell jokes about what happened to John Wayne Bobbitt, but they don't want women doing so.) Men have prostate glands, hysterically enough, and these have a tendency to give out, along with their hearts and, it has to be said, their dicks. This is funny only in male company. For some reason, women do not find their own physical decay and absurdity to be so riotously amusing, which is why we admire Lucille Ball and Helen Fielding, who do see the funny side of it. But this is so rare as to be like Dr. Johnson's comparison of a woman preaching to a dog walking on its hind legs: the surprise is that it is done at all.

The plain fact is that the physical structure of the human being is a joke in itself: a flat, crude, unanswerable disproof of any nonsense about "intelligent design." The reproductive and eliminating functions (the closeness of which is the origin of all obscenity) were obviously wired together in hell by some subcommittee that was giggling cruelly as it went about its work. ("Think they'd wear this? Well, they're gonna *have* to.") The resulting confusion is the source of perhaps 50 percent of all humor. Filth. That's what the customers want, as we occasional stand-up performers all know. Filth, and plenty of it. Filth in lavish, heaping quantities. And there's another principle that helps exclude the fair sex. "Men obviously like gross stuff," says Fran Lebowitz. "Why? Because it's *childish*." Keep your eye on that last word. Women's appetite for talk about that fine product known as Depend is limited. So is their relish for gags about premature ejaculation. ("Premature for *whom?*" as a friend of mine indignantly demands to know.) But "child" is the key word. For women, reproduction is, if not the only thing, certainly the main thing. Apart from giving them a very different attitude to filth and embarrassment, it also imbues them with the kind of seriousness and solemnity at which men can only goggle. This womanly seriousness was well caught by Rudyard Kipling in his poem "The Female of the Species." After cleverly noticing that with the male "mirth obscene diverts his anger"—which is true of most work on that great masculine equivalent to childbirth, which is warfare—Kipling insists:

> But the Woman that God gave him,
> 15   every fibre of her frame
> Proves her launched for one sole issue,
> armed and engined for the same,
> And to serve that single issue,
> lest the generations fail,
> 20   The female of the species must be
> deadlier than the male.

The word "issue" there, which we so pathetically misuse, is restored to its proper meaning of childbirth. As Kipling continues:

> She who faces Death by torture for
> each life beneath her breast
> 25   May not deal in doubt or pity—must
> not swerve for fact or jest.

Men are overawed, not to say terrified, by the ability of women to produce babies. (Asked by a lady intellectual to summarize the differences between the sexes, another bishop responded, "Madam, I cannot conceive.") It gives women an unchallengeable authority. And one of the earliest origins of humor that we know about is its role in the mockery of authority. Irony itself has been called "the glory of slaves." So you could argue that when men get together to be funny and do not expect women to be there, or in on the joke, they are really playing truant and implicitly conceding who is really the boss.

The ancient annual festivities of Saturnalia, where the slaves would play master, were a temporary release from bossdom. A whole tranche of subversive male humor likewise depends on the notion that women are *not* really the boss, but are mere objects and victims. Kipling saw through this:

> So it comes that Man, the coward,
> when he gathers to confer   30
> With his fellow-braves in council,
> dare not leave a place for her.

In other words, for women the question of funniness is essentially a secondary one. They are innately aware of a higher calling that is no laughing matter. Whereas with a man you may freely say of him that he is lousy in the sack, or a bad driver, or an inefficient worker, and still wound him less deeply than you would if you accused him of being deficient in the humor department.

If I am correct about this, which I am, then the explanation for the superior funniness of men is much the same as for the inferior funniness of women. Men have to pretend, to themselves as well as to women, that they are not the servants and supplicants. Women, cunning minxes that they are, have to affect not to be the potentates. This is the unspoken compromise. H. L. Mencken described as "the greatest single discovery ever made by man" the realization "that babies have human fathers, and are not put into their mother's bodies by the gods." You may well wonder what people were thinking before that realization hit, but we do know of a society in Melanesia where the connection was not made until quite recently. I suppose that the reasoning went: everybody does that thing the entire time, there being little else to do, but not every woman becomes pregnant. Anyway, after a certain stage women came to the conclusion that men were actually *necessary,* and the old form of matriarchy came to a close. (Mencken speculates that this is why the first kings ascended the throne clutching their batons or scepters as if holding on for grim death.) People in this precarious position do not enjoy being laughed at, and it would not have taken women long to work out that female humor would be the most upsetting of all.

35   Childbearing and rearing are the double root of all this, as Kipling guessed. As every father knows, the placenta is made up of brain cells, which migrate southward during pregnancy and take the sense of humor along with them. And when the bundle is finally delivered, the funny side is not always immediately back in view. Is there anything so utterly lacking in humor as a mother discussing her new child? She is unboreable on the subject. Even the mothers of other fledglings have to drive their fingernails into their palms and wiggle their toes, just to prevent themselves from fainting dead away at the sheer tedium of it. And as the little ones burgeon and thrive, do you find that their mothers enjoy jests at their expense? I thought not.

Humor, if we are to be serious about it, arises from the ineluctable fact that we are all born into a losing struggle. Those who risk agony and death to bring children into this fiasco simply can't afford to be too frivolous. (And there just aren't that many episiotomy jokes, even in the male repertoire.) I am certain that this is also partly why, in all cultures, it is females who are the rank-and-file mainstay of religion, which in turn is the official enemy of all humor. One tiny snuffle that turns into a wheeze, one little cut that goes septic, one pathetically small coffin, and the woman's universe is left in ashes and ruin. Try being funny about that, if you like. Oscar Wilde was the only person ever to make a decent joke about the death of an infant, and that infant was fictional, and Wilde was (although twice a father) a queer. And because fear is the mother of superstition, and because they are partly ruled in any case by the moon and the tides, women also fall more heavily for dreams, for supposedly significant dates like birthdays and anniversaries, for romantic love, crystals and stones, lockets and relics, and other things that men know are fit mainly for mockery and limericks. Good grief! Is there anything less funny than hearing a woman relate a dream she's just had? ("And then Quentin was there somehow. And so were you, in a strange sort of way. And it was all so peaceful." *Peaceful?*)

For men, it is a tragedy that the two things they prize the most—women and humor—should be so antithetical. But without tragedy there could be no comedy. My beloved said to me, when I told her I was going to have to address this melancholy topic, that I should cheer up because "women get funnier as they get older."

Observation suggests to me that this might indeed be true, but, excuse me, isn't that rather a long time to have to wait?

Analyze

1. According to Hitchens, the need to be funny in women is secondary. What is the primary need by which they are driven? According to Hitchens, what is their "higher calling that is no laughing matter"? Do you agree or disagree?
2. Irony has been called "the glory of _____." What is the missing word and what does that phrase mean?
3. What does Hitchens call "the official enemy of all humor"?
4. How and why does he use the second person in this essay?

Explore

1. Reaction to this piece was swift and incensed, as Hitchens likely hoped. Explore the various reactions you find online. Look especially at the *Vanity Fair* follow-up, and then look at Hitchens's reaction to the reaction (you'll find him on YouTube). Write an essay in which you render the various sides of the debate and then make an argument about what these players/positions/dispositions say about underlying cultural ideas about gender and humor.
2. Hitchens refers to the infamous case of John Wayne Bobbitt. Look into the case and see if you catch his joke. Why would it be okay for a man to make a crack about Bobbitt, but why would a man not want to hear a woman make one?
3. Is the job of comedy to provoke?
4. Comedienne Tig Nataro made a big splash with a monologue based on her cancer diagnosis. Research the buzz on this stand-up routine and the reaction other comics had to it by visiting *The New Yorker*'s blog and NPR. How would Hitchens respond to her performance?

Ellen Finnigan
"Kristen Wiig, Strange Doctor"

Formerly a political columnist for *The Journal Newspapers* in Washington D.C., **Ellen Finnigan** received her Master of Fine Arts degree in creative writing from the University of Montana. Writing in *Kugelmass: A Journal of Literary Humor*, she mourns the departure of Kristen Wiig from the cast of *Saturday Night Live*.

t's official. *Saturday Night Live* has lost something that cannot be replaced. I have made a real effort to reserve judgment in order to give the new female cast members a chance, but I'm sorry, I cannot pretend anymore. It just isn't the same. Some of the new chicks I like: Cecily Strong is very versatile. Kate McKinnon shows real promise. But there was something about Kristen Wiig that went beyond good acting or comedic timing, that made her seem from the very beginning like something singular and special, a star.

What was it? The ancient Greeks had a word for this: *kairos*. Kairos was the Greek god of opportunity. Classical rhetoricians used the word to refer to the right moment, the need to remain aware of the changing circumstances and conditions in which we communicate. Comedy is a kind of communication; so a comedian must have an intuitive understanding of the context in which she performs, including the psychological and emotional makeup of her audience. Wiig was a star from the beginning because she understood her audience and she understood her time. On Saturday nights, I mourn her absence.

When Wiig debuted on *SNL* in 2005, *Sex and the City* had only been off the air for one year. Sex-tape celebutante Paris Hilton was starring in the second season of *The Simple Life*, as reality television was treating us to some real gems. On *The Swan* and *Extreme Makeover*, women deemed unattractive were given free plastic surgery, while "average" guys on *Average Joe* competed for the affections of a hot woman. Inspired by the *Desperate Housewives*, Americans got four million Botox injections in 2005, making it a new $1.4 billion a year industry. Americans got 324,000 nose jobs that year, 98,000 liposuctions, 290,000 boob jobs, 230,000 eyelid lifts, and 135,000 tummy tucks. After allegedly spending almost a quarter of a million dollars on plastic surgery, Demi Moore snagged "hottie" Ashton Kutcher, the kids were all rating each other on the website "Hot or Not," and Paris's catchphrase, "That's hot," was everywhere.

So when Wiig appeared on *SNL* as the Target Lady, a matronly, overly excitable, cashier sporting a so-not-hot bowl cut, and later in a spoof of the *Lawrence Welk Show* as Dooneese, a deranged backup singer with a high, balding forehead, contorted face and tiny, deformed hands, she stuck out like a sore thumb, so to speak. Hollywood.com's Paul Dergarabedian said, "She reminds me of Will Ferrell with her fearlessness and almost complete lack of vanity when it comes to making comedy." A lack of vanity!—and in a woman?—who could imagine it?

Men always say they appreciate a woman with a sense of humor, but if it   5
looks like this? Nobody wants to sleep with that, Kristen. Nobody. And if
you put that out there, who is going to want to sleep with you? And isn't the
whole point of life about trying to get people to want to sleep with you?
That seemed to be what the culture was trying to tell us in the 00's. (That is
always what the culture is trying to tell us: It is one way to create billion-
dollar industries.)

This was a huge part of Wiig's appeal: There was nothing we needed
more in 2005 than an attractive, leggy brunette who was willing to brazenly undermine her would-be hotness. After all, the opposite of "hot" isn't
"average" or even "ugly." "Hotness" isn't about beauty; it's about sex appeal.
So the antonym would be something like *goofy* or just plain *weird*. Wiig
could shed her hotness in an instant; in fact she seemed eager to. But there
was more to her singularity than a lack of vanity as Wiig blazed a trail by
creating a unique brand of comedy that said something about what it is like
to be a woman in this world today.

Who can forget the opening scene of *Bridesmaids*? No man could have
written it. It begins with a late night hook-up between Annie (Kristen
Wiig), an insecure thirty-something, and Ted (Jon Hamm), a quintessen-
tial player.

She says, dreamily, "I love your eyes."

He responds matter-of-factly, "Cup my balls."

"Okay," she says. "I can do that!"   10

"You know what to do!" he calls out, laughing.

Ted is a total jackass who would surely crack up if someone spelled
"BOOBS" on a calculator. He treats Annie like a blow-up doll. Annie is the
picture of accommodation. She once asks meekly, "Can we slow down?"
and later suggests, "Um, I think maybe we're on different rhythms here,"
but her face says it all—not that Ted would notice.

In the morning, Ted tells her that, though he really likes "hanging out,"
he doesn't want a relationship. He then asks her to leave. On her way out she
is forced to climb over the electronic gate at the end of the driveway (in
heels) and when the gate starts to open with Annie straddling atop, we
know the humiliation with Ted will never end.

But Wiig's comedy doesn't stem from any angry, man-bashing femi-
nism. In his classic "Essay on Comedy" published in 1897, Victorian essayist George Meredith mused: "Folly is the natural prey of the Comic, known
to it in all her transformations, in every disguise." Is Wiig concerned here

with the folly committed by a womanizing jerk, or does she have another target in mind? When Annie meets up with her best friend Lillian (Maya Rudolf) later that day, Lillian conveys her disappointment in Annie for hooking up with that "asshole" again. Annie offers the excuse: "But he's so hot." The folly here lies with Annie: Because Ted is "hot" (what we are all supposed to be and want above all else), she is willing to neglect her emotional needs and settle for the occasional orgasm instead. Later in the movie she angles for "more" with Ted, hinting that she wants him to be her date to Lillian's wedding, but he continues to make it clear that he's not interested, openly referring to her as his "fuck buddy" and "number three." The other source of folly is Annie's persistent delusion (common among the fairer sex) that sex with Ted will somehow eventually lead to emotional intimacy with Ted. Annie and Ted are both pathetic, but it is Wiig's character we sympathize with, because we, as women, understand the world she's maneuvering in.

15   This is a post-dating world where men no longer have to compete for women. Instead, women have to compete for men. The "price" of sex is so low that courtship has almost entirely disappeared. In *GQ*, a very candid Siobhan Rosen observed that "a buffet of fetishistic porn available twenty-four/seven has made age-old sexual practices seem unexciting," and "sex itself is like masturbation with a fellow 3D person." Degradation and abuse are considered normal sexual play or innocuous entertainment, and women participate in order to keep their man's attention. Girls learn very early on that relationships are male-centered (as one teenager put it in *New York Magazine*, "They expect you to do things and if you say no they'll be mad") and that they live in a culture where they will be rigorously and relentlessly appraised in terms of their sexual capital.

Now don't get me wrong: I *loved* Tina Fey and Amy Poehler, the female leads on *SNL* before Wiig came along. Tina was a sardonic beauty with brains, Amy an impish tomboy with a wicked cackle. They did skits about Kotex Classics, "mom jeans," pregnancy and other "girl stuff," but those skits struck me as being generically funny or outrageously funny, not funny in a way that was socially critical of gender relations, the way *SNL*'s presidential sketches often expose something about the political milieu. Tina and Amy struck me as tough, just one of the guys, blending in with the largely male troupe of *SNL* and its masculine sensibility even if at times they seemed to be leading it. Sexual politics is a distinct realm in which women's attempts to be just one of the guys (à la Carrie Bradshaw, who famously proclaimed to "have sex like a man") simply do not ring true, and I wonder if that's why they never went there. Kristen bravely did.

Take Shanna, Wiig's ditzy, breathless Marilyn Monroe character. She at first comes across as sexy (in a cartoonish way) and has all the men stuttering and drooling over her, but she soon turns gross, very gross. ("Gross" could be another antonym of "hot.") Our culture prizes hotness in a woman above all else, and Shanna throws it back in our faces. I wasn't surprised when Shanna was voted the second-to-last in a survey of favorite Wiig characters on *Entertainment Weekly's* website, with only 2.9% of the votes. Apparently nobody likes a turd in the cultural punchbowl of the unrelenting sexualization of women (and taking into account the scatological humor Wiig employs in that skit, trust me, that's an apt metaphor). I love Shanna. The theme of "appearance versus reality" makes excellent fodder for comedy because there is no end to our folly when it comes to our tendency to judge things based on appearance, and the disillusion that sets in when the former gives way to the latter. Shanna makes me want to become a waitress at my local "breastaurant" just so I can serve up some wings to men with a lip-glossed smile, then turn around, bend over, and fart all over their food.

When Wiig isn't portraying weirdos and screwballs that would instantly kill any guy's erection, she occasionally capitalizes on her own genetically bequeathed hotness, but she seems to do so only when there is a point. Take Rebecca Larue, Flirting Expert. Here, Wiig embodies the spirit and essence of traditional women's magazines, teaching us how to flirt using a combination of ridiculous physical cues and birdbrain vapidity. The folly exposed here is desperation, a word which has almost completely disappeared from our vocabulary. When I was growing up, I would occasionally hear someone refer to a female as "desperate." It was an insult, but not as mean-spirited as calling someone a "slut." Connotatively, the word "slut" speaks to a woman's sexual activity, while the word "desperate" speaks more to a woman's dignity. A desperate woman would do anything to get a man or to get a man's attention. She trades on her sexual capital. Sex is one thing almost everyone wants, and a body is the one thing everyone has; so what does it say about you if you lead with that?

The thing is: We're *all* desperate now! Take a walk down the street. I'm not talking about women who simply want to look and feel beautiful; I'm talking about the fact that New York City is having trouble enforcing anti-sex-trafficking laws because it is becoming harder to tell who is and who is not a prostitute. Even "serious journalists," if they are going to be on television, are expected to show as much skin as possible at every turn. Ratings rise along with the hemlines. Wiig, of course, takes desperation to extremes: When Larue's antics fail to entice Seth Meyers, she turns to him, throws both feet up in the air, and spreads her legs. Way to cut to the chase, Kristen.

20   Wiig could employ the Gumby-like physicality of a Molly Shannon or the peculiarity of a Rachel Dratch, but she was rarely as creepy as they often were. Her best characters were always endearing, springing as they did from an emotional core, whether of desperation (Rebecca Larue), nervousness (Judy Grimes), or insecurity (Penelope), which, when taken to extremes, made her characters ridiculous and impossible, but at the same time heart-wrenchingly familiar. It was Wiig's ability to capture and exploit the quality of vulnerability in her characters that made her comedy resonate so well with women. Vulnerability is, of course, an inevitable part of the female sexual experience. Vulnerability is also a requirement for emotional honesty, and smart comedy has to be emotionally honest or else it's just screwball, slapstick or ridicule.

Now I admit that perhaps I am giving too much credit to Wiig and not enough credit to her writers, but when you notice recurring patterns in an actor's sensibility, you have to assume she has something to do with it. One of my favorite skits from last season was "Tell Him," an all-female musical number set in a fifties diner where Wiig and company give one of the girls advice on snaring the man she likes. They start by singing:

> *Tell him that you're never gonna leave him*
> *Tell him that you're always gonna love him*
> *Tell him, tell him, tell him, tell him right now.*

25   The confused lover objects, saying, "I did tell him all of those things! On the first date! But he seemed really weirded out!" So they say no, no, no, that *in the beginning* you have to keep things light and casual:

> *Tell him that you don't believe in marriage*
> *Tell him that you never wanna have kids*
> *Tell him, tell him, tell him, tell him all lies.*

In every verse, the advice devolves:

30   > *Tell him that you're open to a three-way*
> *Tell him that you watch porn every day . . .*

Abby Elliot explains, "You need to show him that you're not one of *those* girls."

The confused lover asks, "*What* girls?"

"I mean . . . girls," Elliot says with a shrug.

The absurdity here lies in women denying what are only the most nat-   35 ural of inclinations and desires—for respect, for exclusivity, for marriage, for children, for love—if they want to have any chance of success with men, and in the fact that "success" in our brave new world of relationships would be to have a man call you "chill" . . . and then never call you again. In another age, a man would have to prove himself to a woman in order to win her. Now, a woman has to prove herself to a man: by assuring him that she doesn't expect anything from him whatsoever. This skit did such a brilliant job of exposing the feeling common among women that: hey, it's a man's bed, we're only sleeping in it.

George Meredith wrote that folly is "the daughter of unreason and sentimentalism"; as the "first born of common sense," it is the "vigilant comic's duty to strike down folly where she finds it." We live in a time of confused gender roles and expectations but if we can still collectively identify folly as folly, if we can still laugh at the same things—in ourselves and in our world—it gives me hope that we are not as adrift as we sometimes appear to be. Meredith puts it better:

> *If you believe that our civilization is founded in common-sense (and it is the first condition of sanity to believe it), you will, when contemplating men, discern a Spirit overhead . . . Whenever it sees [men] self-deceived or hoodwinked . . . drifting into vanities, congregating in absurdities; whenever they violate the unwritten but perceptible laws binding them in consideration one to another; the Spirit overhead will . . . cast an oblique light on them, followed by volleys of silvery laughter. That is the Comic Spirit.*

He continues: "To feel its presence and to see it is your assurance that many sane and solid minds are with you in what you are experiencing." This is the assurance Kristen Wiig offered women in her comedy. It is unreasonable to expect a woman to have sex like a man! It is sentimental to think that after years of sexual dallying and womanizing, an aging bachelor's heart will suddenly turn to gold if he meets the right girl! It is cruel to tell a woman that she must repress and deny everything about her that makes her feminine, and thus different from men, that she must never be vulnerable (one of "those" girls), or that she might one day be deemed the "right" girl if only she is hot enough.

Poor Demi. All that plastic surgery and she could only keep Ashton for six years. What now? Back to the cutting board, I guess.

40   *You see Folly perpetually sliding into new shapes in a society possessed of wealth and leisure, with many whims, many strange ailments and strange doctors.*

In our society, folly is clearly sliding into new shapes, but to suggest that the sexual mores of our day may not be an ideal corrective to the notions of the past, to suggest that they may, in fact, have follies of their own, is to risk raising the hackles of a very skeptical public, because anything perceived as "values language" is considered suspect. In this kind of environment, comedy can be an especially effective mode of communication, because it allows for social criticism while withholding moral judgment. Kristen Wiig and other female comedians might be just the "strange doctors" we need. They slip judgment under the door and force us to reckon with something to which we are far more receptive than moral posturing: common sense.

George Meredith wrote: "I do not know that the fly in amber is of any particular use, but the Comic idea enclosed in a comedy makes it more generally perceptible and portable, and that is an advantage." It was to our advantage that Kristen Wiig took the stage every Saturday night for seven years, captured the female experience in a comic idea, and made it easier for everyone to view from a female perspective. I can only hope she will continue to bring her feminine sensibility, her vulnerability, her emotional honesty, her searing wit, and her social criticism to the big screen. Regardless, Kristen Wiig has shown us that female comedians today have a unique power to be able to help men and women to see "the considerable violations of the unwritten but perceptible laws binding them in consideration one to another," thereby exposing the folly which is so often packaged and literally sold, in myriad ways, as progress.

Analyze

1. What is kairos?
2. Finnigan describes a wide range of Wiig's characters. Pick two and describe them to the person sitting next to you.
3. What is an antonym for "hot"?

Explore

1. Screen a few of Wiig's classic performances. What does Finnigan get right? What would you add to her assessment of Wiig's characters? In a brief essay, try to tackle this question: How do Wiig's characters critique our "common sense" notions of beauty, sexuality, and women's power?

2. How is Finnigan's thesis similar to—and different from—Hitchens's argument about female comics? How does Finnigan's description and analysis of Wiig's characters complicate or deepen Hitchens's assessment of the social value of funny women?

3. Finnigan praises Wiig's signature vulnerability. Why is vulnerability a necessary facet to Wiig's comic success? In other words, what is the relationship between vulnerability, emotional honesty, and comedy?

Sean Cunningham
"Why We Owe Gisele an Apology (Particularly God)"

Let's call **Sean Cunningham** diverse: He is a playwright, a screenwriter, a political satirist, and an editor for both *Maxim* and *Maxim for Kids* (really). He has also worked for Esquire.com, *Men's Journal*, and bridal guide *The Knot*. *When Falls the Coliseum* is a blog-like online journal with the subtitle "a journal of American culture (or lack thereof)." It functions as a forum for writers to spout off their opinions and criticisms and witticisms on politics, sporting events, media frenzies, books, movies, and other things.

N FL quarterback/total cutie pie Tom Brady has seen his wife Gisele take some heat for suggesting his teammates failed him and, in the process, cost her husband a fourth Super Bowl ring; some have even termed her New England's own Yoko Ono. While this is an intriguing analogy, as it suggests Tom is about to take football in strange, experimental directions ("What if instead of passing the ball . . . the ball passed *me*?"), it's also deeply unfair to Gisele, who's leggier than Yoko ever was. Additionally, Gisele could never break up the Beatles: she *is* the Beatles.

It's true. When John met Yoko, she didn't go, "You're in the Beatles? How nice! I too am in a band, only my group is better known than yours and sells considerably more records!" The former Ms. Bündchen makes more money than her husband ($45 million to his mere thirty-one in the last *Forbes* celeb rankings) and is undeniably more famous (if I say "Gisele" you know exactly who I mean; when I call out, "Tom!" it could be anyone from "Sawyer" to "Cruise" to "Uncle") (in my case, it's Berenger—*Shoot to Kill* forever, baby). Granted, Tom is taller than Gisele (6'4" to 5'11") . . . but when she's in heels, it's too close for comfort. In this relationship, Gisele is clearly the musician from Liverpool and Tom is an unknown Japanese conceptual artist.

Accordingly, it's time we treat Gisele with the respect she deserves. This is a super model, people. Do you know what that is? It's like a regular model . . . only *super*. They ruled the Earth during the 80s and 90s, when they engaged in behavior including throwing phones at people (Naomi Campbell), using cocaine (Naomi Campbell), throwing phones at people (Naomi Campbell), having a chance to get engaged to a member of U2 and inexplicably choosing the bassist (Naomi Campbell), throwing phones at people (Naomi Campbell), and, perhaps most shockingly, throwing a person *at a phone* (do you need to ask?). Sadly, time has thinned our herd of super models as they got married and had babies and started eating normal-sized meals. Now we're down to a single one . . . and can't we let her angrily swig her bottled water as she leaves her Super Bowl luxury box in peace?

Shame on us.

5   And not just shame on us, but shame on God. Because as we all know, Gisele not only prayed for Tom to win the Super Bowl, but emailed everyone else she knew to pray for him too and then further shared this prayer request by having it leaked to the *New York Post* so they could plaster it on the front page in an attempt to ensure a maximum amount of religious devotion. Yet her one simple hope—that her husband who is almost as rich as she is and slightly taller could receive just one tiny Super Bowl ring to go with the three he already owns—was somehow lost in the backlog of other pleadings with the Almighty. And thus this skinny, skinny woman with unusually large natural breasts that remain surprisingly perky even after giving birth to a beautiful child was forced to turn to the heavens and cry, "WHY HAST THOU FORSAKEN ME!?!"

But here's where some of the blame goes to Gisele. Because she recognized the inherent flaw in the Patriots this season: they have an offense that calls for Tom to throw the ball ... but doesn't allow for him to catch it as well. As a result of this defect, he must rely on other people with hair not nearly so easy to style as his to score touchdowns. These lesser beings— commonly known as "receivers"—have to do nothing more than catch a football and then withstand a bone-shattering tackle from between one and eleven defenders.

Yet they failed at even this simple task as many as three times in a single game.

The key to winning another title is clear: Tom Brady must acquire the ability to throw the ball to himself.

Sometime soon, Gisele has to get down on her knees (and send an email to everyone else in her inner circle to get down on theirs as well) and offer this simple-yet-specific prayer:

> "Lord, please give my husband super powers to both [expletive]   10
> throw the ball and catch the ball so he may win a Super Bowl for the
> fourth time."

And here's where the rest of us come in: until this occurs, we need to stop praying. You're worried about those blood test results? Let it go until Tom wins another Super Bowl. You're concerned about your child shipping out to serve a final tour in Afghanistan? Keep it to yourself until Tom gets ring *quattro*. The monsoon has reached your village and you won't be able to keep your head above the flood waters much longer? DAMMIT, people, how is the Lord supposed to answer Gisele's prayers if you keep distracting Him with your crap?

Everyone, take the pledge now: until the incredibly beautiful and rich Gisele gets that Super Bowl ring for nearly as beautiful and rich and slightly taller Tom Terrific, we give God a break so He can concentrate.

Ideally this will happen next season, so we'll only have to give up Our Savior for a year, and when we get Him back it'll be all the sweeter, knowing we helped restore the faith of a towering Brazilian of German descent.

But if at that point Gisele tries to pray for another Brady Super Bowl ring (or a Super Bowl MVP even), may Our Lord unleash His Wrath on her like Naomi Campbell taking down a personal assistant, because that's just greedy.

Analyze

1. Certain ideas are repeated, like Giselle's being *almost* taller than Tom Brady. Find other examples and consider how (or if) they add humor to the piece.
2. How quickly do you realize the piece is a satire?
3. The American "ideals" of football players and super models are the targets of this satire. Why do we "allow" ourselves to make fun of the same people we idolize?

Explore

1. Look up a few different venues' coverage of this incident. What differences are there between the media portrayal and Cunningham's piece?
2. Comedy is often talked about as having a "shelf life." Let's start there: If you're not familiar with the Giselle/New England Patriots incident, does this piece still contain any humor?
3. On a similar note, what do you know about Yoko Ono and the Beatles? How does that knowledge, or lack thereof, affect your read of the piece?

Ian Frazier
"Laws Concerning Food and Drink"

American writer and humorist **Ian Frazier** is a novelist and an essayist and can be laugh-out-loud funny. "Laws Concerning Food and Drink" originally appeared in *The Atlantic* and was later published as part of a collection of humorous essays called *Lamentations of the Father*. Among Frazier's many talents is his ability to craft and sustain a range of specific, idiosyncratic voices. Note the Biblical diction he adopts in this piece, using it to make us laugh at the daily battles parents wage with their children over table manners, bath time, and behavior. Frazier's generous sensibility and sharp comic timing emanate from these hyper-formal declarations of family "law."

Of the beasts of the field, and of the fishes of the sea, and of all foods that are acceptable in my sight you may eat, but not in the living room. Of the hoofed animals, broiled or ground into burgers, you may eat, but not in the living room. Of the cloven-hoofed animal, plain or with cheese, you may eat, but not in the living room. Of the cereal grains, of the corn and of the wheat and of the oats, and of all the cereals that are of bright color and unknown provenance you may eat, but not in the living room. Of the quiescently frozen dessert and of all frozen after-meal treats you may eat, but absolutely not in the living room. Of the juices and other beverages, yes, even of those in sippy-cups, you may drink, but not in the living room, neither may you carry such therein. Indeed, when you reach the place where the living room carpet begins, of any food or beverage there you may not eat, neither may you drink.

But if you are sick, and are lying down and watching something, then may you eat in the living room.

And if you are seated in your high chair, or in a chair such as a greater person might use, keep your legs and feet below you as they were. Neither raise up your knees, nor place your feet upon the table, for that is an abomination to me. Yes, even when you have an interesting bandage to show, your feet upon the table are an abomination, and worthy of rebuke. Drink your milk as it is given you, neither use on it any utensils, nor fork, nor knife, nor spoon, for that is not what they are for; if you will dip your blocks in the milk, and lick it off, you will be sent away. When you have drunk, let the empty cup then remain upon the table, and do not bite it upon its edge and by your teeth hold it to your face in order to make noises in it sounding like a duck; for you will be sent away.

When you chew your food, keep your mouth closed until you have swallowed, and do not open it to show your brother or your sister what is within; I say to you, do not so, even if your brother or your sister has done the same to you. Eat your food only; do not eat that which is not food; neither seize the table between your jaws, nor use the raiment of the table to wipe your lips. I say again to you, do not touch it, but leave it as it is. And though your stick of carrot does indeed resemble a marker, draw not with it upon the table, even in pretend, for we do not do that, that is why. And though the pieces of broccoli are very like small trees, do not stand them upright to make a forest, because we do not do that, that is why. Sit just as I have told you, and do not lean to one side or the other, nor slide down until you are nearly slid away. Heed me; for if you sit like that, your hair will go into the syrup. And now behold, even as I have said, it has come to pass.

Laws Pertaining to Dessert

5 For we judge between the plate that is unclean and the plate that is clean, saying first, if the plate is clean, then you shall have dessert. But of the unclean plate, the laws are these: If you have eaten most of your meat, and two bites of your peas with each bite consisting of not less than three peas each, or in total six peas, eaten where I can see, and you have also eaten enough of your potatoes to fill two forks, both forkfuls eaten where I can see, then you shall have dessert. But if you eat a lesser number of peas, and yet you eat the potatoes, still you shall not have dessert; and if you eat the peas, yet leave the potatoes uneaten, you shall not have dessert, no, not even a small portion thereof. And if you try to deceive by moving the potatoes or peas around with a fork, that it may appear you have eaten what you have not, you will fall into iniquity. And I will know, and you shall have no dessert.

On Screaming

Do not scream; for it is as if you scream all the time. If you are given a plate on which two foods you do not wish to touch each other are touching each other, your voice rises up even to the ceiling, while you point to the offense with the finger of your right hand; but I say to you, scream not, only remonstrate gently with the server, that the server may correct the fault. Likewise if you receive a portion of fish from which every piece of herbal seasoning has not been scraped off, and the herbal seasoning is loathsome to you, and steeped in vileness, again I say, refrain from screaming. Though the vileness overwhelm you, and cause you a faint unto death, make not that sound from within your throat, neither cover your face, nor press your fingers to your nose. For even now I have made the fish as it should be; behold, I eat of it myself, yet do not die.

Concerning Face and Hands

Cast your countenance upward to the light, and lift your eyes to the hills, that I may more easily wash you off. For the stains are upon you; even to the very back of your head, there is rice thereon. And in the breast pocket of your garment, and upon the tie of your shoe, rice and other fragments are distributed in a manner wonderful to see. Only hold yourself still; hold still, I say. Give each finger in its turn for my examination thereof, and also each thumb. Lo, how iniquitous they appear. What I do is as it must be; and you shall not go hence until I have done.

Various Other Laws, Statutes, and Ordinances

Bite not, lest you be cast into quiet time. Neither drink of your own bath water, nor of bath water of any kind; nor rub your feet on bread, even if it be in the package; nor rub yourself against cars, nor against any building; nor eat sand.

Leave the cat alone, for what has the cat done, that you should so afflict it with tape? And hum not that humming in your nose as I read, nor stand between the light and the book. Indeed, you will drive me to madness. Nor forget what I said about the tape.

Complaints and Lamentations

O my children, you are disobedient. For when I tell you what you must do, 10
you argue and dispute hotly even to the littlest detail; and when I do not accede, you cry out, and hit and kick. Yes, and even sometimes do you spit, and shout "stupid-head" and other blasphemies, and hit and kick the wall and the molding thereof when you are sent to the corner. And though the law teaches that no one shall be sent to the corner for more minutes than he has years of age, yet I would leave you there all day, so mighty am I in anger. But upon being sent to the corner you ask straightaway, "Can I come out?" and I reply, "No, you may not come out." And again you ask, and again I give the same reply. But when you ask again a third time, then you may come out.

Hear me, O my children, for the bills they kill me. I pay and pay again, even to the twelfth time in a year, and yet again they mount higher than before. For our health, that we may be covered, I give six hundred and twenty talents twelve times in a year; but even this covers not the fifteen hundred deductible for each member of the family within a calendar year. And yet for ordinary visits we still are not covered, nor for many medicines, nor for the teeth within our mouths. Guess not at what rage is in my mind, for surely you cannot know.

For I will come to you at the first of the month and at the fifteenth of the month with the bills and a great whining and moan. And when the month of taxes comes, I will decry the wrong and unfairness of it, and mourn with wine and ashtrays, and rend my receipts. And you shall remember that I am that I am: before, after, and until you are twenty-one. Hear me then, and avoid me in my wrath, O children of me.

Analyze
1. What are some of the rules governing the living room?
2. What happens on the first and the fifteenth of the month?
3. What do his kids do to the family cat?

Explore
1. Write a handbook for your classroom decorum in the style of "Laws Concerning Food and Drink."
2. What is funny about the high, formal diction Frazier chooses to use in this piece?
3. How does Frazier's piece wind up creating an image of these kids in our mind's eye? Write a character sketch for one of the children implied by these "laws."

Billy Collins
"Tension"

The New York Times' Bruce Weber called **Billy Collins** "the most popular poet in America." His wit and charm draw a wide range of readers, from poetry aficionados to non-poetry fans. But don't let his accessibility fool you. Collins's poems are often full of mixed messages and surprising nuance. In this poem, Collins takes a swing at some of the conventional wisdom doled out to young and aspiring writers. "Tension" first appeared in The Paris Review, one of America's oldest and most prestigious literary magazines.

"Never use the word *suddenly* just to create tension."
—*Writing Fiction*

Suddenly, you were planting some yellow petunias
outside in the garden,
and suddenly I was in the study
looking up the word *oligarchy* for the thirty-seventh time.

When suddenly, without warning,   5
you planted the last petunia in the flat,
and I suddenly closed the dictionary
now that I was reminded of that vile form of governance.

A moment later, we found ourselves
standing suddenly in the kitchen   10
where you suddenly opened a can of cat food
and I just as suddenly watched you doing that.

I observed a window of leafy activity
and, beyond that, a bird perched on the edge
of the stone birdbath   15
when suddenly you announced you were leaving

to pick up a few things at the market
and I stunned you by impulsively
pointing out that we were getting low on butter
and another case of wine would not be a bad idea.   20

Who could tell what the next moment would hold?
Another drip from the faucet?
Another little spasm of the second hand?
Would the painting of a bowl of pears continue

to hang on the wall from that nail?   25
Would the heavy anthologies remain on their shelves?
Would the stove hold its position?
Suddenly, it was anyone's guess.

The sun rose ever higher.
The state capitals remained motionless on the wall map   30
when suddenly I found myself lying on a couch
where I closed my eyes and without any warning

began to picture the Andes, of all places,
and a path that led over the mountain to another country
with strange customs and eye-catching hats   35
suddenly fringed with little colorful, dangling balls.

Analyze

1. What is the poem's motive?
2. How many times does the word "suddenly" appear?
3. How does this poem break the rule cited in the epigraph and reinforce it simultaneously?

Explore

1. Find a piece of formal writing advice. Write a poem, short story, or personal essay in which you both break the rule and reinforce the need for it.
2. Look for two or three formal features in this poem (repetition, line breaks, etc.). What does Collins do on the page that adds to the humor of the piece? How does the structure of the poem help you think about the structure of a joke?

Donald Barthelme
"In the Morning Post"

The late **Donald Barthelme** is renowned as a postmodernist short fiction writer, and a forerunner of the "flash fiction" form, but he also wrote novels and essays and was a museum director. We shouldn't tell you that he never finished his college degree (oops, we just did). His work "plays" with form and structure, which is part of the humor and fun in itself. "In the Morning Post," a classic piece, is no exception.

In the morning post I received what I regard as a rather astonishing communication from the magazine *Writer's Digest*. The magazine, addressing me by name, disclosed that it was planning, for yearly publication, a cover story "on the link that some people see between writing and drinking" and that it would like to include me "in a roundup piece summarizing the drinking habits of the top writers in America today."

After noting that I had been promoted to Top Writer (gratifying indeed after so many years of corporalship), my second, scandalized reaction was, *"How did they find out?"* I mean, I do take a drink now and again. In fact my doctor, who is the soul of tact, once characterized my consumption as "slightly imprudent." But how the devil did *Writer's Digest* discover this? Does the *whole city* know?

Zizzled with horror, as you may well imagine, I turned next to the magazine's questions, my answers to which they proposed to print (along with a recent photo and a listing of my vodka-soaked work to date). Such is the power of the questionnaire *qua* mechanism that, helplessly, I began penciling in answers, as follows:

1. "How would you describe your own drinking habits? _____ Light _____ Medium _____ Heavy _____ Other?"
   Medium. Light is sissy and Heavy doesn't go down so well with Deans,   5
   Loan Officers and Publishers, and who in the world would want to be Other?
2. "When you feel like having a few drinks, what do you usually have?"
   Zip-Strip on the rocks. Too easy, let us proceed to—
3. "Any favorite hangouts for drinking?"
   Yes, Godot's, but I can't give you the address because you know the place is and I mean we want to keep it that way even though the toppest writers in America "hang out" as you put it there and goodness gracious Elaine's is what we *don't*—Also, in bed, sobbing lightly.
4. "Favorite drinking companions?"   10
   Joe Conrad, Steverino Crane, Pete Hamill and Tom Aquinas.
5. "Heaviest drinkers/writers that you know—or *have* known—of?"
   Oh, this is a mean one, *WD*. I could do a lot of I-didn't-know-what-I-was-doing-my-God-I-didn't-think-they'd-actually-*print*-the-Goddamn-thing damage here, couldn't I? Because I know for a fact that *********** is even more slightly imprudent than I, and that ****** von *****, thought to be sober as white bread, takes a little bang at ten o'clock in the morning, to get himself started. Off the record, I'll tell you nothing.
6. "Do you see any affinity between hard drinking and the writing life? Explain."
   Well, climb up on my knees here, *WD*. When you've been staring at this Billy-by-damn keyboard all your life, decade after decade, you get a little thirsty. The thing is, *the keys don't move.* The "e" is in the same place, every day. The "h" is in the same place, decade in, decade out. The "g" is fixed, eternally. It makes you, like, *thirsty.* Any piano tuner would understand, I think.

Analyze

1. What is the premise of this piece, and does it "work" for you?
2. Who are "Joe Conrad" and "Steverino Crane?"
3. Other than "the morning post" itself, does the piece feel "dated" for you?

Explore

1. Do you read the "speaker" as having two audiences, the *Writers' Digest* questionnaire and an amorphous additional reader who gets to "hear" his thoughts and reactions to the questionnaire itself, or do you read the whole piece as answers to this fictionalized questionnaire? Support your opinion with textual evidence.
2. The "speaker" is both forthright about his alcohol consumption and rationalizing it. How does that dichotomy add to the humor of the piece?
3. Barthelme plays with quite a few social constructs in such a short piece. Find one and discuss its relevance more than thirty years after this piece's original publication.

Christopher Hitchens
"Cheap Laughs: The Smug Satire of Liberal Humorists Debases Our Comedy—and Our National Conversation"

The provocative **Christopher Hitchens** comments on the rising trend of satirical news shows being equated with more legitimate news outlets in the American mind. The boundary between news and entertainment has decidedly blurred. In this review essay, Hitchens focuses on Senator Al Franken's humor and politics, and critiques what he sees as the generally toothless humor of satirical news. This is a typically Hitchens-esque bold critique, in this case a critique of liberal humorists—from *SNL*'s newscasts to Jon Stewart—and it includes a snarky close reading of Al Franken's prose.

The merry month of July 2009 had barely witnessed the spectacle of Al Franken eventually taking his seat as the junior senator from Minnesota when, immediately following the death of Walter Cronkite, *Time* magazine took an online poll to determine who was now "America's most trusted newscaster." Seven percent of those responding named Katie Couric. Nineteen percent nominated Charles Gibson. Twenty-nine percent went for Brian Williams. But the clear winner, garnering 44 percent, was Jon Stewart of *The Daily Show*. Either I missed it, or the poll failed to specify, in that wonderfully reassuring way that polls purport to do, what had been its "margin of error."

A summer debate at the Oxford Union once resolved: "This House believes that the nation is slowly sinking giggling into the sea." Do July's antic politico-media developments mean that undergraduate humor has now triumphed definitively, and that the balance of power is held by the sensibilities of the combined teams of Mr. Stewart and *Saturday Night Live*? Although the answer to the second part of that question is certainly no (the balance of power will continue to be held by opinion polls and those who are in a position to commission and print them), the answer to the first part would appear to be yes. And even the answer to the second part might have to be somewhat qualified: if any one thing crucially undid the candidacy of Senator John McCain for the presidency, it was his nomination of Sarah Palin to be his running mate. And if any one thing undid Governor Palin as a person who could even be considered for the vice presidency, it was the merciless guying of her manner and personality by Tina Fey.

You may conceivably have forgotten that when, after the numbing assault on our civil society in September 2001, Mayor Rudy Giuliani wanted to signal some kind of return to "normalcy," it was to the set of *Saturday Night Live* that he repaired. (They fed him some quite good lines, too: asked with due solemnity "Can we be funny?," he responded, "Why start now?") I distinctly remember wondering what, if they were watching it, the al-Qaeda leadership could possibly be making of this dialogue.

Long before the *Weekly Standard* crew disembarked at Anchorage for its now-historic call upon the lady governor, I myself once sat on a cruise-ship entertainment panel—sponsored off the imposing shores of Alaska by *The Nation* magazine—with Betty Friedan and Al Franken. In the spontaneous-humor stakes, I seem to remember outpointing Betty with relative ease, but I nonetheless noticed with slight envy that some "progressive" women in the front row would start laughing uncontrollably as soon as it was Franken's turn to speak and, indeed, often before he had even opened his mouth. I'd already admired a Mick Jagger impersonation I'd seen him do in Washington (at a benefit for the National Committee for an Effective Congress) and an after-dinner performance he'd given at the White House Correspondents' Dinner in the Clinton era. Franken has a naturally comic face, very, very good dead-pan timing, and an absolutely copper-bottomed, 100 percent, and unironic allegiance to every known tenet of the Democratic Party's version of liberal-ism. In minor conversation at the ship's bar, about the impending campaign of Hillary Clinton for the Senate (or rather, for her unopposed nomination to the Democratic machine's ticket for same), I came to see that Franken's secret asset was that he was really quite a hard-bitten and hard-line partisan.

5   The victory of Stewart in the race for anointment as the new Cronkite surprised me less perhaps than it will have surprised some of you. Not long ago, I was teaching a class on Mark Twain at the New School in New York and someone asked me who, if anybody, would be the equivalent figure for today. I was replying that I didn't think there was one, though the younger Gore Vidal might once have conceivably been in contention, when some-one broke in to say: "What about Jon Stewart?" I was thunderstruck at how many heads nodded, and I replied that I would know better next week, after my upcoming appearance on the show. I recall this now as winning me the most respect I have ever had from any class. The day after my appear-ance, I was at West Point to lecture to the cadets and was stopped every-where I walked by young trainee warriors for America who had caught my act. This sort of thing can become heady.

It also has its vaguely alarming side. "Al Franken for Senator" is one thing (especially when the alternative is or was "Norm Coleman for Senator"). But Jon Stewart for Samuel Langhorne Clemens is quite an-other. What next? Stephen Colbert for Zola? Al Franken for Swift?

Franken very often refers to himself as a "satirist," which is a piece of hubris that comes to him too glibly and naturally. One wants to say, on hearing or reading such a claim, "Actually, sunshine, *we'll* be the judge of that." Swift famously compared satire to a mirror in which people could see every face but their own: if Franken desires to be considered a connoisseur of the satirical, he might want to paste that line into his hat.

The best of his books, which is (I'll call it for brevity's sake) *Lies*, is in fact a fine if accidental illustration of the Swiftian maxim. The necessary clue appears as early as page 37, while Franken is having some easy fun tossing and goring the hapless Bernie Goldberg on the hoary old question of liberal bias in the media. Still, ask yourself who exactly gets himself caught in the following exchange of trick questions:

> Why, Bernie asks, if CBS identifies the Heritage Foundation as a "conservative" think tank, does it not identify the Brookings Institution as a "liberal" think tank?
> I don't know. Bias? Or could it be because the Heritage Foundation's website says their mission is to "promote conservative public policies," while the Brookings website says it is committed to "independent, factual and nonpartisan research"?

10

But Goldberg, as Franken concedes at the outset, does not complain about the identification of Heritage as conservative. He complains about the non-identification of Brookings as liberal. It's hardly a satiric smackdown to cite Brookings itself asking and expecting to be taken—as it is by Franken—at its own "objective" face value. That's Goldberg's accusation to begin with.

The next complaint Franken has is against Goldberg's insistence that Rosie O'Donnell should be described as being as "liberal" as Rush Limbaugh is conservative. Once again, Limbaugh hardly pretends to be otherwise, while Ms. O'Donnell—held harmless by Franken—may well not deserve to be called "liberal" but is partly an apolitical nut and part echo chamber for the more dubious wing of MoveOn.org and even the putrid fringe of the "9/11 Truth" nutbags.

Some of the more tedious moments of my life have been spent on the *Hannity & Colmes* show (I still await the call from Bill O'Reilly), but Franken on page 99 decides to attack Hannity just where he is at his strongest, in a diatribe he broadcast against John Walker Lindh, the so-called American Taliban. Of this pathetic yet sinister character Hannity made the debatable assertion that he "converted from anything-goes liberal agnosticism to hard-core Middle Eastern radical Islam." Whatever may be said against this proposition, Franken notably fails to say it:

> Before reading this, I had never considered the direct line between liberal agnosticism and hard-core, radical Islam. But Hannity has a strong case. So many of my liberal, agnostic women friends from college gradually relinquished their freedoms and decided to spend the rest of their lives in chadors, avoiding the gaze of man.

If this was being intoned on-air by Jon Stewart, the cue for massive studio-audience laughter would have been activated at the word *chadors*, allowing

15

him to beam modestly and likably through the mildly suggestive last four words. On the page, however, it is less easy to hurry us right past the main point. A noticeable swath of campus feminist opinion, which is not alone in this respect, *has* in fact adopted an attitude of cultural relativism toward political Islam, and of decided non-neutrality against its militant female opponents such as Ayaan Hirsi Ali. And the current president of the United States, whom it might not be altogether inaccurate to describe as the Galahad of the *SNL* and Stewart generations, has made exactly one speech about Muslim garb—defining the wearing of the hijab as a human right and indirectly attacking those French secularists who have their misgivings about it.

One could actually write a whole article simply on the Franken-Stewart faction's attitude toward religion. In their world, the expressions *Christian right* or *Moral Majority* are automatic laugh cues, and there is a huge amount of soft-core borscht-belt stuff like this (from Franken) on page 205 of *The Truth*:

> If it hadn't been for Social Security, I never would have met Franni in Boston my freshman year, deflowered her, and gotten her to renounce the Pope. But I digress.

And this, from pages 1 and 2 of Jon Stewart's *Naked Pictures of Famous People* (his book *America* also carries a rib-tickling cover-line promise of Supreme Court justices posing nude) in a painfully unfunny essay/sketch titled "Breakfast at Kennedy's," set this time in Connecticut, at Choate:

> That's where Jack and I bonded. I was the only Jew. My father ran the commissary so I was allowed to attend school there. My room, or the Yeshiva, as Jack called it (he really wasn't prejudiced and would often defend me to the others as a "terrific yid"), was a meeting-place and a hotbed for hatching great pranks . . . I'm sure the ample supply of brisket and whitefish from Dad helped.

20   And in a more goyish form from Stephen Colbert, by no means to be outdone, on page 56 of *I Am America*:

> Now, I have nothing but respect for the Jewish people. Since the Bible is 100% the true Word of God, and the Jews believe in the Old Testament, that means Judaism is 50% right.

If you chance to like this sort of thing, then this is undoubtedly the sort of thing you will like. It certainly works very well with audiences who laugh not because they find something to be funny, but to confirm that they are—and who can doubt it?—cool enough to "get" the joke. What you will not find, in any of this output, is anything remotely "satirical" about the pulpit of the Reverend Jeremiah Wright, or any straight-faced, eyebrow-raising (and studio-audience-thigh-slap-triggering) mention of, say, *The New York Times*'s routine practice of captioning Al Sharpton as "the civil rights activist." Baudelaire wrote that the devil's greatest achievement was to have persuaded so many people that he doesn't exist: liberal platitudinousness must be a bit like that to those who suffer from it without quite acknowledging that there is such a syndrome to begin with.

I myself would have voted for Franken if I lived in Minnesota, if only because he must be among the best-read and best-informed people to have recently run for the upper chamber, as well as one of the very few with whom one might also expect to pass an amusing evening. It took me a while to appreciate the paradox that lies at the center of the senator's so-far published work. He is really quite witty—which is much better than being funny—when he is being purely political. But he is barely even funny when funny is all he is trying to be. See if the following causes you to smile. It's taken from his inaugural address, on page 223 of *Why Not Me?*

> As the *Mandingo* buck, Mede, says in the movie after he has been brought to James Mason's plantation to be used as breeding stock, "Massa, it beez wrong to sell a nigger like a plow horse." He's right. It does beez wrong. It beez *very wrong*. These words are as true today as when Ken Norton said them twenty-six short years ago. And I am here today to say that it was *wrong* to hunt escaped slaves down on horseback; it was *wrong* to boil slaves alive; and it was *wrong* to sell a black woman merely because her breasts had grown too droopy.

Jeepers. Of course the "irony" is that the passage is *supposed* to make you cringe a bit, but this crucially lowered and degraded definition of what is ironic is accidentally confessed a touch later on in the same book, when Franken is writing in his own voice:

> "Ironic distance" is not [Al] Gore's problem. Not that he doesn't have a well-developed sense of irony. He actually has a terrific sense of humor.

See, there's your problem. A sense of irony is to be carefully, indeed strictly, distinguished from the possession of a funny bone. Irony is not air-quote finger-marks, as if to say "Just kidding" when in fact one is not quite kidding. (Does anyone ever say "Just kidding" when in fact only kidding?) Bathos is not irony, though Franken and Stewart and Colbert seem unaware of this. Irony usually partakes of some element of the unintended consequence. How might I give an illustration of the laws of unintended consequences? Let us imagine that Senator Franken composed a chapter about government lying and cover-up, which involved the use of the irresistibly hilarious instance of Sandy Berger, President Clinton's former national security adviser, being caught red-handed as he stuffed his pants with classified papers from the National Archives. In a capital city that witnesses quite frequent alternations of power between the two main parties, what will be the chances that fiasco and corruption occur at the expense of only one of them? Yet meticulous care is taken by the senator to make sure that no such "fair and balanced" laughter is ever evoked, which is quite a sacrifice for a comedian. Consistency of this kind allows no spontaneity, let alone irony. It might even go some way to explaining the howling success of the "Air America" network, the collapsing-scenery rival to the right-wing dictatorship exerted over the rest of the ether.

In the pages of *Lies*, Senator Franken proves himself to have a lethal capacity to deploy wit as a part of a wider political takedown. He does his homework (one can usually guess the Washington outfit that does it for him, such as Citizens for Tax Justice, but he always gives credit) and then, when he is sure he has caught Bill O'Reilly or Ann Coulter, he begins to slow himself down, give himself time, and really milk the kill. If it's not laugh-out-loud funny, it's still pretty good polemical journalism. One has only to repress the thought that his preferred targets are perhaps a bit "fat" or "soft," or as committed as Stewart and Colbert (or indeed O'Reilly and Coulter) to the marketing of instant books with about two dozen words in the title (plus the invariable highlighting of the cabalistic airport-terminal symbol #1).

Stewart, too, has something of a fat-target problem, and seems partly unaware of this problem's source in his own need to please an audience that has a limited range of reference. In *Naked Pictures of Famous People*, when he decides to lampoon Larry King—who in any context is a barn-door-size target—he still manages to make the attack too broad. There's no slight nudge, but a huge dig in the ribs. It needs to be "Adolf Hitler: The Larry

King Interview." And Hitler has to be a guest who has been helped by therapy to become more of a people person. Here's his opening reply to King's
welcome to the show.

> HITLER: (*biting into a bagel*) First of all, Larry, I don't know what   **30**
> I was so afraid of. These are delicious!!!

At whose expense, I wonder, are those three (count them!) exclamation
marks? Who is afraid that who will miss what point? A few of King's characteristic interjections are well-enough parodied ("Lovely man, Bud Fried-
man, very funny"), but Rob Long of *National Review* does King to the very
life three or four times a year with much less reliance on an overdone fantasy guest. Except how can anyone at *National Review* be funny? Weren't
they for Bush, the very mention of whose brain or IQ is enough to ignite
peals of mirth from those in Stewart's studio crowd who just know that
they are smarter than he?

I noticed that both in Senator Franken's *Lies* and in the Stewart team's
America, reference was made to Joseph Welch's famous challenge to Joseph
McCarthy about whether there was any "decency" left at last. In other en-
counters with the same faction and its followers, I have found that this is
one of the "quotes" or "moments" from recent American history that they
can be reliably counted upon to know. Two things seem to be involved here:
an almost nostalgic realization that at one time the hard-right wing believed the entertainment industry was an enemy; and a desire to prove that
it still is. The "American" symbols all over the album-size volumes reviewed
here brilliantly dispel/preempt any charge of being unpatriotic.

Some of the stupid right wing still *does* regard relatively innocuous
mainstream-TV comedy as an enemy, which allows the "ironic" riposte
that mainstream-TV comedy, and the mainstream-TV comedians who wax
fat on it, are really not all that subversive after all. Here's Franken's own
reassurance, from *The Truth*:

> For Dad the rest of religion lay in the ethical teachings of Judaism
> and, to the extent he had absorbed them, of any other faith, West-
> ern, Eastern, or whatever. Again, not so different from our Found-
> ers. In their famous correspondence at the end of their lives, Adams
> and Jefferson wrote a lot about religion. When Adams concluded
> that his personal creed was "contained in four short words, 'Be just

and good'" Jefferson replied, "The result of our fifty or sixty years of religious reading, in the four words, 'Be just and good,' is that in which all our inquiries must end."

35   One might, I suppose, keep this piece of schmaltz handy for the next Judeo-Christian prayer breakfast, but meanwhile, it awakens an appetite to see more of the flashing scalpel and a good deal less of the rubber hammer and the exploding cigar. Almost everything that I have quoted was printed or broadcast at a time when the Democrats were in opposition in both chambers and many state houses, excluded from the White House, and in a minority on the Supreme Court. The rebel humor on offer was rather lame even then. Shall we now be witnesses to a further decline? (This year's African American lesbian comedian at the White House Correspondents' Dinner broke bravely with tradition and chose to roast the absent Rush Limbaugh rather than the incumbent chief executive, to roars of complicit and knowing applause.) A liberal joke, at present, is no laughing matter.

Analyze

1. What is the abbreviated name of Al Franken's book Hitchens uses here?
2. Slow down and dwell on key moments in the text. What does Hitchens mean by this sentence: "Baudelaire wrote that the devil's greatest achievement was to have persuaded so many people that he doesn't exist: liberal platitudinousness must be a bit like that to those who suffer from it without quite acknowledging that there is such a syndrome to begin with."
3. Which, according to Hitchens, is it better to be: funny or witty?
4. How does the title capture Hitchens's major argument?
5. How does Hitchens distinguish between irony and "being funny"? Why does this distinction matter and how does it serve his argument?

Explore

1. How does ironic or satirical news help its readers or viewers "feel smart" about subjects they might not know much about? What other satirical news shows do you watch or have you heard about? Watch a few clips of *The Colbert Report*, *The Daily Show*, or *Onion TV* before you try to answer that question.

2. Hitchens mentions "the guying" of Sarah Palin by *SNL* comic Tina Fey. Her shtick is but one example of *SNL* comics imitating (potential) presidential candidates. Do some research and watch Will Ferrell parody George W. Bush, Darrell Hammond imitate Al Gore, or Chevy Chase impersonate Gerald Ford. Pick the one that makes you laugh most and do a little more research: What exactly does the comic mock? What was the political context for the joke when the sketch was new?

3. Based on your research above, make an argument. Do these sketches have a lifespan outside of their political moment? What made them funny *then*? Do they remain funny *now*? Draw upon evidence from the clips you screen and make your case.

4. In 2008 The Pew Research Center for People & the Press reported that, when asked in a poll to identify their favorite news anchorman, "a comedian showed up at No. 4 on the list." Jon Stewart joined the likes of Tom Brokaw, Dan Rather, and Walter Cronkite in the American mind. What might this suggest about the ever-blurring boundary between news and entertainment in the American political landscape?

5. Hitchens alludes to Jonathan Swift's famous description of satire. "Satire," Swift wrote in *The Battle of the Books and Other Short Pieces*, "is a sort of glass wherein beholders do generally discover everybody's face but their own; which is the chief reason for that kind reception it meets with in the world, and that so very few are offended with it." Swift was writing in the early 1700s in England. How do his ideas apply to twenty-first-century satirical news shows? Write an essay in which you extend, critique, or refine Swift's early insight.

Lizz Winstead
"Sarah Silverman and Me: Fact-Checking US Politics"

Lizz Winstead co-created *The Daily Show*, with Madeleine Smitherberg, and served as head writer. She is an American comedian, radio and television personality, and blogger. *Lizz Free or Die*, her book of essays, was published in 2012.

There has been a barrage of celebrity political videos on TV lately. I have heard a lot of cynicism about whether or not they make a difference—or worse, that celebs are just attention-starved and will do anything to be recognized.

When I hear the apathy, and worse the snark, it always makes me feel a little sick inside. Maybe because I am one of those people who has spent the last 20 years of my life using comedy to shine a light on creeps with power.

So, as we come to the end of this election cycle, I thought it might be helpful to tell you what I have experienced when creative friends get together and make some noise. Change happens. It's not bullshit. It's not self-serving. It is awesome.

It was a natural progression for me to go balls-out into politics as, over the years, my career has developed into more or less "call-and-response" comedy. If it happens, I am reacting either on stage, in videos or on radio and TV.

5   So, when 2011 rolled around and the relentless attacks started on reproductive rights in congress and statehouses across America—oh, like 1,000 bills proposed to curb access to services from Pap smears to abortion—I decided to devote my creative energies touring the country doing comedy shows to benefit Planned Parenthood. I knew humor got people to sit up and take notice. I have built a career using comedy to expose hypocrisy.

But now the rhetoric was escalating at warp speed. It seemed like each week, in every new town, some implausible piece of vaginal invasion legislation was happening. So touring for Planned Parenthood seemed like a no-brainer. The shows were packed and I was helping raise hundreds of thousands of dollars for Planned Parenthood, all across America.

Then, just when I thought the idiocy couldn't get any thicker—BAM! A panel of men were called before Congress to discuss whether religious institutions that employ secular people should be required to cover birth control in their healthcare plans.

Sandra Fluke, a young law student at Georgetown University, one such Catholic institution, who was an advocate for having birth control included in these plans, was not allowed to speak before the panel. So, she took to the airwaves to address the issue. Her appearances on news programs caused a rabid anti-woman backlash, and she was labeled "a slut" and worse by the likes of radio talkshow muculent, Viagrasaurus Rush.

In the heat of all of this, I got a Facebook message from actor and activist Martha Plimpton, asking if I wanted to join forces and do something about all this "slut"-shaming.

The idea was simple: create an advocacy group called "A is For" that has   10
a few goals: first, to launch an amazing website with the most up-to-the-
minute reproductive rights news, which could serve as hub for women and
men to share their stories about why protecting reproductive rights is so
important; and second, to raise money for the groups like pro-choice organization Naral and the Center for Reproductive Rights, which are fighting
the big battles. Our logo would be a scarlet letter "A," reclaiming the sym-
bolism of *The Scarlet Letter,* and our hope was that women and men would
wear the "A" proudly, announcing to the world: "I am a sexual being, I support all aspects of reproductive health and I will not be shamed into silence
about it."

Last March, then, I ventured to LA and met with a group of amazing
women Martha had assembled, and so we started making videos, making
scarlet A's, and defining what our mission would be. And seven months
later, we have women and men walking around all over the country wearing
that scarlet A, proudly declaring their support for women's reproductive
rights.

But I also wanted to expand my reach and make some videos that address issues using the language I speak, that candidly combine truth and
humor, and hit hard just what is at stake in this election. I was inspired by
my pal Sarah Silverman, who, during the 2008 presidential election, made
a huge difference in Florida with her video *The Great Schlep,* creating an
amazing call to action, simply being her. No censorship, no worries about
who it would offend, just Sarah: knowing and trusting that her hilarious
voice and message would generate action. It did.

And then, in 2012, she scissored her dog in the name of introducing to a
whole lot of people who may otherwise have never learned about him a
major GOP money-machine named Sheldon Adelson. And no one but
Sarah would think of calling for arming the elderly in the name of exposing
voter suppression laws. People sat up and took notice. They laughed. Then
they Googled. Then they got angry. Then they got active.

I wanted to do that with my repro rights videos. I raised some money on
Indiegogo, teamed up with the amazing creative team at Revolution Mes-
saging, made six videos and launched Lady Parts Justice.

Our first video, called *It's the Law,* is an uncomfortable, hilarious and   15
real video about a law in some states that forces a woman to pay extra for a
medically unnecessary vaginal probe that takes pictures of her womb before
she can terminate a pregnancy. That video had 635,000 views in 72 hours.

My inbox was flooded with questions asking whether the law was real, or saying that they were shocked to find out that laws like this exist; they asked us if we can please make more videos that expose other pieces of legislation which these creepy politicians are trying to pass.

Some told me they hadn't realized how bad it had gotten and thanked me for the reminder. That was exciting. But when people asked where they could get more information on other awful laws proposed or passed, it felt pretty cool to say, "Go to 'A is For,' " knowing all the detail was there.

But now the assaults on sanity have started to feel like relentless cluster bomb attacks: seems like half of my day is spent slack-jawed staring at the news, gobsmacked as unqualified kook after unqualified kook keeps getting elected spouting things like women no longer die during childbirth, or that the chunks of toxic bilge that spew from antiquated factories have nothing to do with our melting earth, or maybe the weirdest of all, that more than a few folks, some of whom sit on the US supreme court, believe a bunch of cells in a woman's body *and* Walmart are people.

But when I talked to people about what affected them the most, it was not about a specific issue, rather the epidemic of how a lie gets repeated over and over again—and how the media seemed pretty lax at calling out the bull, and thus these lies were starting to become truths. Someone needed to correct the record. And who better to do that than comedians?

So, in one phone call with comedian and fellow troublemaker Elon James White, and FilmAid executive director and make-it-happenist Liz Manne, we came up with the concept of "Actually." Our plan was make series of videos using clips of some of the most egregious political lies, and then we turn to our most trusted information sources—comedians—to correct the record. Each rebuttal starts with the word "Actually": the word that so many of us say right before opening a can of whoop-ass.

20   We wanted to do it right, so to produce them, we called the folks at Schlep Labs who had made all the wonderful videos Sarah Silverman had done. We pitched the idea to American Bridge to see if they wanted to finance the project. They were in, and in less than a month, and for way less than the millions poured into rightwing political ads that push lie after lie, we had Rosie Perez, W. Kumau Bell, Elon James White and Jay Smooth all doing amazing videos setting the record straight.

The best part for me was that Sarah and I, who usually spend our limited time together laying in a hotel bed with a few dogs and some junk food, watching a *Law and Order* marathon, teamed up and took on that hideous notion that "Corporations Are People." Voila, Actually.org was born: a fact-checking website with added fun. Could there be a better public service?

Now you have some answers about whether or not these celebrity ads work. They do wake people up, and using humor backed up with facts is an amazing one-two punch for re-energizing some folks who have been feeling deflated about politics. And there is one other thing you should know: many of the celebs you see in these ads face opposition from managers or agents who tell us not to step up because it may offend some conservative network executive, or alienate the viewers of certain cable channels. They warn we will be branded as partisan.

Hell, I've already been branded as a whore and worse because I dare speak out about the radical notion that because women are sexual beings they should have all the access they need to affordable healthcare. I'll take "partisan."

I tell you this because when you see ads where someone famous sticks their neck out for a cause, they are taking a risk that they may lose fans and work.

Actually, they do it because they believe in something greater than them- 25 selves. So, when you feel like shitting all over a celebrity for speaking out and taking a stand, remember they don't have to; they are choosing to do something for the greater good, and are willing to take a hit for it.

All I ask is that if your first response to seeing a celeb talking about an issue is "What an asshole," think about what they are saying. Then, think again.

Analyze

1. What is "call-and-response comedy"?
2. What is a "muculent"?

Explore

1. Lizz Winstead has been called the "founder of satirical news." Look into her career and biography. How might her career and her brand of humor counter Hitchens's claims about women comics, also in this book?
2. If you "reclaim the scarlet letter A" you are announcing to the world: "I am a sexual being, I support all aspects of reproductive health and I will not be shamed into silence about it." What is *The Scarlet Letter?* How does this classic text figure in contemporary debates about women's reproductive rights?

Jason Schneiderman
"Wester"

Jason Schneiderman earned an MFA from New York University and a PhD from CUNY. He is the author of the poetry collections *Sublimation Point* (2004) and *Striking Surface* (2010), winner of the 2009 Richard Snyder Publication Prize from Ashland Poetry Press. His essays have appeared in the *American Poetry Review* and elsewhere. In "Wester" Schneiderman has fun with voice and logic.

We're leaving the subway and Karen says
"We're going to 10th Avenue," and I say,
"So we'll be going wester?" and Karen says,
being all mean about it, "No, we're not
5   going 'wester' because 'wester' isn't a word"
and I say "Well it should be" and Bill says
"'Wester' isn't a word because there's no
'westest'. Like if I were in China and you
were here, we'd both be west of each other,
10   and besides, west only exists on earth, like
astronauts are never west of the earth or
east of each other," and I say, "Yeah, but
when we get where we're going, we'll be
more west than we are now," and Karen says,
15   "Yeah," and Bill says "Yeah," and I say
"Wester."

Analyze

1. The poem uses reported speech. How many voices does it characterize?
2. How many sentences make up the poem?
3. Where are they walking?

Explore

1. *The New York Times Magazine* has a blog called "That Should Be a Word." Check out the definitions for "showverdose" (binge-watching

serial TV episodes) or "bagriculture" (the "practice of saving shopping bags"). Invent a word that somehow captures an as-yet-unnamed cultural object or practice. Submit an entry.

2. Comedian Rich Hall coined the term "sniglets" back in the 1980s. A regular feature of his show *Not Necessarily the News,* "sniglets" are the granddaddy to both Schneiderman's "Wester" and the blog above. Screen a clip of Hall's "sniglets" (you'll find him on YouTube). In the style of Schneiderman's poem or Hall's "sniglets," make a case for the legitimacy of the word you invent. Justify your definition of the entry above with concrete evidence.

Gary Shteyngart
"Only Disconnect"

Gary Shteyngart is a fiction writer, essayist, and blurber (blurbs are those back-of-the-book author endorsements; Shteyngart is so infamous for blurbing he has given readings of his blurbs). He frequently writes about technology, sometimes almost prophetically, as the novel *Super Sad True Love Story* will attest. His celebrity-filled trailer for his recent memoir *Little Failure* epitomizes Shteyngart's ability to make a career out of self-deprecation. In an interview with *The New York Times*, where the essay below was originally published, he said that he likes books in which people suffer: "If there's no suffering, I kind of tune out."

Since fiscal year 2008, I have been permanently attached to my iTelephone. As of two weeks ago, I am a Facebooking twit. With each post, each tap of the screen, each drag and click, I am becoming a different person—solitary where I was once gregarious; a content provider where I at least once imagined myself an artist; nervous and constantly updated where I once knew the world through sleepy, half-shut eyes; detail-oriented and productive where I once saw life float by like a gorgeously made documentary film. And, increasingly, irrevocably, I am a stranger to books, to the long-form text, to the pleasures of leaving myself and inhabiting the free-floating consciousness of another. With each passing year, scientists estimate that I lose between 6 and 8 percent of my humanity, so that by the close of this decade you will be able to quantify my personality. By the first quarter of 2020 you will be able to understand who I am through a set of metrics as simple as those used to measure the torque of the latest-model Audi or the spring of some brave new toaster.

"This right here," said the curly-haired, 20-something Apple Store glamnerd who sold me my latest iPhone, "is the most important purchase you will ever make in your life." He looked at me, trying to gauge whether the holiness of this moment had registered as he passed me the Eucharist with two firm, unblemished hands. "For real?" I said, trying to sound like a teenager, trying to mimic what all these devices and social media are trying to do, which is to restore in us the feelings of youth and control.

"For real," he said. And he was right. The device came out of the box and my world was transformed. I walked outside my book-ridden apartment. The first thing that happened was that New York fell away around me. It disappeared. Poof. The city I had tried to set to the page in three novels and counting, the hideously outmoded boulevardier aspect of noticing societal change in the gray asphalt prism of Manhattan's eye, noticing how the clothes are draping the leg this season, how backsides are getting smaller above 59th Street and larger east of the Bowery, how the singsong of the city is turning slightly less Albanian on this corner and slightly more Fujianese on this one—all of it, finished. Now, an arrow threads its way up my colorful screen. The taco I hunger for is 1.3 miles away, 32 minutes of walking or 14 minutes if I manage to catch the F train. I follow the arrow taco-ward, staring at my iPhone the way I once glanced at humanity, with interest and anticipation. In my techno-fugue state I nearly knock down toddlers and the elderly, even as the strange fiction and even stranger reality of New York, from the world of Bartleby forward, tries to reassert itself in the form of an old man in a soiled guayabera proudly, openly defecating on Grand Street. But sorry, *viejo*, you're not global enough to hold my attention. "Thousands of Uzbeks Flee Violence in Kyrgyzstan." "Gary, what do we want to do about Turkish rights?" "G did u see the articl about M.I.A. + truffle fries = totes messed up." I still have to eat, and when I finally get to my destination that taco tastes as good as my iPhone said it would. But I am not dining alone. The smartphone, my secret sharer, is in my other hand. Even as the pico de gallo is dribbling down my chin I am lost to the restaurant, the people, the commerce around me, my thumb pressing down the correct quadrants of the screen to tell the world just how awesome this taco is, even as "Kyrgyz Authorities Order Uzbeks to Remove Barriers," while "A Third Filipino Journalist Is Killed," and, over "In Eritrea, the Young Dream of Leaving."

I dream of leaving, too. Heading upstate in the summertime with a trunk full of books, watching Roosevelt Island sweep by in a rainstorm, I wake up from the techno-fugue state and remember who I am, the 37 analog years that went into creating this particular human being. Upstate I will train for my vocation, novel-writing, by tearing through the Russian classics that gave me my start, reading up on those frigid lovelorn Moscow and Petersburg winters while summer ants crawl up my shins. In the meantime, I will start conjuring my next book, one that with any luck may still be read on paper by live human beings five years from now. In my quest for calm, I have a surprising ally. As far as I'm concerned, American Telephone & Telegraph has done more for the art of reading and introspection than all the Kindles and Nooks ever invented. Because up in the exalted summer greenery of the mid-Hudson Valley, completing an AT&T call is like driving a Trabant from New York to Los Angeles: technically feasible but not really going to happen.

I am sitting underneath a tree beside a sturdy summer cottage rebuilt by 5 an ingenious Swedish woman. The birds are twittering, but in a slightly different way than my New York friends. I open a novel, *A Short History of Women,* by Kate Walbert, a book I will grow to love over the coming week, but at first my data-addled brain is puzzled by the density and length of it (256 pages? how many screens will that fill?), the onrush of feeling and fact, the surprise that someone has let me not into her Facebook account but into the way other minds work. I read and reread the first two pages understanding nothing. Big things are happening. World War I. The suffragist movement. Out of instinct I almost try to press the text of the deckle-edged pages, hoping something will pop up, a link to something trivial and fast. But nothing does. Slowly, and surely, just as the sun begins to swoon over the Hudson River and another Amtrak honks its way past Rhinebeck, delivering its digital refugees upstream, I begin to sense the world between the covers, much as I sense the world around me, a world corporeal and complete, a world that doesn't need the press of my thumb, because here beneath the weeping willow tree my input is meaningless.

Soon my friends will get off that Amtrak, they will help me roast an animal and some veggies, even as they point their iTelephones at the sky, praying for rain. Their prayers will not be answered. *Connecting. . . .* will flash impotently on the screen, but they will not connect. In the meantime, something "white nights" will be happening out there; the sun has set and yet it has not. With the animal safely in our stomachs, with single malts and beers before us, we can read or talk softly about what we're reading, about the glory and sadness of finding ourselves *this* close to the middle of our existence (cue the Chekhov, cue the Roth) and as we do so the most important purchases we have ever made in our lives are snugly holstered in the pockets of our shorts, useless, as we commune in some ancient way, laughing and groaning, passing around lighted objects and containers of booze while thoroughly facebooking one another for real in the fading summer light.

Analyze

1. What is a Trabant?
2. To what does Shteyngart liken the Apple store salesman passing forward the phone? Is the comparison heavy-handed or does it work?
3. If you own a smartphone, how has it transformed your life?
4. What is the first thing Shteyngart uses his phone to do?

Explore

1. Have you ever given up technology, your phone, or even just a form of social media by choice (or force!)? What was the experience like for you?
2. If you own a cell phone, recall any days or moments when your phone died or you did not have service. Did you have anxiety or were you more relaxed?
3. What are some differences between your generation and those who did not come of age with digital communication?
4. What, if any, do you see as possible long-term ramifications of our need to be digitally "connected"?

Researching and Writing About Humor
Barbara Rockenbach and Aaron Ritzenberg[1]

Research-based writing lies at the heart of the mission of higher education: to discover, transform, and share ideas. As a college student, it is through writing and research that you will become an active participant in an intellectual community. Doing research in college involves not only searching for information but also digesting, analyzing, and synthesizing what you find in order to create new knowledge. Your most successful efforts as a college writer will report on the latest and most important ideas in a field as well as make new arguments and offer fresh insights.

It may seem daunting to be asked to contribute new ideas to a field in which you are a novice. After all, creating new knowledge seems to be the realm of experts. In this guide, we offer strategies that demystify the research and writing process, breaking down some of the fundamental steps that scholars take when they do research and make arguments. You'll see that contributing to scholarship involves strategies that can be learned and practiced.

Throughout this guide we imagine doing research and writing as engaging in a scholarly conversation. When you read academic writing, you'll see that scholars reference the studies that came before them and allude to the studies that will grow out of their research. When you think of research as engaging in a conversation, you quickly realize that scholarship always has a social aspect. Even if you like to find books in the darkest corners of

1 Barbara Rockenbach, Director of Humanities & History Libraries, Columbia University; Aaron Ritzenberg, Associate Director of First-Year Writing, Columbia University.

the library, even if you like to draft your essays in deep solitude, you will always be awake to the voices that helped you form your ideas and to the audience who will receive your ideas. As if in a conversation at a party, scholars mingle: They listen to others and share their most recent ideas, learning and teaching at the same time. Strong scholars, like good conversationalists, will listen and speak with an open mind, letting their own thoughts evolve as they encounter new ideas.

You may be wondering, "What does it mean to have an open mind when I'm doing research? After all, aren't I supposed to find evidence that supports my thesis?" We'll be returning to this question soon, but the quick answer is: To have an open mind when you're doing research means that you'll be involved in the research process well before you have a thesis. We realize this may be a big change from the way you think about research. The fact is, though, that scholars do research well before they know any of the arguments they'll be making in their papers. Indeed, scholars do research even before they know what specific topic they'll be addressing and what questions they'll be asking.

When scholars do research, they may not know exactly what they are hunting for, but they have techniques that help them define projects, identify strong interlocutors, and ask important questions. This guide will help you move through the various kinds of research that you'll need at the different stages of your project. If writing a paper involves orchestrating a conversation within a scholarly community, there are a number of important questions you'll need to answer: How do I choose what to write about? How do I find a scholarly community? How do I orchestrate a conversation that involves this community? Whose voices should be most prominent? How do I enter the conversation? How do I use evidence to make a persuasive claim? How do I make sure that my claim is not just interesting but important?

GETTING STARTED

You have been asked to write a research paper. This may be your first research paper at the college level. Where do you start? The important thing when embarking on any kind of writing project that involves research is to find something that you are interested in learning more about. Writing and research are easier if you care about your topic. Your instructor may have given you a topic, but you can make that topic your own by finding something that appeals to you within the scope of the assignment.

Academic writing begins from a place of deep inquiry. When you are sincerely interested in a problem, researching can be a pleasure, since it will satisfy your own intellectual curiosity. More important, the intellectual problems that seem most difficult—the questions that appear to resist obvious answers—are the very problems that will often yield the most surprising and most rewarding results.

Presearching to Generate Ideas

When faced with a research project, your first instinct might be to go to Google or Wikipedia, or even to a social media site. This is not a bad instinct. In fact, Google, Wikipedia, and social media can be great places to start. Using Google, Wikipedia, and social media to help you discover a topic is what we call "presearch"—it is what you do to warm up before the more rigorous work of academic research. Academic research and writing will require you to go beyond these sites to find resources that will make the work of researching and writing both easier and more appropriate to an academic context.

Google   Let's start with Google. You use Google because you know you are going to find a simple search interface and that your search will produce many results. These results may not be completely relevant to your topic, but Google helps in the discovery phase of your work. For instance, you are asked to write about the impact of social media on relationships.

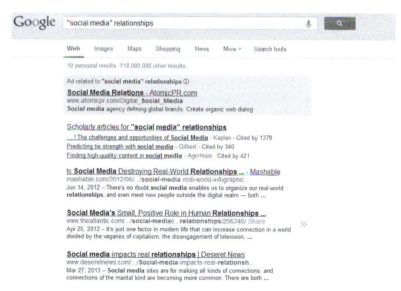

A standard Google search.

This Google search will produce articles from many diverse sources—magazines, government sites, and corporate reports among them. It's not a bad start. Use these results to begin to home in on a topic you are interested in pursuing. A quick look through these results may yield a more focused topic such as how social media is affecting the ways people relate in school or the workplace, or how the nature of friendship is evolving because of tools like Facebook and Twitter.

Wikipedia   A Wikipedia search on social networking services and relationships will lead you to several articles that address both concepts. The great thing about Wikipedia is that it is an easy way to gain access to a wealth of information about thousands of topics. However, it is crucial to realize that Wikipedia itself is not an authoritative source in a scholarly context. Even though you may see Wikipedia cited in mainstream

References

1. ^ Ahlqvist, Toni; Bäck, A., Halonen, M., Heinonen, S (2008). "Social media road maps exploring the futures triggered by social media". *VTT Tiedotteita - Valtion Teknillinen Tutkimuskeskus* (2454): 13.

2. ^ Kaplan Andreas M., Haenlein Michael, (2010), Users of the world, unite! The challenges and opportunities of social media, Business Horizons, Vol. 53, Issue 1 (page 61)

3. ^ *a b c d e f g h i j* H. Kietzmann, Jan; Kristopher Hermkens (2011). "Social media? Get serious! Understanding the functional building blocks of social media". *Business Horizons* **54**: 241–251.

4. ^ *a b* Agichtein, Eugene; Carlos Castillo. Debora Donato, Aristides Gionis, Gilad Mishne (2008). "Finding high-quality content in social media". *WSDM'08 - Proceedings of the 2008 International Conference on Web Search and Data Mining*: 183–193.

5. ^ *a b c d e f g h* Nigel Morgan; Graham Jones; Ant Hodges. "Social Media" 🔖. *The Complete Guide to Social Media From The Social Media Guys*. Retrieved 12 December 2012.

References section on Wikipedia.

newspapers and popular magazines, academic researchers do not consider Wikipedia a reliable source and do not consult or cite it in their own research. Wikipedia itself says that "Wikipedia is not considered a credible source . . . This is especially true considering that anyone can edit the information given at any time." For research papers in college, you should use Wikipedia only to find basic information about your topic and to point you toward scholarly sources. Wikipedia may be a great starting point for presearch, but it is not an adequate ending point for research. Use the References section at the bottom of the Wikipedia article to find other, more substantive and authoritative resources about your topic.

Using Social Media   Social media such as Facebook and Twitter can be useful in the presearch phase of your project, but you must start thinking about these tools in new ways. You may have a Facebook or Twitter account and use it to keep in touch with friends, family, and colleagues. These social networks are valuable, and you may already use them to gather information to help you make decisions in your personal life and your workplace. Although social media is not generally useful to your academic research, both Facebook and Twitter have powerful search functions that can lead you to resources and help you refine your ideas.

After you log in to Facebook, use the "Search for people, places, and things" bar at the top of the page to begin. When you type search terms into this bar, Facebook will first search your own social network. To extend beyond your own network, try adding the word "research" after your search terms. For instance, a search on Facebook for "social media research" will lead you to a Facebook page for the Social Media Research Foundation. The posts on the page link to current news stories on social media, links to other similar research centers, and topics of interest in the field of social media research. You can use these search results as a way to see part of the conversation about a particular topic. This is not necessarily the scholarly conversation we referred to at the start of this guide, but it is a social conversation that can still be useful in helping you determine what you want to focus on in the research process.

Twitter is an information network where users can post short messages (or "tweets"). While many people use Twitter simply to update their friends ("I'm going to the mall" or "Can't believe it's snowing!"), more and more individuals and organizations use Twitter to comment on noteworthy events or link to interesting articles. You can use Twitter as a presearch tool

Facebook page for the Social Media Research Foundation.

because it aggregates links to sites, people in a field of research, and noteworthy sources. Communities, sometimes even scholarly communities, form around topics on Twitter. Users group posts together by using hashtags—words or phrases that follow the "#" sign. Users can respond to other users by using the @ sign followed by a user's Twitter name. When searching for specific individuals or organizations on Twitter, you search using their handle (such as @barackobama or @whitehouse). You will retrieve tweets that were created either by the person or organization, or tweets that mention the person or organization. When searching for a topic to find discussions, you search using the hashtag symbol, #. For instance, a search on #globalization will take you to tweets and threaded discussions on the topic of globalization.

There are two ways to search Twitter. You can use the search book in the upper right-hand corner and enter either a @ or # search as described above. Once you retrieve results, you can search again by clicking on any of words that are hyperlinked within your results, such as #antiglobalization.

If you consider a hashtag (the # sign) as an entry point into a community, you will begin to discover a conversation around topics. For instance, a search on Twitter for #socialmedia leads you to Social Media Today (@socialmedia2day), a community that explores new developments and emerging technologies in social media and how it is used in government, education, business, advertising, and other areas. Major news sources from around the world are also active in Twitter, so articles, video, interviews, and other resources from the news media will be retrieved in a search. Evaluating information and sources found in social media is similar to how you evaluate any information you encounter during the research process. And, as with Wikipedia and Google searches, this is just a starting point to help you get a sense of the spectrum of topics. This is no substitute for using library resources. Do not cite Facebook, Twitter, or Wikipedia in a research paper; use them to find more credible, authoritative sources. We'll talk about evaluating sources in the sections that follow.

Create a Concept Map

Once you have settled on a topic that you find exciting and interesting, the next step is to generate search terms, or keywords, for effective searching. Keywords are the crucial terms or phrases that signal the content of any given source. Keywords are the building blocks of your search for information. We have already seen a few basic keywords such as "social media" and "relationships." One way to generate keywords is to tell a friend or classmate what you are interested in. What words are you using to describe your research project? You may not have a fully formed idea or claim, but you have a vague sense of your interest. A concept map exercise can help you generate more keywords and, in many cases, narrow your topic to make it more manageable.

A concept map is a way to visualize the relationship between concepts or ideas. You can create a concept map on paper, or there are many free programs online that can help you do this (see, for instance http://vue.tufts .edu/, http://wisemapping.org, or http://freeplane.sourceforge.net). There are many concept mapping applications available for mobile devices; the concept map here was created using the app SimpleMind.

Here is how you use a concept map. First, begin with a term like "social media." Put that term in the first box. Then think of synonyms or related words to describe social media such as "relationships," "Web 2.0," "friendship," "communication," "alienation," and "loneliness." This brainstorming process will help you develop keywords for searching. Notice that keywords can also be short phrases.

After some practice, you'll discover that some phrases make for excellent keywords and others make for less effective search tools. The best keywords are precise enough to narrow your topic so that all of your results are

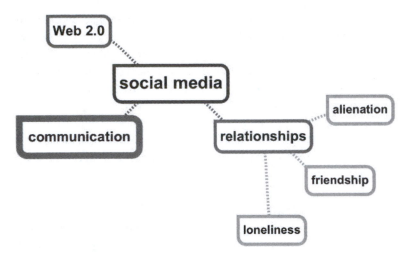

A concept map.

relevant, but are not so specific that you might miss helpful results. Concept maps created using apps such as SimpleMind allow you to use templates, embed hyperlinks, and attach notes, among other useful functions.

Keyword Search

One of the hardest parts of writing is coming up with something to write about. Too often, we make the mistake of waiting until we have a fully formed idea before we start writing. The process of writing can actually help you discover what your idea is, and most important, what is interesting about your idea.

Keyword searches are most effective at the beginning stages of your research. They generally produce the most results and can help you determine how much has been written on your topic. You want to use keyword searches to help you achieve a manageable number of results. What is manageable? This is a key question when beginning research. Our keyword search in Google on "social media and relationships" produced almost 3 million results. The same search in JSTOR.org produces almost 200 results. These are not manageable results sets. Let's see how we can narrow our search.

Keyword searches, in library resources or on Google, are most effective if you employ a few search strategies that will focus your results.

1. Use AND when you are combining multiple keywords. We have used this search construction previously:

"social media" AND relationships

The AND ensures that all your results will contain both "social media" and "relationships." Many search engines and databases will assume an AND search, meaning if you type

"social media" language

the search will automatically look for all terms. However, in some cases the AND will not be assumed and "social media language" will be treated as a phrase. Worse yet, sometimes the search automatically assumes an OR. That would mean that all your results would come back with either social or media or language. This will produce a large and mostly irrelevant set of results. Therefore, use AND whenever you want two or more words to appear in a result.

2. Using OR can be very effective when you want to use several terms to describe a concept, such as:

relationships OR friendships OR communication

A search on social media and relationships can be broadened to include particular kinds of relationships between people. The following search casts a broader net because results will come back with social media and either relationships, friendship, or communication:

"social media" AND (relationships OR friendship OR communication)

Not all of these words will appear in each record. Note also that the parentheses set off the OR search indicating that "social media" must appear in each record and then either relationships, friendship, or communication needs to appear along with social media.

3. Use quotation marks when looking for a phrase. For instance, if you are looking for information on social media and communication in

multinational corporations you can ensure that the search results will include all of these concepts and increase the relevance by using the following search construction:

"social media" AND communication AND
"multinational corporations"

This phrasing will return results that contain both the word *globalization* and the phrase "multinational corporation."

4. Use NOT to exclude terms that will make your search less relevant. You may find that a term keeps appearing in your search that is not useful. Try this:

"social media" NOT technology

If you are interested in the relational side of this debate, getting a lot of results that discuss the technological details of social media may be distracting. By excluding the keyword "technology," you will retrieve far fewer sources and ideally more relevant results.

Researchable Question

In a college research paper, it is important that you make an argument, not just offer a report. In high school you may have found some success by merely listing or cataloging the data and information you found; you might have offered a series of findings to show your teacher that you investigated your topic. In college, however, your readers will not be interested in data or information merely for its own sake; your readers will want to know what you make of this data and why they should care.

To satisfy the requirements of a college paper, you'll need to distinguish between a topic and a research question. You will likely begin with a topic, but it is only when you move from a topic to a question that your research will begin to feel motivated and purposeful. A topic refers only to the general subject area that you'll be investigating. A researchable question, on the other hand, points toward a specific problem in the subject area that you'll be attempting to answer by making a claim about the evidence you examine.

"Social media and relationships" is a topic but not a researchable question. It is important that you ask yourself, "What aspect of the topic is most interesting to me?" It is even more important that you ask, "What aspect of the topic is it most important that I illuminate for my audience?" Ideally, your presearch phase of the project will yield questions about social media and relationships and language that you'd like to investigate.

A strong researchable question will not lead to an easy answer, but rather will lead you into a scholarly conversation in which there are many competing claims. For instance, the question, "What are the official languages of the United Nations?" is not a strong research question, because there is only one correct answer and thus there is no scholarly debate surrounding the topic. It is an interesting question (the answer is: Arabic, Chinese, English, French, Russian, and Spanish), but it will not lead you into a scholarly conversation.

When you are interested in finding a scholarly debate, try using the words "why" and "how" rather than "what." Instead of leading to a definitive answer, the words "why" and "how" will often lead to complex, nuanced answers for which you'll need to marshal evidence in order to be convincing. "Why did Arabic become an official language of the UN in 1973?" is a question that has a number of complex and competing answers that might draw from a number of different disciplines (political science, history, economics, linguistics, and geography, among others). If you can imagine scholars having an interesting debate about your researchable question, it is likely that you've picked a good one.

Once you have come up with an interesting researchable question, your first task as a researcher is to figure out how scholars are discussing your question. Many novice writers think that the first thing they should do when beginning a research project is to articulate an argument, then find sources that confirm their argument. This is not how experienced scholars work. Instead, strong writers know that they cannot possibly come up with a strong central argument until they have done sufficient research. So, instead of looking for sources that confirm a preliminary claim you might want to make, look for the scholarly conversation.

Looking at the scholarly conversation is a strong way to figure out if you've found a research question that is suitable in scope for the kind of paper you're writing. Put another way, reading the scholarly conversation can tell you if your research question is too broad or too narrow. Most novice writers begin with research questions that are overly broad. If your question is so broad that there are thousands of books and articles participating in the scholarly conversation, it's a good idea for you to focus your question so that you are asking something more specific. If, on the other hand, you are asking a research question that is so obscure that you cannot find a corresponding scholarly conversation, you will want to broaden the scope of your project by asking a slightly less specific question.

Keep in mind the metaphor of a conversation. If you walk into a room and people are talking about globalization and language, it would be out of place for you to begin immediately by making a huge, vague claim, like, "New technology affects the way that people speak to each other around the world." It would be equally out of place for you to begin immediately by making an overly specific claim, like, "Social media usage in Doha is a strong indicator of Facebook's growing strength in Qatar." Rather, you would gauge the scope of the conversation and figure out what seems like a reasonable contribution.

Your contribution to the conversation, at this point, will likely be a focused research question. This is the question you take with you to the library. In the next section, we'll discuss how best to make use of the library. Later, we'll explore how to turn your research question into an argument for your essay.

Your Campus Library

You have probably used libraries all your life, checking out books from your local public library and studying in your high school library. The difference between your previous library experiences and your college library experience is one of scale. Your college library has more stuff. It may be real stuff like books, journals, and videos, or it may be virtual stuff, like online articles, ebooks, and streaming video. Your library pays a lot of money every year to buy or license content for you to use for your research. By extension, your tuition dollars are buying a lot of really good research material. Resorting to Google and Wikipedia means you are not getting all you can out of your college experience.

Not only will your college library have a much larger collection, it will have a more up-to-date and relevant collection than your high school or community public library. Academic librarians spend considerable time acquiring research materials based on classes being taught at your institution. You may not know it, but librarians carefully monitor what courses are being taught each year and are constantly trying to find research materials appropriate to those courses and your professor's research interests. In many cases, you will find that the librarians will know about your assignment and will already have ideas about the types of sources that will make you most successful.

Get To Know Your Librarians!

The most important thing to know during the research process is that there are people to help you. While you may not yet be in the habit of going to the library, there are still many ways in which librarians and library staff can be helpful. Most libraries now have an email or chat service set up so you can ask questions without even setting foot in a library. No question is too basic or too specific. It's a librarian's job to help you find answers, and all questions are welcome. The librarian can even help you discover the right question to ask given the task you are trying to complete.

Help can also come in the form of consultations. Librarians will often make appointments to meet one-on-one to offer in-depth help on a research paper or project. Chances are you will find a link on your library website for scheduling a consultation.

Among the many questions fielded by reference librarians, three stand out as the most often asked. Because librarians hear these questions with such regularity, we suggest that students ask these questions when they begin their research. You can go to the library and ask these questions in person, or you can ask via email or online chat.

1. How Do I Find a Book Relevant to My Topic?   The answer to this question will vary from place to place, but the thing to remember is that finding a book can be either a physical process or a virtual process. Your library will have books on shelves somewhere, and the complexity of how those shelves are organized and accessed depends on factors of size, number of libraries, and the system of organization your library uses. You will find books by using your library's online catalog and carefully noting the call number and location of a book.

Your library is also increasingly likely to offer electronic books or ebooks. These books are discoverable in your library's online catalog as well. When looking at the location of a book, you will frequently see a link for ebook versions. You will not find an ebook in every search, but when you do the advantage is that ebook content is searchable, making your job of finding relevant material in the book easier.

If you find one book on your topic, use it as a jumping-off point for finding more books or articles on that topic. Most books will have bibliographies either at the end of each chapter or at the end of the book in which the author has compiled all the sources he or she used. Consult these bibliographies to find other materials on your topic that will help support your claim. You can also return to the book's listing in your library's online catalog. Once you find the book, look carefully at the record for links to subjects. By clicking on a subject link, you are finding other items in your library

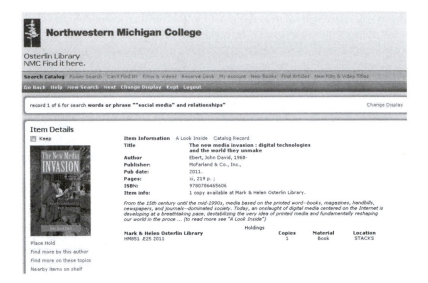

College library online catalog search.

on the same subject. For instance, on the Northwestern Michigan College library catalog, individual listings include the following links: "Find more by this author," "Find more on this topic," and "Nearby items on shelf."

2. What Sources Can I Use as Evidence in My Paper?   There are many types of resources out there to use as you orchestrate a scholarly conversation and support your paper's argument. Books, which we discussed earlier, are great sources if you can find them on your topic, but often your research question will be something that is either too new or too specific for a book to cover. Books are very good for historical questions and overviews of large topics. For current topics, you will want to explore articles from magazines, journals, and newspapers.

Magazines or periodicals (you will hear these terms interchangeably) are published on a weekly or monthly schedule and contain articles of popular interest. These sources can cover broad topics, like the news in magazines such as *Newsweek*, *Time*, and *U.S. News and World Report*. They can also be more focused for particular groups like farmers (*Dairy Farmer*) or photographers (*Creative Photography*). Articles in magazines or periodicals are by professional writers who may or may not be experts. Magazines typically are not considered scholarly and generally do not contain articles with bibliographies, endnotes, or footnotes. This does not mean they are not good sources for your research. In fact, there may be very good reasons to use a magazine article to help support your argument. Magazines capture the point of view of a particular group on a subject, like how farmers feel about increased technology of food production. This point of view may offer support for your claim or an opposing viewpoint to counter. Additionally, magazines can highlight aspects of a topic at a particular point in time. Comparing a *Newsweek* article from 1989 on Japan and globalization to an article on the same topic in 2009 allows you to draw conclusions about the changing relationship between the United States and Japan over that 20-year period.

Journals are intended for a scholarly audience of researchers, specialists, or students of a particular field. Journals such as *Technology and Health*, *Modern Language Journal*, or *Anthropological Linguistics* are all examples of scholarly journals focused on a particular field or research topic. You may hear the term "peer-reviewed" or "referred" in reference to scholarly journals. This means that the articles contained in a journal have been reviewed by a group of scholars in the same field before the article is published in the journal. This ensures that the research has been vetted by a group of peers before it is published. Articles from scholarly journals can help provide some authority to your argument. By citing experts in a field you are bolstering your argument and entering into the scholarly conversation we talked about at the beginning of this guide.

Newspaper articles are found in newspapers that are generally published daily. There is a broad range of content in newspapers, ranging from articles written by staff reporters, to editorials written by scholars, experts, and general readers, to reviews and commentary written by experts. Newspapers are published more frequently and locally than magazines or journals, making them excellent sources for very recent topics and events as well as those with regional significance. Newspaper articles can provide you with a point of view from a particular part of the country or world (how do Americans feel about social media vs. the Chinese); or a strong opinion on a topic from an expert (a school psychologist writing an editorial on the effects of Facebook bullying on adolescents).

A good argument uses evidence from a variety of sources. Do not assume you have done a good job if your paper only cites newspaper articles. You need a broad range of sources to fill out your argument. Your instructor will provide you with guidelines about the number of sources you need, but it will be up to you to find a variety of sources. Finding two or three sources in each of the categories above will help you begin to build a strong argument.

3. Where Should I Look for Articles on My Topic?   The best way to locate journal, magazine, or newspaper articles is to use a database. A database is an online resource that organizes research material of a particular type or content area. For example, *PsycINFO* is a psychology database where you would look for journal articles (as well as other kinds of sources) in the discipline of psychology. Your library licenses or subscribes to databases on your behalf. Finding the right database for your topic will depend upon what is available at your college or university because every institution has a different set of resources. Many libraries will provide subject or research guides that can help you determine what database would be best for your topic. Look for these guides on your library website. Your library's website will have a way to search databases. Look for a section of the library website on databases, and look for a search box in that section. For instance, if you type "language" in a database search box, you may find that your library licenses a database called *MLA International Bibliography* (Modern Language Association). A search for "history" in the database search box may yield *American History and Life* or *Historical Abstracts*. In most instances, your best bet is to ask a librarian which database or databases are most relevant to your research.

When using these databases that your library provides for you, you will know that you are starting to sufficiently narrow or broaden your topic when you begin to retrieve thirty to fifty sources during a search. This kind of narrow result field will rarely occur in Google, which is one of the reasons why using library databases is preferable to Google when doing academic research. Databases will help you determine when you have begun to ask a manageable question.

When you have gotten down to thirty to fifty sources in your result list, begin to look through those results to see what aspects of your topic are being written about. Are there lots of articles on social media, bullying, and adolescents? If so, that might be a topic worth investigating since there is a lot of information for you to read. This is where you begin to discover where your voice might add to the ongoing conversation on the topic.

Using Evidence

The quality of evidence and how you deploy the evidence is ultimately what will make your claims persuasive. You may think of evidence as that which will help prove your claim. But if you look at any scholarly book or article, you'll see that evidence can be used in a number of different ways. Evidence can be used to provide readers with crucial background information. It can be used to tell readers what scholars have commonly thought about a topic (but which you may disagree with). It can offer a theory that you use as a lens. It can offer a methodology or an approach that you would like to use. And finally, evidence can be used to back up the claim that you'll be making in your paper.

Novice researchers begin with a thesis and try to find all the evidence that will prove that their claim is valid or true. What if you come across evidence that doesn't help with the validity of your claim? A novice researcher might decide not to take this complicating evidence into account. Indeed, when you come across complicating evidence, you might be tempted to pretend you never saw it! But rather than sweeping imperfect evidence under the rug, you should figure out how to use this evidence to complicate your own ideas.

The best scholarly conversations take into account a wide array of evidence, carefully considering all sides of a topic. As you probably know, often the most fruitful and productive conversations occur not just when you are talking to people who already agree with you, but when you are fully engaging with the people who might disagree with you.

Coming across unexpected, surprising, and contradictory evidence, then, is a good thing! It will force you to make a complex, nuanced argument and will ultimately allow you to write a more persuasive paper.

Other Forms of Evidence

We've talked about finding evidence in books, magazines, journals, and newspapers. Here are a few other kinds of evidence you may want to use.

Interviews   Interviews can be a powerful form of evidence, especially if the person you are interviewing is an expert in the field that you're investigating. Interviewing can be intimidating, but it might help to know that many people (even experts!) will feel flattered when you ask them for an interview. Most scholars are deeply interested in spreading knowledge, so you should feel comfortable asking a scholar for his or her ideas. Even if the scholar doesn't know the specific answer to your question, he or she may be able to point you in the right direction.

Remember, of course, to be as courteous as possible when you are planning to interview someone. This means sending a polite email that fully introduces yourself and your project before you begin asking questions. Email interviews may be convenient, but an in-person interview is best, since this allows for you and the interviewee to engage in a conversation that may take surprising and helpful turns.

It's a good idea to write down a number of questions before the interview. Make sure not just to get facts (which you can likely get somewhere else). Ask the interviewee to speculate about your topic. Remember that "why" and "how" questions often yield more interesting answers than "what" questions.

If you do conduct an in-person interview, act professionally. Be on time, dress respectfully, and show sincere interest and gratitude. Bring something to record the interview. Many reporters still use pens and a pad, since these feel unobtrusive and are very portable.

Write down the interviewee's name, the date, and the location of the interview, and have your list of questions ready. Don't be afraid, of course, to veer from your questions. The best questions might be the follow-up questions that couldn't have occurred to you before the conversation began. You're likely to get the interviewee to talk freely and openly if you show real intellectual curiosity. If you're not a fast writer, it's certainly OK to ask the interviewee to pause for a moment while you take notes. Some people like to record their interviews. Just make sure that you ask permission if you choose to do this. It's always nice to send a brief thank-you note or email after the interview. This would be a good time to ask any brief follow-up questions.

Images   Because we live in a visual age, we tend to take images for granted. We see them in magazines, on TV, and on the Internet. We don't often think about them as critically as we think about words on a page. Yet a critical look at an image can uncover helpful evidence for a claim. Use Google Image search or flickr.com to find images using the same keywords you used to find books and articles. Ask your instructor for guidance on how to properly cite and acknowledge the source of any images you wish to use. If you want to present your research outside of a classroom project (for example, publish it on a blog or share it at a community event), ask a research librarian for guidance on avoiding any potential copyright violations.

Multimedia   Like images, multimedia such as video, audio, and anima-
tions are increasingly easy to find on the Internet and can strengthen your
claim. For instance, if you are working on globalization and language, you
could find audio or video news clips illustrating the effects of globalization
on local languages. There are several audio and video search engines available, such as Vimeo (vimeo.com) or Blinkx (blinkx.com), a search engine
featuring audio and video from the BBC, Reuters, and the Associated Press
among others. As with images, ask your instructor for guidance on how to
properly cite and acknowledge the source of any multimedia you wish to use.
If you want to present your research outside of a classroom project (for example, publish it on a blog or share it at a community event), ask a research
librarian for guidance on avoiding any potential copyright violations.

Evaluating Sources

A common problem in research isn't a lack of sources, but an overload of
information. Information is more accessible than ever. How many times
have you done an online search and asked yourself the question: "How do I
know what is good information?" Librarians can help. Evaluating online
sources is more challenging than traditional sources because it is harder to
make distinctions between good and bad online information than with
print sources. It is easy to tell that *Newsweek* magazine is not as scholarly as
an academic journal, but online everything may look the same. There are
markers of credibility and authoritativeness when it comes to online information, and you can start to recognize them. We'll provide a few tips here,
but be sure to ask a librarian or your professor for more guidance whenever
you're uncertain about the reliability of a source.

1. **Domain**—The "domain" of a site is the last part of its URL. The domain
   indicates the type of website. Noting the web address can tell you a lot.
   A .edu site indicates that an educational organization created that content. This is no guarantee that the information is accurate, but it does
   suggest less bias than a .com site, which will be commercial in nature
   with a motive to sell you something, including ideas.
2. **Date**—Most websites include a date somewhere on the page. This date
   may indicate a copyright date, the date something was posted, or the
   date the site was last updated. These dates tell you when the content on
   the site was last changed or reviewed. Older sites might be outdated or
   contain information that is no longer relevant.

3. **Author or editor**—Does the online content indicate an author or editor? Like print materials, authority comes from the creator or the content. It is now easier than ever to investigate an author's credentials. A general Google search may lead you to a Wikipedia entry on the author, a LinkedIn page, or even an online résumé. If an author is affiliated with an educational institution, try visiting the institution's website for more information.

Managing Sources

Now that you've found sources, you need to think about how you are going to keep track of the sources and prepare the bibliography that will accompany your paper. Managing your sources is called "bibliographic citation management," and you will sometimes see references to bibliographic citation management on your library's website. Don't let this complicated phrase deter you—managing your citations from the start of your research will make your life much easier during the research process and especially the night before your paper is due when you are compiling your bibliography.

EndNote and RefWorks   Chances are your college library provides software, such as EndNote or RefWorks, to help you manage citations. These are two commercially available citation management software packages that are not freely available to you unless your library has paid for a license. EndNote or RefWorks enables you to organize your sources in personal libraries. These libraries help you manage your sources and create bibliographies. Both EndNote and RefWorks also enable you to insert endnotes and footnotes directly into a Microsoft Word document.

Zotero   If your library does not provide EndNote or RefWorks, a freely available software called Zotero (Zotero.org) will help you manage your sources. Zotero helps you collect, organize, cite, and share your sources, and it lives right in your Web browser where you do your research. As you are searching Google, your library catalog, or library database, Zotero enables you to add a book, article, or website to a personal library with one click. As you add items to your library, Zotero collects both the information you need for you bibliography and any full-text content. This means that the content of journal articles and ebooks will be available to you right from your Zotero library.

To create a bibliography, simply select the items from your Zotero library you want to include, right click and select "Create Bibliography from Selected Items . . .," and choose the citation style your instructor has asked you to use for the paper. To get started, go to Zotero.org and download Zotero for the browser of your choice.

Taking Notes   It is crucial that you take good, careful notes while you are doing your research. Not only is careful note taking necessary to avoid plagiarism, but it can also help you think through your project while you are doing research.

While many researchers used to take notes on index cards, most people now use computers. If you're using your computer, open a new document for each source that you're considering using. The first step in taking notes is to make sure that you gather all the information you might need in your bibliography or works cited. If you're taking notes from a book, for instance, you'll need the author, the title, the place of publication, the press, and the year. Be sure to check the style guide assigned by your instructor to make sure you're gathering all the necessary information.

After you've recorded the bibliographic information, add one or two keywords that can help you sort this source. Next, write a one- or two-sentence summary of the source. Finally, have a section on your document that is reserved for specific places in the text that you might want to work with. When you write down a quote, remember to be extra careful that you are capturing the quote exactly as it is written—and that you enclose the quote in quotation marks. Do not use abbreviations or change the punctuation. Remember, too, to write down the exact page numbers from the source you are quoting. Being careful with small details at the beginning of your project can save you a lot of time in the long run.

WRITING ABOUT HUMOR

In your writing, as in your conversations, you should always be thinking about your audience. While your most obvious audience is the instructor, most college instructors will want you to write a paper that will be interesting and illuminating for other beginning scholars in the field. Many students are unsure what kind of knowledge they can presume of their audience. A good rule of thumb is to write not only for your instructor but also for other students in your class and for other students in classes similar to yours. You can assume a reasonably informed audience that is curious but also skeptical.

Of course it is crucial that you keep your instructor in mind. After all, your instructor will be giving you feedback and evaluating your paper. The best way to keep your instructor in mind while you are writing is to periodically reread the assignment while you are writing. Are you answering the assignment's prompt? Are you adhering to the assignment's guidelines? Are you fulfilling the assignment's purpose? If your answer to any of these questions is uncertain, it's a good idea to ask the instructor.

From Research Question to Thesis Statement

Many students like to begin the writing process by writing an introduction. Novice writers often use an early draft of their introduction to guide the shape of their paper. Experienced scholars, however, continually return to their introduction, reshaping it and revising it as their thoughts evolve. After all, since writing is thinking, it is impossible to anticipate the full thoughts of your paper before you have written it. Many writers, in fact, only realize the actual argument they are making after they have written a draft or two of the paper. Make sure not to let your introduction trap your thinking. Think of your introduction as a guide that will help your readers down the path of discovery—a path you can only fully know after you have written your paper.

A strong introduction will welcome readers to the scholarly conversation. You'll introduce your central interlocutors and pose the question or problem that you are all interested in resolving. Most introductions contain a thesis statement, which is a sentence or two that clearly states the main argument. Some introductions, you'll notice, do not contain the argument, but merely contain the promise of a resolution to the intellectual problem.

Is Your Thesis an Argument?

So far, we've discussed a number of steps for you to take when you begin to write a research paper. We started by strategizing about ways to use presearch to find a topic and ask a researchable question, then we looked at ways to find a scholarly conversation by using your library's resources. Now we'll discuss a crucial step in the writing process: coming up with a thesis.

Your thesis is the central claim of your paper—the main point that you'd like to argue. You may make a number of claims throughout the paper; when you make a claim, you are offering a small argument, usually about a piece of evidence that you've found. Your thesis is your governing claim, the central argument of the whole paper. Sometimes it is difficult to know if you have written a proper thesis. Ask yourself, "Can a reasonable person disagree with my thesis statement?" If the answer is no, then you likely have written an observation rather than an argument. For instance, the statement, "There are six official languages of the UN" is not a thesis, since this is a fact. A reasonable person cannot disagree with this fact, so it is not an argument. The statement, "Arabic became an official language of the UN for economic reasons" is a thesis, since it is a debatable point. A reasonable person might disagree (by arguing, for instance, that "Arabic became an official language of the UN for political reasons"). Remember to keep returning to your thesis statement while you are writing. Not only will you be thus able to make sure that your writing remains on a clear path, but you'll also be able to keep refining your thesis so that it becomes clearer and more precise.

Make sure, too, that your thesis is a point of persuasion rather than one of belief or taste.

"Chinese food tastes delicious" is certainly an argument you could make to your friend, but it is not an adequate thesis for an academic paper, because there is no evidence that you could provide that might persuade a reader who doesn't already agree with you.

Organization

For your paper to feel organized, readers should know where they are headed and have a reasonable idea of how they are going to get there. An introduction will offer a strong sense of organization if it:

- introduces your central intellectual problem and explains why it is important;
- suggests who will be involved in the scholarly conversation;
- indicates what kind of evidence you'll be investigating; and
- offers a precise central argument.

Some readers describe well-organized papers as having a sense of flow. When readers praise a sense of flow, they mean that the argument moves easily from one sentence to the next and from one paragraph to the next. This allows your reader to follow your thoughts easily. When you begin writing a sentence, try using an idea, keyword, or phrase from the end of the previous sentence. The next sentence, then, will appear to have emerged smoothly from the previous sentence. This tip is especially important when you move between paragraphs. The beginning of a paragraph should feel like it has a clear relationship to the end of the previous paragraph.

Keep in mind, too, a sense of wholeness. A strong paragraph has a sense of flow and a sense of wholeness: not only will you allow your reader to trace your thoughts smoothly, but you will ensure that your reader understands how all your thoughts are connected to a large, central idea. Ask yourself, as your write a paragraph: What does this paragraph have to do with the central intellectual problem that I am investigating? If the relationship isn't clear to you, then your readers will likely be confused.

Novice writers often use the form of a five-paragraph essay. In this form, each paragraph offers an example that proves the validity of the central claim. The five-paragraph essay may have worked in high school, since it meets the minimum requirement for making an argument with evidence. You'll quickly notice, though, that experienced writers do not use the five-paragraph essay. Indeed, your college instructors will expect you to move beyond the five-paragraph essay. This is because a five-paragraph essay relies on static examples rather than fully engaging new evidence. A strong essay will grow in complexity and nuance as the writer brings in new evidence. Rather than thinking of an essay as something that offers many examples to back up the same static idea, think of an essay as the evolution of an idea that grows ever more complex and rich as the writer engages with scholars who view the idea from various angles.

Integrating Your Research

As we have seen, doing research involves finding an intellectual community by looking for scholars who are thinking through similar problems and may be in conversation with one another. When you write your paper, you will not merely be reporting what you found; you will be orchestrating the conversation that your research has uncovered. To orchestrate a conversation involves asking a few key questions: Whose voices should be most prominent? What is the relationship between one scholar's ideas and another scholar's ideas? How do these ideas contribute to the argument that your own paper is making? Is it important that your readers hear the exact words of the conversation, or can you give them the main ideas and important points of the conversation in your own words? Your answers to these questions will determine how you go about integrating your research into your paper.

Using evidence is a way of gaining authority. Even though you may not have known much about your topic before you started researching, the way you use evidence in your paper will allow you to establish a voice that is authoritative and trustworthy. You have three basic choices to decide how best you'd like to present the information from a source: summarize, paraphrase, or quote. Let's discuss each one briefly.

Summary   You should summarize a source when the source provides helpful background information for your research. Summaries do not make strong evidence, but they can be helpful if you need to chart the intellectual terrain of your project. Summaries can be an efficient way of capturing the main ideas of a source. Remember, when you are summarizing, to be fully sympathetic to the writer's point of view. Put yourself in the scholar's shoes. If you later disagree with the scholar's methods or conclusions, your disagreement will be convincing because your reader will know that you have given the scholar a fair hearing. A summary that is clearly biased is not only inaccurate and ethically suspect, but it will make your writing less convincing because readers will be suspicious of your rigor.

Let's say you come across the following quote that you'd like to summarize. Here's an excerpt from *The Language Wars: A History of Proper English*, by Henry Hitchings:

> No language has spread as widely as English, and it continues to spread. Internationally the desire to learn it is insatiable. In the twenty-first century the world is becoming more urban and more middle class, and the adoption of English is a symptom of this, for increasingly English serves as the lingua franca of business and popular culture. It is dominant or at least very prominent in other areas such as shipping, diplomacy, computing, medicine and education. (300)

Consider this summary:

> In *The Language Wars*, Hitchings says that everyone wants to learn English because it is the best language in the world (300). I agree that English is the best.

If you compare this summary to what Hitchings actually said, you will see that this summary is a biased, distorted version of the actual quote. Hitchings did not make a universal claim about whether English is better or worse than other languages. Rather, he made a claim about why English is becoming so widespread in an increasingly connected world.

Now let's look at another summary.

> According to Hitchings, English has become the go-to choice for global communications and has spread quickly as the language of commerce and ideas (300).

This is a much stronger summary than the previous example. The writer shortens Hitchings'original language, but he or she is fair to the writer's original meaning and intent.

Paraphrase   Paraphrasing involves putting a source's ideas into your own words. It's a good idea to paraphrase if you think you can state the idea more clearly or more directly than the original source does. Remember that if you paraphrase you need to put the entire idea into your own words. It is not enough for you to change one or two words. Indeed, if you only change a few words, you may put yourself at risk of plagiarizing.

Let's look at how we might paraphrase the Hitchings quote that we've been discussing. Consider this paraphrase:

> Internationally the desire to learn English is insatiable. In today's society, the world is becoming wealthier and more urban, and the use of English is a symptom of this (Hitchings 300).

You will notice that the writer simply replaced some of Hitchings's original language with synonyms. Even with the parenthetical citation, this is unacceptable paraphrasing. Indeed, this is a form of plagiarism, because the writer suggests that the language is his or her own, when it is in fact an only slightly modified version of Hitchings's own phrasing.

Let's see how we might paraphrase Hitchings in an academically honest way:

> Because English is used so frequently in global communications, many people around the world want to learn English as they become members of the middle class (Hitchings 300).

Here the writer has taken Hitchings's message but has used his or her own language to describe what Hitchings originally wrote. The writer offers Hitchings's ideas with fresh syntax and new vocabulary, and the writer is sure to give Hitchings credit for the idea in a parenthetical citation.

Quotation

The best way to show that you are in conversation with scholars is to quote them. Quoting involves capturing the exact wording and punctuation of a passage. Quotations make for powerful evidence, especially in humanities papers. If you come across evidence that you think will be helpful in your project, you should quote it. You may be tempted to quote only those passages that seem to agree with the claim that you are working with. But remember to write down the quotes of scholars who may not seem to agree with you. These are precisely the thoughts that will help you build a powerful scholarly conversation. Working with fresh ideas that you may not agree with can help you revise your claim to make it even more persuasive, since it will force you to take into account potential counterarguments. When your readers see that you are grappling with an intellectual problem from all sides and that you are giving all interlocutors a fair voice, they are more likely to be persuaded by your argument.

To make sure that you are properly integrating your sources into your paper, remember the acronym ICE: Introduce, Cite, and Explain. Let's imagine that you've found an idea that you'd like to incorporate into your paper. We'll use a quote from David Harvey's *A Brief History of Neoliberalism* as an example. On page 7, you find the following quote that you'd like to use: "The assumption that individual freedoms are guaranteed by freedom of the market and of trade is a cardinal feature of neoliberal thinking, and it has long dominated the US stance towards the rest of the world."

1. The first thing you need to do is **introduce** the quote ("introduce" gives us the "I" in ICE). To introduce a quote, provide context so that your readers know where it is coming from, and you must integrate the quote into your own sentence. Here are some examples of how you might do this:

> In his book *A Brief History of Neoliberalism*, David Harvey writes . . .
> One expert on the relationship between economics and politics claims . . .
> Professor of Anthropology David Harvey explains that . . .
> In a recent book by Harvey, he contends . . .

Notice that each of these introduces the quote in such a way that readers are likely to recognize it as an authoritative source.

2. The next step is to **cite** the quote (the C in ICE). Here is where you indicate the origin of the quotation so that your readers can easily look up the original source. Citing is a two-step process that varies slightly depending on the citation style that you're using. We'll offer an example using MLA style. The first step involves indicating the author and page number in the body of your essay. Here is an example of a parenthetical citation that gives the author and page number after the quote and before the period that ends the sentence:

> One expert on the relationship between economics and politics claims that neoliberal thinking has "long dominated the US stance towards the rest of the world" (Harvey 7).

Note that if it is already clear to readers which author you're quoting, you need only to give the page number:

> In *A Brief History of Neoliberalism*, David Harvey contends that neoliberal thinking has "long dominated the US stance towards the rest of the world" (7).

The second step of citing the quote is providing proper information in the works cited or bibliography of your paper. This list should include the complete bibliographical information of all the sources you have cited. An essay that includes the quote by David Harvey should also include the following entry in the works cited:

> Harvey, David. *A Brief History of Neoliberalism.* New York: Oxford UP, 2005. Print.

3. Finally, the most crucial part of integrating a quote is **explaining** it. The E in ICE is often overlooked, but a strong explanation is the most important step to involve yourself in the scholarly conversation. Here is where you will explain how you interpret the source you are citing, what aspect of the quote is most important for your readers to understand, and how the source pertains to your own project. For example:

> David Harvey writes, "The assumption that individual freedoms are guaranteed by freedom of the market and of trade is a cardinal feature of neoliberal thinking, and it has long dominated the US stance towards the rest of the world" (7). As Harvey explains, neoliberalism suggests that free markets do not limit personal freedom but actually lead to free individuals.

Or:

> David Harvey writes, "The assumption that individual freedoms are guaranteed by freedom of the market and of trade is a cardinal feature of neoliberal thinking, and it has long dominated the US stance towards the rest of the world" (7). For Harvey, before we understand the role of the United States in global politics, we must first understand the philosophy that binds personal freedom with market freedom.

Novice writers are sometimes tempted to end a paragraph with a quote that they feel is especially compelling or clear. But remember that you should never leave a quote to speak for itself (even if you love it!). After all, as the orchestrator of this scholarly conversation, you need to make sure that readers are receiving exactly what you'd like them to receive from each quote. Notice, in the above examples, that the first explanation suggests that the writer quoting Harvey is centrally concerned with neoliberal philosophy, while the second explanation suggests that the writer is centrally concerned with U.S. politics. The explanation, in other words, is the crucial link between your source and the main idea of your paper.

Avoiding Plagiarism

Scholarly conversations are what drive knowledge in the world. Scholars using each other's ideas in open, honest ways form the bedrock of our intellectual communities and ensure that our contributions to the world of thought are important. It is crucial, then, that all writers do their part in maintaining the integrity and trustworthiness of scholarly conversations. It is crucial that you never claim someone else's ideas as your own, and that you always are extra careful to give the proper credit to someone else's thoughts. This is what we call responsible scholarship.

The best way to avoid plagiarism is to plan ahead and keep careful notes as you read your sources. Remember the advice (above) on Zotero and taking notes: find the way that works best for you to keep track of what ideas are your own and what ideas come directly from the sources you are reading. Most acts of plagiarism are accidental. It is easy when you are drafting a paper to lose track of where a quote or idea came from; plan ahead and this won't happen. Here are a few tips for making sure that confusion doesn't happen to you.

1. Know what needs to be cited. You do not need to cite what is considered common knowledge such as facts (the day Lincoln was born), concepts (the Earth orbits the sun), or events (the day Martin Luther King was shot). You do need to cite the ideas and words of others from the sources you are using in your paper.
2. Be conservative. If you are not sure if you should cite something, either ask your instructor or a librarian, or cite it. It is better to cite something you don't have to than not cite something you should.
3. Direct quotations from your sources need to be cited as well as anytime you paraphrase the ideas or words from your sources.
4. Finally, extensive citation not only helps you avoid plagiarism, but it also boosts your credibility and enables your reader to trace your scholarship.

Citation Styles

It is crucial that you adhere to the standards of a single citation style when you write your paper. The most common styles are MLA (Modern Language Association, generally used in the humanities), APA (American Psychological Association, generally used in the social sciences), and Chicago (*Chicago Manual of Style*). If you're not sure which style you should use, you must ask your instructor. Each style has its own guidelines regarding the format of the paper. While proper formatting within a given style may seem arbitrary, there are important reasons behind the guidelines of each style. For instance, while MLA citations tend to emphasize author names, APA citations tend to emphasize the date of publications. This distinction make sense, especially given that MLA standards are usually followed by departments in the humanities and APA standards are usually followed by departments in the social sciences. While papers in the humanities value original thinking about arguments and texts that are canonical and often old, papers in the social sciences tend to value arguments that take into account the most current thought and the latest research.

There are a number of helpful guidebooks that will tell you all the rules you need to know in order to follow the standards for various citation styles. If your instructor hasn't pointed you to a specific guidebook, try the following online resources:

Purdue Online Writing Lab: owl.english.purdue.edu/Internet Public Library: www.ipl.org/div/farq/netciteFARQ.html

Modern Language Association (for MLA style): www.mla.org/style

American Psychological Association (for APA style): www.apastyle.org/

The Chicago Manual of Style Online: www.chicagomanualofstyle.org/tools_citationguide.html

SAMPLE STUDENT RESEARCH PAPER

Brittany MacLean

Beyond Serious: How Internal Monologue Creates
Humor in George Saunders' "Victory Lap"

Introduction

There's a saying that the only difference between a tragedy
and a comedy is a happy ending. That is certainly true in the
case of George Saunders' "Victory Lap." However, there is
another important device that Saunders uses, without which
the humor of the piece would be lost. That device is internal
monologue. As many critics have noted, point of view is
crucial. For instance, Charles Yu, writing in the *LA Review of
Books*, states: "Alternating in point of view between a violent
predator, his would-be victim, and the teenage boy who
comes between them, the story cycles through each character's view of the events, the way that view has been formed
for each by his or her personal history, their respective lives
to that point."

But Saunders helps the reader find humor by making
each voice entirely genuine in its ruminations via internal
monologue. This authenticity lends sincerity to the character
which in turn causes the reader to identify or empathize with
them. Many of the internal thoughts that Saunders makes
the reader privy to are funny, and as the reader grows to
know the characters and their thoughts, there is more humor

to be found in each individual's voice even while much of the subject matter surrounding the action of the story is serious.

From the start of the piece, the reader is thrust into the humorous ruminations of almost-15-year-old Alison, specifically her conversations with imaginary suitors and her hyperbolic love for everything around her. For Alison and Kyle, their happy endings center on the triumph over their oppressors: Alison's would-be abductor and Kyle's strict parents. In Kyle's character, the reader finds an individual who has been suffocated by his upbringing, which, despite its serious implications, renders his internal thoughts humorous. Maureen Corrigan, writing for NPR, agrees, saying, "By the end of "Victory Lap," nerdy Kyle has faced down evil, while his parents who sought to cosset him are the ones who need to be told reassuring fictions."

He is constantly worried about breaking silly rules, and the oppression he feels manifests itself with comic strings of uncontrollable cursing. Kyle's ending is happy in that he does not bring the rock down on the would-be abductor and kill him, which renders him free from guilt.

After the reader is introduced and attached to Alison and Kyle's characters, the serious nature of the plot begins. However, there is even humor to be found in the internal monologue of Alison's would-be abductor. If the reader wasn't aware of his internal thoughts, he would be merely sinister. While on the outside he is a violent man meaning to abduct and injure an adolescent girl, his thoughts paint him as an inept criminal who was subjected to a childhood filled with abuse. As Yu says, "there are whole histories floating just under the surface of the story" because Saunders "can do this with just a drop of concentrated empathy." Although the reader does not agree with the attacker's actions, there is some sympathy to be felt, and humor to be found in his incompetence as an abductor. For the reader, the happy ending surrounding the would-be abductor is his capture and the implication that justice is served.

Alison

Right away we are thrust into the internal thoughts of almost-15-year-old Alison Pope, and we quickly discern she is engaging in internal, fictional dialogues with imaginary suitors. From the first introduction of Alison, her whimsy and good humor are apparent, as the fictional nature of the scenario of the suitors is contrasted with the incredibly pragmatic dialogue she invents. She names her first imagined suitor "Mr. Small Package" because that's how he describes her in an imagined exchange. Insulted, she quickly moves on to the next suitor who, trying to be suave, misspeaks and suggests the two go stand on the moon. "Had he said, *Let us go stand on the moon?*" Alison reflects. "If so, she would have to be like, {eyebrows up}. And if no wry acknowledgment was forthcoming, be like, Uh, I am not exactly dressed for standing on the moon, which, as I understand it, is super-cold?" (Saunders 4). This internal exchange creates humor because there is an authenticity in it as well as the juxtaposition of how pragmatic she is in her fantasy life. We are charmed by the sound of her inner voice.

MacLean   4

Her imagined suitor scene is interrupted when she starts thinking about getting to dance class, which reveals a hyperbolic love of everyone:

> Although actually she loved Ms. C. So strict! Also loved the other girls in class. And the girls from school. *Loved* them. Everyone was so nice. Plus the boys at her school. Plus the teachers at her school. All of them were doing their best. Actually, she loved her whole town. That adorable grocer, spraying his lettuce! Pastor Carol, with her large comfortable butt! The chubby postman, gesticulating with his padded envelopes! (Saunders 4–5)

Not only is this over-the-top love of everyone humorous, the genuine way in which it is delivered makes the reader smile. Her mind runs from one "love" to another, adding to the animated nature of her thoughts. In this way, Saunders crafts what we can imagine to be the actual spinning mind of a 15-year-old girl. This passage creates humor because of the fervor and conviction with which Alison expresses her love. These positive, running thoughts are a striking characteristic of Alison's internal monologue. Later, when she asks herself if she is special, she runs through a list of special women, thinking, "Helen Keller had been awesome; Mother Teresa was amazing; Mrs. Roosevelt was quite chipper in spite of her husband, who was handicapped, which, in addition, she had been gay, with those big old teeth, long before such time as being gay and First Lady was even conceptual" (7). The strength of Alison's convictions, along with word choices like "awesome" and "amazing" captures the characteristic jargon of teenagers. Saunders authentically imitates the mind and voice of a 15-year-old.

Although she is surely changed, which can be seen by the lack of bubbliness in her internal monologue after the attempted abduction, ultimately the humor the reader encountered in her monologue before the abduction is not effaced. Alison was not abducted, nor did she (despite having nightmares to the contrary) watch Kyle kill the would-be abductor.

Kyle

The reader is first introduced to Kyle through the eyes of Alison, who regards him with a pitying disinclination. Alison shares that Kyle's parents "didn't let him do squat" (8); however, the reader doesn't truly start to understand the nature of that comment until he or she is in Kyle's mind. When the internal monologue switches from Alison to Kyle, the first glimpse inside Kyle's house reveals the use of the Family Status Indicator. When Kyle gets home he finds that "the big clocklike wooden indicator was set at All Out. Other choices include Dad Out; Kyle Out; Mom & Kyle Out; Dad & Kyle Out; and All In" (10). We start to see the importance of order and discipline in the house, not to mention the fact that Kyle is an only child. Kyle then thinks to himself, "Why did they even need All In? Wouldn't they know when they were All In? Would he like to ask Dad that? Who, in his excellent, totally silent downstairs woodshop, had designed and built the Family Status Indicator?" (11). This internal thought is humorous because it calls attention to the silliness of this quirky family instrument. This is not the only system the family employs that seems ridiculous, and Kyle's thoughts about such systems are funny because to him they are givens. Other examples are the geode his father tasks him with placing in the yard and Kyle's obsessive cleaning because of the microbes he leaves behind. While Alison might not be interested in Kyle, the reader feels for him. Saunders achieves this connection via the access he gives us to Kyle's thoughts.

There is still humor even as the serious action draws closer, particularly when Kyle notices the van of the would-be abductor pull up to Alison's house. We learn that Kyle's father has tasked him with recording the comings and goings of vehicles in the neighborhood, which Kyle says serves "the dual purpose of (1) buttressing Dad's argument that Father Dmitri should build a soundproof retaining wall and (2) constituting a data set for a possible Science Fair project for him, Kyle, entitled, by Dad, 'Correlation of Church Parking Lot Volume vs. Day of Week, with Ancillary Investigation of Sunday Volume Throughout Year'" (15). The introduction of the would-be abductor also brings out the humor of Kyle's internal monologue when, after recording the arrival of the stranger in his traffic log, he laments, "That sucked. Stank, rather. The guy being a stranger, he, Kyle, now had to stay inside until the stranger left the neighborhood. Which totally futzed up his geode placing. He'd be out there until midnight. What a detriment!" (15). It is not merely funny that this is a rule in Kyle's house; rather, the humor lies in the fact that Kyle is so accepting of it and how he can only think of the geode placing. His familial life has conditioned him so that he does not even consider the possibility of his father not making him work all night to place the geode.

His use of the exclamatory "detriment" ties into another important aspect of Kyle's internal monologue, his language. On the one end of the spectrum, Kyle uses words like "Gar," "Yoinks," and "holy golly." There's also the mix of technical terminology and slang like "Way verboten," the frequent use of which is humorous. Despite this rather tame exclamatory language, the endearing nature of which makes it funny, Kyle also rattles off chains of curses in his head. This cursing seems uncontrollable, which only lends to the humor. Kyle, who is so set on following the rules, has an (internal) dirty mouth that he can't control. While the curses themselves are humorous in their inventiveness, it is ultimately the dual nature of Kyle's internal monologue that creates humor. On the one hand he is complying with the ridiculous rules that his parents have, while on the other he is cursing (internally) until he's (figuratively) blue in the face. After Kyle goes off on one such internal rant, he thinks about the disappointment his parents would feel. Particularly humorous, however, is when his squeaky clean demeanor is explored in the same sentence as such cursing chains, like when he ponders how his parents could even possibly "brag" about his bad habit: "They thought so highly of him, sending weekly braggy emails to both sets of grandparents, such as: Kyle's been super-busy keeping up his grades while running varsity cross-country though still a sophomore, while setting aside a little time each day to manufacture such humdingers as cunt-swoggle rear-fuck—What was wrong with him?" (13). The juxtaposition of the obedient son with the boy who has the mouth of a sailor is apparent in this passage. It shows that the cursing is out of character from the boy his parents see. But it's more humorous because it is both striking on the page, and it is funny to imagine his parents sending such a letter to his grandparents.

Once the action starts and Kyle struggles with the decision whether or not to help Alison, the seriousness of his own situation becomes apparent. While his parents' rules are funny because of how ridiculous they are, they have also crippled Kyle immensely. Because of his parents' rules, he actually considers not helping Alison, letting her get abducted, and simply returning to normal life as if nothing had happened. More importantly, he thinks that his parents would be proud of him for not doing anything and for following their rules. The tragedy of Kyle's situation does not efface the comedy because his narrative, too, ultimately has a happy ending. Not only does he end up saving Alison, but doing so also seems to liberate him from the controlling voices of his parents in his head. Lastly, Alison stops him from bringing the rock down and killing her would-be abductor, thus saving him from a lifetime of regret. Kyle's ending, like Alison's, is a happy one—he does not commit a crime and he protects his loved ones.

258   appendix

MacLean   9

Alison's would-be abductor

Although Alison's would-be abductor is committing a horren-dous act that does not put him in good favor with the reader, Saunders "widens the field of vision, showing us not just what the monster does, but who the monster is" (Yu). He does this by creating a comic internal monologue that allows for sympathy to develop. Alison's would-be attacker has some horrible things in mind when he takes her, but his in-ability to smoothly execute his plan leads to a humorous in-ternal monologue, starting when he brings Alison back to the van, only to find that it's locked: "Fucksake. Side door of the van was locked. How undisciplined was that. Ensuring that the door was unlocked was clearly indicated on the pre-mis-sion matrix" (Saunders 19). Coming back to a locked car door and immediately thinking, "Fucksake" is relatable and comic, despite the circumstances. Here is an abductor who just can't get the planning right.

He does have a plan for the van, however, as he decides that if the abduction goes well he'll get on the freeway and "Basically steal the van. It was Kenny's van. He'd borrowed it for the day. Screw Kenny. Kenny had once called him stupid. Too bad, Kenny, that remark just cost you a van" (20). Despite the dark nature of these plans because he would have Alison with him, his attitude toward Kenny is funny. Even his attitude about things going wrong is humorous, as he decides that he'll "go buy corn, return van to Kenny, say, Hey, bro, here's a shitload of corn, thanks for the van, I never could've bought a suitable quantity of corn in my car" (20). While the reality of

MacLean   10

what he would have done to Alison is horrific, the idea of so much corn, and for some reason, corn specifically, is funny.

Nonetheless, he is still psychotic; he attempts to kidnap Alison and also the hints at what he plans to do with her. There is also the darkness of his childhood and the implication that his stepfather, Melvin, was abusive to him. While this does not excuse his violent behavior, it does make room for sympathy. His mother and stepfather did irreversible damage. He fantasizes about being the king and about dominating women, not to mention the nonchalant way in which he talks about disposing of Alison if things go wrong. Despite all this, there is a happy ending, not for the abductor per se, but for the reader. There is a gratification at the thought of him being captured, which allows for the humor of his incompetency (and the thoughts surrounding the abduction) to stand. Ultimately, the reader is able to infer that justice is served.

Conclusion

While the seriousness of the subject matter in "Victory Lap" cannot be ignored, neither can the humor of its three main characters. Each monologue is humorous in its own way; Alison is a bubbly, fierce 15-year-old; Kyle is obsessed with following his parents' silly rules; and the attacker is ineffectual. Overall, the three internal monologues paired with the happy ending teach us that humor and seriousness are not mutually exclusive. In fact, they cannot only exist but can even thrive together. This darkness is instrumental to seeing the piece as humorous because without the lows of the characters, we would not be able to climb so high to a happy ending.

Works Cited

Corrigan, Maureen. "George Saunders Lives Up to the Hype."
    Fresh Air. NPR, 15 Jan. 2013. Web. 29 July 2014.

Saunders, George. "Victory Lap." *Tenth of December.*
    New York: Random House, 2013. 3–27. Print.

Yu, Charles. "A Drop of Concentrated Empathy: On Broken-
    ness and Beauty in the Stories of George Saunders."
    Los Angeles Review of Books, 28 Feb. 2013. Web.
    29 July 2014.

credits

Chapter 1: Expository

Page 2 O'Shannon, Dan. Excerpted from *What Are you Laughing At?: A Comprehensive Guide to the Comedic Event* by Dan O'Shannon. © Dan O'Shannon, 2012. Published by Continuum US. Reprinted by permission of Bloomsbury Publishing, Inc.

Page 21 Clay, Felix. "6 Weirdly Specific Characters That Are in Every Sitcom Ever" by Felix Clay, originally published on *Cracked.com*. © Demand Media, Inc. All rights reserved. Reprinted by permission of *Cracked.com*.

Page 28 Nissan, Colin. "The Ultimate Guide to Writing Better Than You Normally Do," originally published in *The Best of McSweeney's Internet Tendency*. Reprinted by permission of the author.

Page 31 Weiner, Jonah. "Jerry Seinfeld Intends to Die Standing Up" by Jonah Weiner, from *The New York Times*, Dec. 20, 2012. Copyright © 2012, The New York Times Company. Reprinted by permission.

Page 45 Burgess, Katie. "How to Read a Poem," originally published at *The Rumpus* (therumpus.net), June 11, 2013. Reprinted by permission of the author.

Page 48 Knox, Jennifer L. "The Best Thanksgiving Ever," published in *Painted Bride Quarterly*, 68: Poetry (http://pbq.drexel.edu/). Reprinted by permission of the author.

Page 50 Somers, Erin. "Modern Vice," originally published at *The Rumpus* (therumpus.net), April 2, 2013. Reprinted by permission of the author.

Page 52 Ephron, Nora. "A Few Words About Breasts" from *Crazy Salad: Some Things About Women* by Nora Ephron. © 1972 by Nora Ephron. Used by permission of ICM. All rights reserved.

Page 61 Treece, Will. "Abu Dhabi Named #1 in List of Cities Ranked Alphabetically," draft, by Will Treece, copyright © 2013, Will Treece. Reprinted by permission of the author.

Page 63 Logan, Brian. "Funny Foreigners: How Overseas Comics Are Storming Edinburgh" by Brian Logan, from *The Guardian*, August 17, 2010. Copyright Guardian News & Media Ltd 2010. Reprinted by permission.

Page 67 Stein, Scott. "Garghibition" was originally published in *Liberty*, 1999. Reprinted by permission of the author.

Page 71 Martone, Michael. "On Anesthesia," from *Seeing Eye* by Michael Martone. Reprinted by permission of the author.

Chapter 2: Analytical

Chapter 3: Persuasive

Page 189 Cunningham, Sean. "Why We Owe Gisele an Apology (Particularly God)" posted at *When Falls the Coliseum* (whenfallsthecoliseum.com), February 10, 2012. Reprinted by permission of Sean Cunningham.

Page 192 Frazier, Ian. "Laws Concerning Food and Drink" by Ian Frazier. Copyright © 1997 by Ian Frazier, originally appeared in *The Atlantic Magazine*, used by permission of The Wylie Agency LLC.

Page 196 Collins, Billy. "Tension" from *Ballistics: Poems* by Billy Collins, copyright © 2008 by Billy Collins. Used by permission of Random House, an imprint and division of Random House LLC. All rights reserved.

Page 198 Barthelme, Donald. "In the Morning Post" from *Not-Knowing* by Donald Barthelme. Copyright © 1997 by the Estate of Donald Barthelme, used by permission of The Wylie Agency LLC.

Page 200 Hitchens, Christopher. "Cheap Laughs: The Smug Satire of Liberal Humorists Debases Our Comedy—and Our National Conversation" by Christopher Hitchens. © 2009 The Atlantic Media Co., as first published in *The Atlantic Magazine*. All rights reserved. Distributed by Tribune Content Agency, LLC and reprinted by permission.

Page 209 Winstead, Lizz. "Sarah Silverman and Me: Fact-Checking US Politics—the Fun Way" by Lizz Winstead, from *The Guardian*, October 22, 2012. Copyright Guardian News & Media Ltd 2012. Reprinted by permission.

Page 214 Schneiderman, Jason. "Wester" from *Striking Surface* by Jason Schneiderman. Copyright 2010 by Jason Schneiderman. Reprinted by permission of Ashland Poetry Press.

Page 215 Shteyngart, Gary. "Only Disconnect" by Gary Shteyngart, from *The New York Times*, July 18, 2010. Copyright © 2010, The New York Times Company. Reprinted by permission.

index